DEVELOPING EXPERT SYSTEMS

DEVELOPING EXPERT SYSTEMS

A KNOWLEDGE ENGINEER'S HANDBOOK FOR RULES & OBJECTS

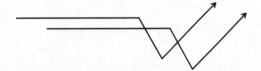

Edmund C. Payne
Robert C. McArthur

John Wiley & Sons, Inc.
New York / Chichester / Brisbane / Toronto / Singapore

Library of Congress Cataloging in Publication Data:

Payne, Edmund C.
    Developing expert systems : a knowledge engineer's handbook for
rules & objects / Edmund C. Payne, Robert C. McArthur.
        p.   cm.
    Includes bibliographical references.
    1. Expert systems (Computer science)   I. McArthur, Robert C.
II. Title.
QA76.76.E95P29   1990
006.3'3—dc20   89-27383
    ISBN 0-471-51413-6   CIP

Printed in the United States of America

10 9 8 7 6 5 4 3 2

CONTENTS

PART TWO: BUILDING
THE PROTOTYPE: FORWARD CHAINING 69

PART FOUR: MODELING THE ENVIRONMENT 271

PREFACE

As with so many new technologies, the introduction of "Artificial Intelligence" initially appeared to many people to herald a breakthrough in accomplishing a laborious task, "programming for nonprogrammers." Tales of greatly improved programmer productivity and rapid prototyping only encouraged this attitude. However, although implementing expert systems allows us to tackle new types of problems, the reality is that the requirements inherent to any large project remain: a clear methodological approach and some basic know-how.

We have likened the process of learning expert-system–building skills to that of acquiring house-building skills. An individual might begin by exploring written material about house construction and perhaps discover that the mysteries of their construction are difficult to penetrate. The next step is classes or seminars that teach how to use the tools of the trade: hammers, saws, and so on. Perhaps work is then done on a small project such as a dog house (the proverbial "toy" project). Inevitably, individuals find themselves on their own and faced with building something real, such as a house, and with the realization that the training covered the simple mechanics of applying the tools, but not the know-how necessary to build something at all complex. Each step of this analogy can be applied to building an expert system with a commercial shell—given an understanding of the basic tools, what next?

Over the years, as we have implemented expert systems, we've noted a thread common to all the approaches we were using and to the questions and problems of the novice. Facility with the features of a tool did not correlate with an understanding of design and structure. Studying fully implemented systems and textbook case histories provided novices with few clues as to why design decisions were made or the order and process of the implementation. Toy examples, while showing off shell features, could not be scaled up, because large problems require different approaches from small problems.

Our solution to the problem of structuring the knowledge-engineering process was to craft several working applications at successive stages of development, enabling step-by-step exploration of implementation details. The expert systems, which combine all of the major AI paradigms, are composites of actual case studies. These examples demonstrate alternate solutions to a given problem and provide concrete examples of how those alternative techniques may be implemented by the user.

In addition to using this technique in seminars and consulting assignments, we developed an on-line teaching/development tool, AXLE (the

Albathion eXpert System Learning Environment). AXLE combines text with a working, fully implemented version of our example expert systems to provide step-by-step guidance in constructing expert systems. This text incorporates the philosophy of the AXLE product in providing a step-by-step, detailed description of the expert-system–building process.

Without the AXLE product, this book would not be possible. For their help in implementing the examples and serving as a testing ground for the general methodology we wish to thank individuals at the Information Technology Institute of the Singapore National Computer Board, particularly Lim Joo Hong. We wish to also thank Judy Bolger, Yehudah Fredundlich, Bharat Charan, and Wyndell Smith for their help with testing and developing the examples and text for AXLE, which were later modified for use in this book.

In addition, we wish to thank Liss Fain for her proofing, editing, commenting, and encouraging; Udomsri Kumkem, whose moral support and common sense were crucial to getting the book finished and out the door; and the expert system shell companies—IntelliCorp, AION, AICORP, Level Five Research, and Gold Hill Computers—for their cooperation in gathering information for the tables in the appendices. Finally, we would like to thank Karl Wiig for years of inspiration.

San Francisco, California   EDMUND C. PAYNE

Bangkok, Thailand   ROBERT C. MCARTHUR
January 1990

INTRODUCTION

The field of artificial intelligence (AI) has progressed in a relatively short time from an academic discipline to a commercially viable technology. In particular, *the area of expert systems has generated many adherents because it offers the opportunity to organize human expertise and experience into a form that the computer can manipulate.* However, the technology is complex and not easily mastered. Users of AI technology have quickly been disabused of the notion that the function of programmers has been displaced. True, a user with very little computer knowledge can, using AI representation strategies such as rules and frames, accomplish much more than was previously possible. Nonetheless, there remains a need for individuals skilled in manipulating the technology—traditional programmers, using languages such as Lisp or C, as well as individuals practicing a new discipline, knowledge engineering.

The primary aim of this book is to combine theory and practice to demonstrate how a "real" expert system is built. Much as a consultant would, we lead the reader through the steps that were taken to build a typical diagnostics system, using the proven "learning by example" approach. Guidance is given to the reader concerning specific design and implementation techniques. Although the running theme of the book is the theory of expert system implementation, all of the theory is turned into practice by pointed examples. We have chosen as our model the case-study approach; we take a single real-world example and decompose it into a set of chronological stages. These stages are presented to the reader with alternative approaches and rationales for each design decision.

No particular knowledge of programming or of a specific commercial shell is required for using this book. Many of the examples and illustrations in the book are taken from AXLE (the Albathion eXpert System Learning Environment). The Entrypaq product can be used in conjunction with this book as an aid to building your own applications. If you have a Macintosh with 1 megabyte of memory and HyperCard, you can obtain Entrypaq, Albathion's expert system shell, for hands-on participation with the examples described in this book.

The examples provided in this book have been designed to work in most commercial shell environments. The original work on these systems was done in IntelliCorp's Knowledge Engineering Environment (KEE) and Lisp. The applications were subsequently re-implemented in Gold Hill's GoldWorks. Finally, for this book, the bulk of the applications were again re-implemented using an object-shell implemented by Albathion in Apple's HyperCard and the accompanying scripting language HyperTalk (which can, in turn, be converted into C, Lisp, Pascal, etc.). Appendices in the back of the book provide tables translating book terminology and formats into a number of popular commercial shells.

To implement the HyperCard versions, we have constructed a simple expert-system shell (the shell contains a frame and rule-building environment and a forward chainer). This shell, along with the HyperCard scripts and functions described in this book, are available from Albathion at a nominal cost (see the card at the back of this book for details).

AUDIENCE

The book has been designed to meet the needs of several different audiences. For *students* taking intermediate and advanced AI courses at the university level, this book provides a comprehensive methodology for identifying the need for an expert system and then designing and implementing the system. The availability of large numbers of examples showing specific techniques, decision points, and decision rationales provides a practical guide to the actual building of a system. Although this is only one of many ways such a system could be built, the book provides a comprehensive methodology that has been tested and refined in a large number of practical client situations.

For *individuals at a corporation* assigned the task of building an expert system, the book serves as both a methodology handbook and a practical implementation guide. Using the same philosophy as the AXLE product embodies, we provide many examples of problem-solving techniques both for the commonly available expert system shells such as KEE and Gold-Works and for computer languages such as Lisp and C.

For *managers*, the first part of the book provides an overview of how a problem can be assessed and resources allocated to the project. The second part of the book can also be a useful guide to the potential costs and time requirements of such a project.

Finally, this book is intended for those *individuals* exploring expert system techniques on their own. We have provided examples (and Entrypaq, a sample development environment containing these examples on floppy disk) that can be used on the Apple Macintosh with HyperCard. These HyperTalk examples provide access to these concepts for those of you who may not have a practical need to use these systems immediately but still have either a desire to keep informed or a need to assess the technology for possible future needs.

PART

1

PROJECT ASSESSMENT, PLANNING, INITIATION

1

Assessing the Problem

Our book begins where all expert systems begin—with a perceived problem that is difficult to solve using traditional computing methods. What are the components of the problem that have led us to believe that an expert system is required? How do we decide if the project is both feasible and cost effective? Is it a technical or a political decision? Will people use the system once it is built? By starting with these questions we are facing the political reality of any applied, commercial expert system project (and even those that are done for purely research purposes will often require a long-range justification).

The questions we have just asked are for the most part not unique to expert system projects. They are (or should be) asked about any proposed computer software system. Expert systems are only an extension of the array of tools that computers provide. We'll begin our exploration of the expert system building process by looking at how a problem in quality control was discovered in our example—a canning plant.

Throughout the book, we will accompany a pair of experienced consultants as they implement an expert system. Subjects are introduced in the same order that they would appear, and be dealt with, in a typical project. This ordering of subject matter provides a logical framework for learning new concepts as well as providing more experienced users with a quick means of identifying chapters referencing specific implementation paradigms.

Four types of information are provided in the book:

- the theory and background surrounding each major topic area
- the actual implementation approach, including the knowledge representation or code required
- alternatives to the primary approach (for example, rules vs. a programming language)
- the rationale for the approach taken

These four information types are illustrated using an analytic case study.

Analytical problems have been around for hundreds of years, ever since people began developing things that could break; diagnostic skills have developed in tandem with these problems. Many of the skills that true experts possess in analyzing and repairing problems are still learned by apprenticeship—the process of one person working closely with another who has acquired these skills. However, as problems have become more complex, and thus increasingly formalized, analytic tasks are accompanied by ever-growing mountains of documentation.

The next step in the evolution of problem analysis is the development of expert advisory systems. These systems are computer programs that can represent the knowledge of an expert and then serve as a tool for less-experienced people. Expert systems have the potential to assist users in ways that paper documentation never could, by

- presenting users with only the questions they need to answer, based on previous answers and direct reading of external data
- incorporating the knowledge of experienced users, including the special cases that make many problems so difficult to solve

APPLICABILITY TO OTHER PROBLEM DOMAINS

Expert systems have been applied to problems in many domains. To date, the majority of work has been in the area of problem analysis, with planning a close second. The application of expert systems to problem analysis can be further broken down by industry and analysis type.

The application used in the book is the analysis of solutions for quality control problems in a canning plant. This application is ideal for the following reasons.

- Problem analysis is the most common of all subjects for expert systems.

- The problems being analyzed in the example manufacturing environment are easily understood even by those unfamiliar with manufacturing.

- The example problem is sufficiently complex to require the use of a variety of expert-systems techniques.

- The use of a detailed factual study provides meaningful details lost in small, derived examples.

- Most importantly, the approaches illustrated in the book are applicable to a broad range of problem domains.

At the plant, problems in can quality have been detected, and the company is searching for ways to make problem detection and correction more consistent. Two sets of expert knowledge exist: how to detect a quality problem in a can, and what types of mechanical problems can lead to quality problems. The goal of our system will be to combine engineering knowledge with operator experience to build a system that can diagnose problems and suggest corrective procedures.

The methodology for building expert systems presented in this book is typical for a large number of domains—for example, deciding about the relative merit of insurance claims, investigating problems in switching circuits, or detecting failures in a communications satellite. To facilitate the association between the detailed problem solution described here and the implementation of this methodology in other fields, Chapter 7 takes you step by step through the relationships between the manufacturing example and applications in other disciplines:

- communications
- aerospace
- insurance
- finance

STRUCTURE

As you read this book, you will encounter specific topics in the same order that you would typically encounter them while building an expert system: discovery and assessment of a problem; assessment of the tools and resources required; implementation of prototype solutions; and, finally, the testing and fielding of the completed system. Figure 1-1 shows the steps involved in implementing an expert system, classified according to the four major implementation phases. At the end of each phase, the project is reevaluated, and either progresses to the next set of tasks or is terminated.

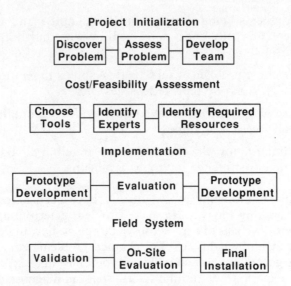

FIGURE 1-1. The process of expert system implementation

This book describes the system-building process starting at day 1, showing each decision made, along with the rejected options and the rationale for the decision. This chronological progression is disaggregated into sets of expert system paradigms and building blocks (e.g., the introduction of alternate rule forms, object graphics, or frames).

The first section is a general introduction to the processes that lead to a requirement for an expert system. It begins with the perception of a problem, examining how expert systems present one possible solution. From perceived need, the book next shows how a group can assess the utility of an expert system, develop criteria with which to evaluate a project's feasibility, and finally identify the resources and tools required to start the project. Then you will observe the team as it begins implementation of the expert system—the process of knowledge engineering and the implementation of an initial rule-based system. Through this first level of prototype building, we assume that the user has no programming knowledge—thus, although the end result of this first half of the book is a functioning, useful expert system, it contains no requirement or use of any computer programming languages.

In the second half of the book HyperTalk, HyperCard's programming language, has been used for the examples because the code reads so much like descriptive English statements. We have also provided selected examples of these same functions, written in Lisp, in the appendices. Chapters that include some programming examples are marked in the table of contents with a plus(+), and chapters that require some interest in programming are marked with an asterisk(*). In this half the book is rich in implementation techniques as well as general methodology. Then, the book examines solutions to the problem of testing and validating the completed expert system. Finally, you can explore how an expert system can be interfaced to the external environment, including data bases, sensors, and multimedia devices.

PROBLEM DESCRIPTION

The techniques for building an expert system presented in this book are applicable to many different types of expert systems. Paradigms and technical approaches will be presented in the order that they typically occur in the system building process. From time to time through the course of the book, we will return to the team at the canning plant as it implements its advisory system for plant operators. These plant visits will illustrate our theoretical treatment of an AI paradigm by demonstrating the actual practices and pitfalls that occur in the development of an expert system. Although events and individuals have been modified to some extent, these narratives are based on real-world events that occurred during the process of implementing expert systems. We'll begin now with some background on the events at the canning plant that led up to the decision to build an expert system (throughout the text, these narratives will be indicated by a smaller font delineated with vertical bars).

Discovering the Problem

Three years before the start of the expert system project, a beverage maker discovered unpleasant "off-notes" in certain batches of beer following the canning process. An investigation was begun to discover the source of the problem. Eventually, a team of taste testers was formed to investigate consistency fluctuations in large batches of the canned beverages.

We visited the taste team in the role of consultants evaluating the possibilities for computer support of the investigative effort. As we waited, three men and two women entered the room and took their places at a round formica table, a performance they would repeat three or four times each week. Each individual on the panel was a professional taste tester, employed by the manufacturer to help track down persistent problems with the flavor of its most popular brand of beer.

Arranged on the table were a large number of cans of beer, distinguished one from another only by large, black numbers scrawled on their sides with a marking pen. As they took their places, one of the men opened the first can of beer and poured equal amounts into glasses placed in front of each person. This process was performed for each can. All the beers distributed, the five people began sampling;

each sample was assigned a number between 1 and 8, and was evaluated for qualities including mouth feel, off notes, and metallic aftertaste.

The numbers were later analyzed in a search for statistically significant variations in the overall flavor of the beers. Ultimately, the manufacturer discovered that the problems were not being caused by brewing irregularities but by the can manufacturing process at a particular plant.

Investigating the Problem

With the discovery of a particular canning plant problem, the team switched its operations to examine the actual processes that occur during the manufacture of the cans. The taste testing was now used to determine which parts of the production line might be causing the problems with the final product. The tasters were instructed to search for flavors, or "notes," in the beer that would point to possible locations in the production process where flavor problems might be occurring. A metallic taste, for example, might indicate problems in the integrity of the plastic coating sprayed onto the interior of the cans, while a chemical taste might be related to improper washing of the cans prior to being filled with beverage.

Figure 1-2 shows a more detailed look at the canning plant, illustrating inputs and outputs for one of the canning lines.

On the canning line, the cans start as sheets of metal. Disks are cut from the metal and pressed into cans; the cans are washed, coated, and finally filled with the beverage. In addition to the sheet metal and beverage, principal raw materials include a coating applied to the inside of the cans and a wash mix that is used to clean the cans as they move down the line. Operators track the current status of the line and control the machinery. At various points along the line, samples are taken for delivery to trained inspectors. The final output is filled and sealed cans of beverage, ready to be shipped to customers.

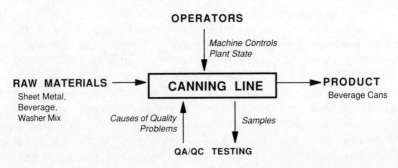

FIGURE 1-2. Operations of the canning line

Three major categories of quality-related problems were identified:

1. mechanical problems in the line, such as a washer becoming clogged

2. problems with the raw materials, such as the plastic can coating or the washer mix

3. operator errors

The taste team methodically investigated each of these problems. At each stage of the process, the team soaked the metal pieces in the beer and then tasted the beer. This process eventually led to a set of taste "signatures" assigned to different parts of the can manufacturing process. The study ended with a report that pointed to various places in the process where quality problems could occur because of failure of physical processes. The study was of particular interest to management, because the tasters had found several links between quality problems and marginal machine failure that had puzzled operators for some time. The report also created questions about how this new information would be disseminated to the operators.

Causal Links

A major problem confronting workers in any field is the lack of a good conceptual model for the functioning of the system with which they work. All too often, operators in a manufacturing system operate the plant through a control panel, with few visual links to the activities they are controlling. In a similar manner, office workers often are interpreting policies whose actual intent and implementation are unclear. Thus, our first indication that an expert system might be appropriate comes from the fact that the intermediate links between the symptoms of a problem and the problem's causes are not clearly evident.

In the plant, although many production-related problems were easily detected, it was often difficult for operators to link observations of quality problems to their cause. Through the work of the taste testers, a set of causal links was now identified. One aim of the plant-improvement project was to spread this knowledge to the operators, creating awareness of the relationship between quality problems and mechanical problems on the production line.

NEED FOR EXPERT-SYSTEMS TECHNOLOGY

Situations such as the one described above are common occurrences. A set of new information filled in gaps in the operators' model of connections between machine failure and poor quality. However, the application of new knowledge is not always so easily facilitated.

First of all, the actual "failures" in equipment (or policies or systems) are often combinations of degraded performance in several components and not the result of one obvious single failure. Second, these data are only a portion of a large volume of information on possible failures. Solutions for consistently providing usable information have been only somewhat successful in the past.

How do you know when you have a problem requiring an expert system? For that matter, how do you know you have a real expert available? There exist some fairly good guidelines for determining if an expert system is appropriate.

- Is a discrete unit of a business consistently outperforming all others (department, factory, branch office, etc.)? Is there a single, experienced person leading this effort?

- Are one or two individuals always sought out when a really tough problem crops up?

- Is the amount of information coming to the potential end-user of the system overwhelming? Is all of it needed at some time, but only small portions for any given problem?

There are many other criteria, of course. However, as you proceed through this application, try to think of our examples as analogies to types of problems—not exact blueprints for implementing your own application, but rather guidelines for addressing different situations, such as:

- fault diagnosis from sensor data

- solving quality-control problems

- building end-user interfaces for extracting data about a problem

- simulation and data collection/analysis

Very often, expert systems are proposed as one element of a larger project. The expert system proposed at the canning plant was part of a series of efforts to improve the quality of cans being produced at the plant. Expert systems introduced as components of larger systems have a much higher chance of success than those that are appended to systems already in place. They are more likely to succeed, because the expert system will be more fully integrated into the environment, both procedurally (e.g., integrated with maintenance scheduling) and mechanically (database links, sensor hookups, etc.).

Project Champion

How do expert systems come to be considered as a possible solution to a problem? Almost always there is a project champion, an individual who is willing to shepherd the expert system through management. While this is not too different from more traditional systems, all new technologies require an extra boost. This was true of mainframes when they were first introduced, even more true of time-shared systems when they began to challenge the batch systems, and particularly true of the introduction of personal computing. In our plant, one such individual recognized that several pieces of specialized knowledge existed in the heads of a few individuals. By sharing this information with every operator in the plant, a giant gain in quality consistency could be achieved.

Let's look at the team that will build and use the system. The expert-system building process is often thought of as having several major players:

- the project champion

- management

- the developer—you, the person who will build the expert system

- the expert(s)—the people with the domain knowledge

- the end-user—the person who will make use of a delivered system (perhaps a new operator or a less experienced plant engineer)

Of course, any one person might wear more than one hat. Conversely, there may be more than one person filling a single role (particularly that of end-user).

> Three years after the taste work was completed, while plans were being made to modernize the plant, the vice president of quality assurance/quality control realized that a new technology—expert systems—provided a possible solution to automating the information discovered during the taste-testing work. The parent corporation had developed a capability for building expert systems and would provide initial support for the project. First, however, the plant would need to do a reevaluation of the current QA/QC process, with specific recommendations on how an expert system for operators could be integrated into the plant.
>
> The vice president realized that a fair amount of up-front analysis would have to be done, including a justification for not using more traditional methods. Luckily, justification would not prove all that difficult because of the highly anecdotal nature of the information that would have to be integrated into the system. Even with corporate support, however, the project still needed a clear set of goals.

SYSTEM GOALS

From the start, the problems in building an expert advisory system are quite evident: a relatively untried technology (as is any technology with less than five to ten years of fielded applications), a still-developing method for implementation, and a high cost of entry in terms of the combined hardware, software, and required human resources.

The term "expert system" covers a wide range of techniques and paradigms that, taken together, offer users a new set of tools for tackling previously unmanageable problems. This approach allows us to capture and apply the expertise that has previously been the sole domain of an individual who has excelled in his or her field of endeavor.

Our goal, then, is to build a system that will enable the operators in our manufacturing plant to perform at a level of reliability equal to that of the plant's most skillful engineer and most experienced operator working in tandem. More realistically, we can only hope to capture some of the experts' skills for a very focused set of problems. Even this more modest goal, however, will result in unique capabilities for training less experienced operators as well as increasing performance consistency for all workers— even experts have bad days.

Project Rationale

Expert-systems technology has two target areas: jobs that are quite complex and require a high degree of skill, and jobs that are quite idiosyncratic and require a high degree of experience (of course many systems contain both of these elements, for example, the control room at a nuclear power plant). Academic education primarily prepares individuals for the theoretical aspects of their work, not the practical aspects. Similarly, vocational training instructs individuals in the normal operations performed on a job, but fails to teach the details unique to a particular job. Traditionally, no substitute for on-the-job experience has existed.

Expert systems provide a vehicle for training individuals to better perform their jobs by showing them on a daily basis how the experts perform. They also enable companies to preserve the expertise of those individuals (often described as "corporate jewels") who have excelled in manipulating their environments. The benefits of expert systems are thus threefold:

1. to preserve knowledge

2. to communicate that knowledge to less experienced employees

3. to apply that knowledge for more consistent and higher quality performance

Let's now look at how the decision to go forward unfolded at the canning plant.

Failure of Traditional Systems

Although operations at the plant were in general satisfactory, the taste team's analysis had pinpointed the fact that only the best operators were able to detect the more subtle nuances of early machine failure, and even the best operators had specialty areas that did not always overlap with others'. For new or less diligent operators, quality problems occurred because of marginal equipment failure undetectable by straightforward sensor data interpretation. Clearly, the consistency of the product could be enhanced by sharing expertise among all operators.

The problem, of course, was not so simple as writing yet another manual. The fault detection and repair manuals were not faulty in themselves, but rather were unable to capture in an easy-to-use form the complexities of the interaction among variations in operationa ɔarameters and quality problems. A simple relation such as a clogged washer nozzle leading to improper washing was easy to detect. However, a chain of events such as that shown in Figure 1-3 was a difficult relationship to recognize.

The problem of fault recognition would, of course, still be fairly simple if a fault were indicated any time a sensor showed an abnormal value. However, many tolerances in the plant could be exceeded without requiring corrective action— regularly scheduled maintenance could take care of it. In other cases, however, that same abnormality in conjunction with one or more similar slight abnormalities could lead to serious quality problems.

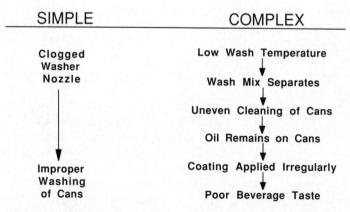

SIMPLE	COMPLEX
Clogged Washer Nozzle	Low Wash Temperature
↓	↓
	Wash Mix Separates
	↓
	Uneven Cleaning of Cans
	↓
	Oil Remains on Cans
	↓
Improper Washing of Cans	Coating Applied Irregularly
	↓
	Poor Beverage Taste

FIGURE 1-3. Comparison of a simple and a complex reasoning path

> NOTE: Interactions of insignificant abnormal conditions can result in a signifi-
> cant problem. Systems must have enough built-in intelligence to indicate a fail-
> ure only when the combination of abnormal conditions creates a significantly
> aberrant state.

The requirements of the system were beginning to come clear. First, the system should note slight abnormalities and compare them, using a set of heuristics, to any other existing abnormalities in the plant. Second, using all of this evidence, one or more hypotheses should be generated concerning possible actions to be taken. These might range from scheduling early maintenance to a full shutdown and repair. Finally, it would be nice if the system had the capability of providing the operator with detailed repair instructions for discovered problems. These could range from references to the proper operations manuals, to excerpts from these manuals, to an integrated text and video disc presentation showing in detail how to perform the indicated maintenance. Ultimately, the system was seen as an important potential contributor to the company's plant modernization plan. The system held the potential to integrate operations and maintenance by automatically collecting historical data on the plant's operations and using this information to anticipate problems before they occurred (Figure 1-4).

Let's summarize the goals:

- provide operators with notice of imminent mechanical problems requiring equipment maintenance or shutdown

- help isolate specific mechanical causes of poor beverage quality

- aid operators in repairing the problem

The system had two distinct but related roles in the plant's operation. First, the expert system would support the operators currently running the canning line by interpreting sensor readings taken from the plant's machinery. When a mechanical fault in the canning line was discovered, the system would identify all possible consequences to other canning line components and make recommendations for corrective action.

Second, the system would capture the senior operator's knowledge about identifying and correcting the causes of typical can-coating problems. The expert system, emulating this experienced operator, would begin with a suspected prob-lem, such as a bubbly can coating, and then work backward to isolate the cause. The knowledge extracted from the expert would be supplemented with the results discovered in the taste-testing work. Using starting conditions and the built-in expertise, the system could advise the operator on possible causes of the problem. This system would be integrated with the first part of the system—the sensor inter-pretations—to provide a unified diagnostic and fault correction system.

FIGURE 1-4. An expert system in the factory floor control room

The team was ready to go ahead and rebuild all major systems in the plant. At this point in the planning, top management called a temporary halt. While agreeing that the plans were quite laudable, and indeed, if successfully implemented, would greatly benefit the company, they pointed out that a phased development was desirable, so that each step could be carefully tested and evaluated before the next step was attempted.

In order to get the most benefit from the effort, and to ensure the continuity of the project, management requested that several different approaches be generated and evaluated. Each approach was to reflect a different aspect of the quality problem that the plant was currently experiencing.

SETTING APPLICATION CONTEXT:
TYPES OF EXPERT SYSTEMS

Before we continue, let's look at where our example system fits into a classification of expert systems. Two areas have been the primary foci of **expert systems development: analysis and synthesis (Figure 1-5).**

The example application used in this book will illustrate most of the approaches shown under the analysis category. We begin with a pure diagnosis

Figure 1-5   Problem Types for expert systems

Analysis	Diagnosis	determining problem causes
	Corrective Action	determining solutions to diagnosed problems
	Prediction	determining outcomes to situations
	Filtering	eliminating unimportant information
	Monitoring	tracking information and triggering responses
	Instruction	interpreting user actions and providing guidance
Synthesis	Scheduling	constraining the type and order of actions
	Design	configuring objects with constraints
	Planning	meeting goals and satisfying constraints

problem, and then, through the addition of new components and expansion of existing information, we look at aspects of filtering, repair, and prediction.

Most complex problems are actually modular in solution. That is, they are ultimately composed of integrated modules, each of which solves one of these problem types. For example, a system might have both a diagnostic module and a repair module that uses the information gathered by the diagnostic module. A simpler system might have just the diagnostic component; the repair would use conventional methods.

Although every project has unique aspects, once a need has been established, determining all possible options is necessary before a specific approach is elected. For example, in work that was done for a large transportation facility, a need for an expert system was determined and a team put together. The team was composed of a couple of the company's top operations people, a programmer experienced in conventional languages, and an individual with a Ph.D. in artificial intelligence. Unfortunately for the team, they quickly decided on an approach and began madly implementing, only to find, six months later, that the theoretical approach they had been implementing was not the only possible approach to solving the problem. In fact, their approach required resources far beyond the means of the project.

How does one generate alternatives and choose among them? As we have done in our example, you begin with a requirement for a system. Once a set of project goals has been set, you must determine what type of application you are building.

Identifying Alternative Problem-Solving Techniques

Typically, a single problem is composed of several sub-problems, each of which can be attacked using one of several types of approach. Ultimately, of course, several or all of the sub-problems may be addressed, but initially we wish to limit the scope of the problem by picking one approach and, if necessary, solving only those components of the problem for which this approach is appropriate.

Once we have identified the alternative approaches, we need to look at the type of strategy that approach will use. The choice of a strategy is dictated by a number of factors, including the *type of data* that will drive the system, the *reliability of the data*, and the *data and search space size* (the number of possibilities that the system must evaluate). The following table (Figure 1-6) illustrates each of these categories with references to systems that have solved the related problems. (Many of these solutions are worthy of a book in themselves; therefore, we have provided suggested readings in place of a detailed description of each technique).

Initially, these characteristics of the problem can be used to set bounds on the scope. For example, the simplest type of problem is one in which the solution is deterministic, the data and search spaces are small, the data are static, and the data reliability is high. These characteristics might be thought of as constraints—by relaxing the constraints one at a time, a realistic assessment of an approach can be made.

To determine which constraints will be relaxed, cost, resource, and risk factors can be assigned to these different characteristics of the problem. In this way, logical decisions can be made about which scenarios will be reasonable. For example, in the canning plant, we have varying types of data (ranging from operator observations to direct sensor input) with varying reliability. We also have a potentially huge data space. Clearly, using anecdotal operator observations requires the use of an expert operator, while using sensor data requires the use of an expert engineer. Here, the issues involved are which expert will be used in building the system and what are the required resources for testing (we'll need more operator input to test the anecdotal cases).

What we'll need to do is organize a structured approach that first assesses the categories our problem falls into and then sets priorities on those categories by assigning and evaluating criteria such as cost and risk.

The team then began generating a list of alternatives. Altogether, over twenty possible approaches and system types were considered. The alternatives that were seriously considered by the project planning team included:

- a system that would *monitor the operating history* of each plant component and attempt to detect, as early as possible, any mechanical problems that might affect production

- a system that would emulate the process used by the engineers in *planning the maintenance schedule*

Figure 1-6. Factors governing expert-systems strategy

Type of Data[a]	
Real-time monitoring	Continuous stream of data changing with time
Historical	Static data that will never change over time
Static	Data that may change but not within time frame of the reasoning process
Time-dependent	Data whose reliability changes with time
State-triggered	Data dependent on other data

[a] Solutions to the use of time-varying data include *situational calculus* (McCarthy and Hayes 1969), and *simulation* (Faught 1980; Payne 1985).

Reliability of Data[b]	
High	Usually the case where data can be verified
Medium	Often, the case for time-dependent data with moderately rapid changes over time
Low	Often the case where decisions must be made quickly, for example, monitoring or state triggered

[b] Solutions addressing data reliability include *certainty factors* (Shortliffe and Buchanan 1975), and *fuzzy logic* (Zadeh 1979).

Data and Search Space Size[c]	
Infinite	Must be bounded by sub-goals in the expert system
Very large	Must be bounded by sub-goals in the expert system
Large	Should be broken into smaller modules
Medium	Will require modularization in some cases
Small	May later be expanded as system grows

[c] Solutions to large search spaces include *reasoning by elimination, generate and test* (McDermott 1980), and *subproblems* (Sacerdoti 1974, 1975).

Solution Characteristics[d]	
Deterministic	A specific situation will always result in the same outcome
Stochastic	A specific situation may result in different outcomes at different times as a function of some random element

[d] Solutions to systems involving alternative outcomes include *what-if modeling* over a range of possible solutions (Rosenfield, et al. 1985).

- a system that would aid in *diagnosing the causes of quality-control problems* in the plant

- a system that would offer operators advice on *repair of faulty systems*

The approach chosen for the initial project would be determined based on a careful evaluation of all aspects of the project.

Approach Rationale

Eventually, it was decided to go ahead with a diagnostic system that would include some simple repair advice. It is useful to review the rationale behind the choice of diagnostics as the system's problem domain.

A system for early detection of mechanical problems in the plant would be based on the expertise of three groups—engineering, operations, and quality assurance—and include mechanics and engineers, several of whom were nearing retirement. The primary benefit of the system would be to substitute routine maintenance for emergency repairs that typically resulted in a shutdown of part or all of the production line. The system would anticipate developing problems, based on heuristics developed over the years by the most experienced operations personnel combined with information on previously unsuspected causal links between beer quality and marginally faulty mechanical components. As envisioned by the planning team, such a system would involve the complete computerization of all repair and maintenance records in the plant, which were then being stored on a bewildering variety of paper forms.

A system for helping with maintenance planning was also seriously considered by the project planning team. It was to be based on the experience of the plant's management and planning staff. The primary benefit of the system would be to decrease the time required for maintenance and emergency repair, but, it would also provide better scheduling of required and recommended maintenance needs. When this maintenance occurs, various equipment changes have to be made, as well as adjustments to other equipment on the plant floor, often requiring a shutdown of one or more production lines. Sequencing problems are common because of the need to calibrate different pieces of the production line independently during the maintenance process.

As for diagnosing quality-control problems in the plant, several domain areas were considered as candidates for the system:

- raw materials irregularities

- substandard equipment performance

- inconsistent operator calibration of operations parameters

The first two options were seen as direct causes of poor product quality in the plant. Moreover, it was believed that most of the low-quality batches could be traced directly either to raw materials that failed to meet specification or to poor performance of the plant's equipment during production. The third option for a diagnostic system, machine repair, was included largely because it seemed such a natural problem domain for an expert system in the canning plant.

SUMMARY

This chapter began by describing the case example that will be used throughout the book to illustrate issues of expert-systems design and implementation. Using this example, the believed needs for an expert system and the goals that the systems implementation must meet were discussed in the context of different expert-system problem solving strategies.

READINGS

Hayes-Roth, F., D. A. Waterman, and D. B. Lenat. 1983. *Building expert systems*. Reading, MA: Addison-Wesley.

Malin, J. T., and N. Lance. 1987. Processes in construction of failure management expert systems from device design information. *IEEE Transactions on Systems, Man, and Cybernetics*. SMC-17:956–967.

McCarthy, J. , and P. J. Hayes. 1969. Some philosophical problems from the standpoint of artificial intelligence. In *Machine Intelligence*, vol. 4, B. Meltzer and D. Michie, ed., 463–502, Edinburgh: Edinburgh University Press.

McDermott, J. 1980. R1: An expert in the Computer Systems Domain. *AAAI* 1:269–271.

Rosenfield, D. B., W. Copacino, and E. C. Payne. 1985. Logistics planning and evaluation using "what-if" simulation. *J. of Business Logistics* 6, No. 2:89–109.

Shortliffe, E. H., and B. G. Buchanan. 1975. A model of inexact reasoning in medicine. *Mathematical Biosciences* 23:351–379.

Winston, P. H. 1984. *Artificial Intelligence*. Reading, MA: Addison-Wesley.

Zadeh, L. A. 1965. Fuzzy sets. *Information and Control* 8:338–353.

Zadeh, L. A. 1979. A theory of approximate reasoning. In *Machine Intelligence*, vol. 9, ed. J. E. Hayes, D. Michie, and L. I. Mikulich. New York: John Wiley and Sons.

2

PLANNING THE PROJECT

E xpert systems develop through a series of steps:

- Discovery of a problem

- Evaluating alternative solution domains
    - scoping the system
    - identifying appropriate experts

- Choosing an implementation environment
    - designing the knowledge structures
    - extracting knowledge and formulating rules
    - prototyping
    - validation and extension
    - field testing

Before any type of computer implementation can begin, project assessment and design must be completed. This chapter begins by examining how alternative approaches can be identified and evaluated against a standard set of criteria. Once an approach has been chosen, the system's scope is defined as a function of the implementation team's experience and resources. Finally, we begin the project by identifying the expert(s) whose knowledge the system will encapsulate.

EVALUATING ALTERNATIVE SOLUTION DOMAINS

We've already looked at the different types and characteristics of expert systems. Using this information we were able to generate a set of distinct approaches to the generic problem of increasing quality in the plant. In this section, we'll look at how we can go about choosing among the different solution domains. To do this, we begin by defining a set of criteria on which the various approaches can be either quantitatively or qualitatively evaluated. We are of course starting with a big assumption—that a decision about the project has not already been made by top management, for reasons that have little to do with the intrinsic worth of the project. That assumption made, we are going to do our best to choose the single best option available.

How Are Criteria Chosen?

Two sets of criteria exist—standard measures that apply to almost all problems and measures particular to each individual project. The old standbys are predicated on measuring the size of the project: overall scope, budget, and required resources. Another set is used to determine the value of the project: cost savings or non-cost–related benefits. In addition to these, a number of other measures can be looked at: Risk level can be measured by a number of criteria, such as quality of the experts or the company's experience in doing similar projects. The success potential of the project is similar to risk, but takes into account more political factors, such as how critical top management's assessment will be. Finally, considerations must be made about resources available to the project—are the people available, is the hardware and expertise for using it available, etc.

What Makes Criteria Valid?

Once an initial list of criteria has been established, the criteria must be evaluated as to their actual relevance and validity for assessing the proposed project. The strongest measure of a criterion's relevance is the availability (and reliability) of data that support its use. For example, if availability of resources is a criterion, but you cannot get any managers to absolutely commit their people or hardware, then the relevance of that criterion is low. On the other hand, you do now have some data on the success potential of the project.

Are All Criteria Given Equal Weight?

While few people would argue that all criteria should be given equal weight, the weight they are given will often depend on the point of view of the evaluator. Someone who really desires to experiment with AI technology would weight potential risk quite low, reasoning that this is research and thus assumed to be risky. On the other hand, a high-level manager in this same company may feel that the department must show a success to be allowed to continue pursuing expert system implementation. To this individual, the lower the risk and higher the success potential, the better. The conclusion is that weights will vary for criteria, but the assignment of those weights may be somewhat arbitrary. The best path is to try and reach a consensus of all parties privy to the decision-making process.

Qualitative versus Quantitative

In any comparative study of this nature, a decision must be made as to whether quantitative or qualitative data will be used. Two major factors are involved here.

First, are quantitative data available? If a project like the one being contemplated has never been attempted, assigning real numbers to costs, risk factors, etc. can be difficult or impossible. Extrapolation from similar types of projects is of course possible, for example, previous software projects, but because of the many unique characteristics of building expert systems (such as the top experts' direct interaction with the implementation effort), historical information may be invalid.

Second, are quantitative values required? In most situations, it is more time consuming to apply quantitative values than qualitative ones. And often, when comparison of like objects is involved, qualitative values are just as valuable and accurate. In many cases, where different levels of decision makers are involved, assigning a risk level designated simply as "high" may be enough information when compared with a "low" risk problem. In other cases, of course, values such as "high cost" may be quite deceiving; for example, where the cost is negligible, the relatively high cost of one option may not be a significant comparison criterion.

Criteria for the Canning Plant

In choosing the project's problem domain, a set of criteria was developed with which to compare and contrast the various options. Because no project like this had been attempted at the plant, these criteria were not quantitative but rather were used as qualitative guides for comparing the different types of projects that had been discussed previously. Later, when more of these projects had been undertaken, quantitative data would be available. The criteria were defined so as to reflect a number of concerns in the company. The criteria and their related "ideal" scoring are summarized in Figure 2-1.

Notice that the criteria reflect several types of concerns: financial, risk-related, and future investment. The most obvious criterion is that of "Cost Savings": How much money will this system save, either in terms of reduced operational costs or increased production time? Ideally, one would like to simply add up the expected

FIGURE 2-1. Qualitative evaluation of project criteria

	High	Medium	Low
Scope		√	
Feasibility	√		
Budget		√	
Resources			√
Success Potential		√	
Expansibility	√		
Cost Savings	√		
Risk	√		

benefits, subtract the expected costs for each project option, and then choose the option that has the highest expected value. Unfortunately, nothing quite so simple is possible because of the uncertainties involved.

The company wished to find the project that most closely matched the scores shown in Figure 2-1. Because of the state of the technology being applied, no one doubted that this project would have fairly high risk. Any situation where off-the-shelf software is not available will always have an above-average risk of failure. However, to compensate for the risk, a relatively narrow initial scope was desired. At the same time, if the project was indeed a success, the company wished to avoid a mistake that had been made famous by a particular insurance company. The success there had been much greater than anyone had expected, and its management had faced the embarrassment of having to kill the project because no options had existed for expanding the system into a field-deployable version. Finally, the company wanted to pick a system that would provide a reasonable return. There was no sense in creating a successful system that did not provide some significant savings. These savings were called cost in the evaluation, but were not necessarily monetary. They also considered the slightly less tangible benefits of increased quality as measured by consistent flavor in the beverages.

Analyzing the Criteria

The criteria here are in no way unique to this problem, or even to this domain. Each problem will have some unique criteria, and scoring these criteria will always proceed in a distinctive way. In general, however, the criteria listed here are a good starting point.

First to be considered is the overall *scope* of the project—does the size of the chosen problem make sense? A standard rule heard over and over about the proper scope for an exploratory expert system is that the problem should take an expert from one to eight hours to solve. While this is not a hard-and-fast rule, the general idea is to pick a problem that can be bounded without losing meaning. If the problem is too small, the project will go nowhere. If the problem is too big and not modular, the system will never be completed. However, if the problem is a reasonable size, or a single module can be used as a starting point, then the scope is probably right. Evaluating what is "reasonable" will vary from project to project, but in general it will be a function of the available resources and the experience of the team.

Feasibility can be looked at in several different ways, both as a measure of the state of the technology as applied to the problem and as a measure of availability of know-how on possible development and implementation teams. For example, a project may in all ways look perfect, except that the computation time required to solve the problem is longer than the time in which an operator must make a decision.

Next is *budget*—how much does the project need and how much has been allocated? If these are not the same, can the project be reduced in scope and still be meaningful? Alternatively, if the scope cannot realistically be reduced, is there enough justification for the project to expand the budget? Rating this criterion is thus partially a measure of how much the project will cost in relation to what is available and partly a measure of how flexible the cost requirements for the project are.

Availability of resources includes both hardware and software for implementation and availability of individuals with expertise in the targeted areas. Traditionally, the development of an expert system has been contingent on the existence of at least one expert who performs a task significantly better than his or her peers. However, many initial systems must prove themselves conceptually before they are allowed the use of such valuable resources. Thus, part of the resource criterion is to pick a project where other resources can be combined so as to minimize the early-on need for the "best" engineer or operator.

With software projects, uncertainty translates into financial risk because of the dangers of schedule slippage and cost overruns. This represents a trade-off between potential cost savings and feasibility. Relatively easy implementation of software implicitly requires the use of known and proven techniques; if it can be deployed quickly, this implies that the system is relatively small and simple. If a good expert (or experts) is available, this will ease the knowledge engineering burdens.

These criteria should reflect a realistic caution within a project planning team concerning the team's ability to build and deploy the system in a timely fashion. Past experience with software projects shows that delays and unexpected difficulties are the norm rather than the exception. Seen in this light, each of the criteria above reflects a desire to minimize the cost penalty of a project failure.

The criteria of *expansibility* and *success potential* are more concerned with the project's long-term benefit to the company:

- Expansibility
    the ability of the expert system to be extended to meet all
        present and future challenges
    integration with existing systems

- Success Potential
    applicability to other domain choices
    political viability with other departments

If the system does not integrate well with the environment into which it will be installed, duplication of effort is certainly possible. On the other hand, if the techniques used can be re-used later, a good investment will have been made for the future. Finally, if other groups or, even worse, the target user group, has a high level of resistance to the project, then ultimate delivery and use will be infeasible no matter how successful the technical effort.

The Evaluation Process—Applying the Criteria

Let's now look at how three of the proposed approaches faired in the evaluation process. Note that the diagnosis problem was further split into two related but smaller options. The checks show the actual rating for the option being discussed, and the black dots indicate the ideal scoring when different.

Component monitoring

This option had acceptable ratings in only half of the categories. A major objection to this option was the potential delay in deployment while a new communications network was installed in the plant. The new network was part of the overall plant-improvement project, but would not be installed immediately. In addition, a new tracking system was being devised for the plant using conventional software technology. The decision was made to wait and see if the new tracking system would alleviate many of the problems that the expert system might have solved.

	High	Medium	Low
Scope		✓	
Feasibility	●	✓	
Budget		✓	
Resources			✓
Success Potential		✓	
Expansibility	●	✓	
Cost Savings		●	✓
Risk	✓	●	

Maintenance planning

The project planning team rejected this option because it was viewed as too risky for the inexperienced development team, given the uncertain financial benefits. In general, solving planning problems with expert systems technology was known to be relatively difficult. Moreover, it was not clear that the benefits would be clearly measurable after the system was finished and deployed, given the other changes that were being made in the way the plant operated. Measuring the benefits was important in any case, but especially so in a pilot program that was to aid in determining how far this new technology would be introduced into the company.

	High	Medium	Low
Scope		✓	
Feasibility	●		✓
Budget	✓	●	
Resources			✓
Success Potential		✓	
Expansibility	●	✓	
Cost Savings		●	✓
Risk	✓	●	

Diagnostics — raw materials analysis

This option rated close to the ideal scoring on every criterion except one: feasibility. It was impossible to evaluate the availability of expertise, because the people who knew the most about such analysis were constantly traveling about the country to the company's various plants. Although there was local expertise available, it would have to be supplemented by knowledge gathered elsewhere, and the ease of obtaining sufficient access to that additional expertise could not be evaluated.

	High	Medium	Low
Scope		√	
Feasibility	●		√
Budget		√	
Resources			√
Success Potential		√	
Expansibility	√		
Cost Savings	√		
Risk	√	●	

Diagnostics — substandard equipment performance

This option also rated close to the ideal scoring on every criterion. However, this option also did not appear to be feasible. Integration with other plant-improvement activities was felt to be quite risky, because it was believed that changes in the plant's operation could change the way this particular system would be deployed. In particular, because of changes in the responsibilities of plant personnel, it was not clear whether the system's users would be the plant's QC personnel or the plant's line operators. (See Table on the following page.)

Eventually, the decision was made to go ahead with the last option—an expert system to diagnose quality-control problems caused by substandard performance of the plant's mechanical components. Even though organizational changes might occur after commencement of the project, it appeared that the underlying knowledge base would be unaffected, and superficial changes could be incorporated into the software in sufficient time to avoid a delay in the system's deployment. Details of the presentation of information to the user would be different, of course, but the basic expertise being captured would remain the same in either case.

	High	Medium	Low
Scope		√	
Feasibility	●		√
Budget		√	
Resources			√
Success Potential		√	
Expansibility	√		
Cost Savings		√	
Risk	√	●	

SETTING PROBLEM SCOPE

How is scope set? This is the hardest part of every software project because of the impossibility of predicting where problems will occur. Thus, too large a scope is often chosen, often with disastrous consequences, such as when unexpected problem nuances create larger than planned demands on resources and funds.

Another benefit of setting the proper scope is better design. If a problem has been properly analyzed and appropriate boundaries set, the resulting system should be representative of a larger system. The prototype will then provide a strong starting platform for later expansion.

Setting the problem scope consists of several steps:

1. *Ensure that the problem can be bounded.* Some problems are intractable with the resources that are available. For example, the computational power of the development environment may be inadequate for certain types of search problems. In other cases, too many situations must be addressed to have any meaningful solution in a reduced scope. This has often been the case with medical diagnosis systems.

2. *Decompose the problem into modules.* This is the approach of choice if a small problem cannot be chosen. Instead of trying to do an incomplete portion of the whole, it is preferable to divide the problem into smaller, stand-alone segments that can be implemented individually. Then, if the project is to continue, the individual modules can be integrated to form a larger system. Even if the whole project is to be done, this is a desirable approach because the smaller modules are easier to debug and maintain.

3. *Choose only those modules that form a representative set for the problem.*
    Even if the problem can be reduced to a set of modules, the tempta-
    tion is often to try implementing too many of these simultaneously.
    Usually implementing two or three will provide the proof that they
    can be integrated.

4. *Decompose chosen modules into physical components* and choose only
    those components that form a representative set for solving the
    problem within that module. Within each module further reduc-
    tion of scope can often be achieved. In the plant example, we do
    not need to represent all of the canning lines or even all of a single
    canning line—representing just those interconnected portions that
    affect the quality control aspects of can production will be enough.
    For example, we do not need to examine all of the electrical con-
    nections on the line.

5. Finally, after going through these steps, *evaluate how far the problem
    has been reduced*. A significant size reduction indicates a well-chosen
    problem. The chosen information, once implemented, will form a
    robust framework from which the system can, if successful, be
    expanded. Also, the success of this initial prototype should be
    representative of how the full-blown system will fair if a truly
    representative sample has been selected.

Once the problem domain had been chosen, the next step for the project team
was to define the precise scope of the project. Although the overall subject matter
(mechanically-based quality control problems) had been chosen, the team had yet
to narrow down the system as to:

• which quality-control problems would be analyzed

• which machines would be included

The plant was simply too complex, and the number of QC problems too large,
to include them all.

Identifying the Problem Domain: Pumps and Sprayers

It was decided that the initial focus would be on problems associated with pumps
and spraying devices. The plant possessed a wide variety of different pumps, most
of which were rather old and cantankerous. Many of the pumps were vital to
the plant's operation, because they provided pressure to mainline components.
The failure of many of these mainline components could then cause the entire
production line to be shut down.

In addition, most pump-related problems were relatively easy to identify and repair. This relative simplicity also attracted the project team to making pump-related problems the major focus of the system.

Identifying Problem Focus: Flavor Off-Notes

Identifying which QC problems would be tackled was somewhat more difficult. Many of the mechanical QC problems were either too easy to diagnose (such as leaks caused by a poor seal) or were only indirectly related to mechanical difficulties (such as foaming in a wash tank caused by a bad batch of wash solution).

In the end, it was decided that the main focus should be on oily and soapy residues in the cans. Unpleasant off-notes in the packaged beverage flavor had been traced to these residues by the taste team and constituted a continuing problem. Once this particular QC problem had been solved using the expert system, it could then be extended to other, similar QC problems faced by the canning plant.

Narrowing the subject matter was only one small part of determining the scope of the system, however. The project team felt that many potential difficulties could be forestalled by being much more precise about describing exactly what the initial version of the system should do. In particular, this description focused on two related sets of questions:

1. Given that the system will undergo an evolution from simple to more complex as the project goes along, what are the functions and goals for the system at each stage of its development?

2. Again for the various stages of the system's development, what would be a typical usage scenario at each stage?

The project team agreed that if these two sets of questions could be answered before work commenced, even if only partially, there would be much less danger of the project getting out of control or experiencing delays and cost overruns.

IDENTIFYING EXPERTS

Once you have decided on the domain for the expert system, it is time to identify the most appropriate experts. Some of the process described here will no doubt take place during the feasibility evaluation, so this is something of an iterative process.

Identification of experts can sometimes be simple; many fields have a small number of people who are clearly world-class experts, with skills far above the normal practicioner. In a similar fashion, many companies have a few individuals who stand out above all the other employees in some aspect of their work. However, in many cases, choosing the expert is a difficult task. Several reasons for this come to mind:

- The task may require expertise in more than one area—a single "expert" may not exist, particularly if the problem is in a new area such as factory automation.

- No outstanding expert may be available, at least in the early phases of the project. Thus one or more individuals must be chosen to play the expert role.

- Choosing one expert over another may be a very touchy subject, especially if the chosen expert is lower than the other (organizationally) or has lower status in some way (operator vs. engineer, foreman vs. manager, etc.).

- The expert must have not only ability but also a willingness to communicate that ability.

Domain Expertise

A critical part of an expert system project is, logically enough, the identification of the expert or experts who will provide information on manipulation of the domain. Let's look first, however, at the requirement for general knowledge about the domain.

An important distinction must be made here. To build the system, we will need to have a thorough knowledge of the domain itself, **declarative knowledge.** For this we indeed need expertise, but in most cases not the expertise of our expert. If the expert is truly expert, he or she will be a valued resource whose time is quite valuable. Thus, we don't wish to occupy that person's time if the information we need can be obtained from another source.

Once an expert has been identified, we must find one or more individuals with declarative or **domain expertise**—not the traditional expertise in expert system building, but equally important. Such a person or persons can supply us with the jargon and background information that the expert will assume we know.

Background knowledge about the domain will serve as a foundation for our expert's **procedural knowledge**—the expertise on how to identify problems and fix them. The individuals with knowledge about the general domain of the plant will provide us with the background information that we need both to become intelligent interrogators of the expert and to construct whatever models of the actual domain are required to support the expert's rules.

Experts themselves come in two basic flavors: the expert with deep **theoretical knowledge**, extensive education, and practical—but usually high-level—experience; and the expert with primarily apprentice-style training, little formal education, but many years of **practical, hands-on experience**. Examples of this contrast in type of expertise may be seen by comparing the plant engineer with the plant operator or an architect with an experienced construction supervisor. Depending on the type of system being implemented, one or both of these individuals may be required. As we will see, conflicts between these two types of expertise often arise. The knowledge engineering problems are also different for the two situations.

A special case exists: Knowledge engineers are sometimes experts in their own right. On occasion, the knowledge engineer will have experience in the domain itself, as is the case where an expert is the initiator of a project and also takes on the role of both expert and knowledge engineer. While a dual role may seem ideal, such a situation is actually fraught with problems, lack of perspective being the major one. However, more commonly, the knowledge engineer will need to learn the basic terminology of the domain as well as specifics of the environment around which the expert system is to be built.

Characteristics of the Expert

Most often the process of identifying candidates for the position of expert occurs during the project assessment phase. Several criteria are applied during this selection process. First, an expert should be able to perform in a way that stands out from the norm. Second, an expert should bring personal motivation to the project. People's feelings about this vary, but most people seem more than willing to take on the title of expert. If they are the best, these types of projects are certainly no threat to their own jobs.

Sometimes, in situations where there is some overlap of talents, several possible experts exist. Sometimes the best expert is not available. A second set of criteria can now be applied to reduce this selection. These include:

- an evaluation of the person's ability to communicate what they know—perhaps an ability to work with abstract concepts (This is important because it will speed the project to have an expert who can quickly learn to interpret the information that is put into the computer.)

- orientation (Can this person's experience be brought to bear in solving the problems that will be faced by the system's users?)

- granularity of knowledge (Does the level of detail at which this expert works correspond to that of the users?

- a familiarity with computers or a willingness to learn (While not critical, computer friendliness will greatly accelerate the process, particularly in the areas of review and editing of the unfolding system.)

We let on earlier that we were going to use two different experts, an engineer with expertise in mechanical failure and an operator with expertise on identifying quality problems. These decisions are not usually very clear, however, until the actual selection process begins. And even with a careful plan of action, the politics of the situation must be taken into account. Let's see what occurred in the selection process at our plant, starting with the first hurdle, management.

Dealing with Management

Choosing an expert for the project team at the canning plant was complicated. In the beginning, we required an understanding of the plant's operation that was as broadly-based as possible. This entailed interviewing over a dozen individuals in various parts of the plant, ranging from line operators to foremen. In addition, spending considerable time with plant management was absolutely essential to understanding the business implications of the completed system.

The importance of the time spent with plant management personnel cannot be overestimated, because they provided the project with a mission and sense of direction. Most of the discussions with management concerned the planning and delineation of the project: what the problem domain of the system would be, who should and should not be involved, and so forth.

In a very real sense, our first knowledge engineering task was to understand the problems faced by plant management in sufficient detail for us to delineate and plan the project. Many expert system projects are doomed to failure because they do not pay enough attention to the concerns of management and therefore attempt to solve the wrong problem.

Many Experts

Even after the project was launched (with management's blessing), and after two individuals had been chosen as the project's official experts, we were still forced to spend considerable time with other individuals in the plant. Part of this time was needed for practical reasons: We were still unfamiliar with many aspects of the plant's operation, and we wanted to make sure that we had a reasonably good grasp on how things worked.

Much of this time, however, was needed for political and psychological reasons. First, we felt it was important to meet and talk with as many people in the plant as possible. Second, we wanted people to feel involved in the project and to feel that their opinions were valued. Third, we wanted to mollify those individuals who were *not* chosen as project experts.

By speaking with a wide range of individuals throughout the plant, several things were accomplished:

- Nearly everyone understood precisely what we were trying to accomplish by building the system.

- People grew accustomed to our presence at the plant.

- We made people feel that they were part of the project team, even though they were unable to contribute in a technical sense.

Many of these people later went out of their way to help us. Toward the end of the project, their support was crucial in convincing management that the system should be deployed in the plant.

Expert Selection Process

For diagnosing mechanical causes of QC problems, there was not too much difficulty identifying the candidate experts. The possible choices for appropriate experts were quickly reduced to the following individuals:

- Nancy, a highly trained engineer responsible for nearly all of the analytical tools used by the QC staff

- George, the most experienced of all the QC staff, who has limited education and analytical skills

- Frank, the head foreman in charge of overall line operations

Expertise is not always the sole factor in choosing the expert. The issues mentioned previously, such as availability and the ability to work easily with others, also play a factor (see Figure 2-2). As we will see, composite experts must also sometimes be constructed; that is, we must sometimes use several experts for complementary parts of the knowledge domain.

FIGURE 2-2. Evaluating the experts

	Nancy	George
Knowledge Source	Theoretical	Practical
Quality Control Techniques	Analytical	Intuitive
Computer Literate?	Yes	No

Of the three, Frank was the most desirable expert, because of his intimate familiarity with almost all details of the plant's operation. Moreover, Frank possessed good analytical skills and was not afraid of using a computer. Unfortunately, Frank's time was too limited to allow his participation in the project except in a review and advisory capacity.

That left Nancy and George. Nancy's theoretical knowledge of how QC problems arose was seen as important. She had already solved a few QC-related mysteries that had stumped all of the other available experts, including George. Also, she was comfortable around computers–not that she had any programming skills as such, but she had worked with them in the past and understood to some degree the inherent requirements for structure when using them. The main drawback to using Nancy as the primary expert was that she was seen as a little too impractical. Her exacting intellectual standards, while appropriate to her job, were seen as a detriment to the timely completion of the project.

George was ideal from a number of standpoints. Like Frank, George was familiar with virtually every detail of the plant's operation. He had come up through the plant organization the hard way, having started some 20 years before as a line operator. In addition, George had been directly involved in tracking down almost every kind of QC problem observed in the plant, and he had personally repaired most of the plant's equipment at one time or another. In fact, George's expertise was somewhat legendary; it was said that he could identify the causes of most QC problems simply by sniffing the contents of a beverage sample, even while eating a pastrami sandwich!

The difficulty with using George as the primary expert was his lack of analytical skills. George had never tried to organize what he knew and was uncomfortable with the use of computers. He was also a little cantankerous, especially if he felt people were looking down on him because of his lack of education. Ultimately, it was decided that the project team would somehow have to codify the expertise of both Nancy and George. It seemed impossible to ignore one and use only the skills of the other.

NOTE: The use of multiple experts is quite common when building diagnostic systems. It often turns out that there are individuals whose skills roughly correspond to those of Nancy and George: one an analytically minded trained practitioner and the other an experienced, relatively uneducated veteran. Nearly as often, it turns out to be difficult to build a useful system by using the expertise of only one type of individual.

To minimize the difficulties associated with involving both Nancy and George, the project team decided to split their responsibilities so that Nancy was responsible for formulating any logic that required numerical observations, such as those for temperature and pressure. George, on the other hand, was responsible for logic that involved qualitative observations such as smell and sound. In this way, it was hoped, the knowledge of the two experts could be cleanly separated, minimizing any disagreements that might arise in the future.

STAGES OF EXPERT SYSTEMS DEVELOPMENT

We previously discussed the political beginnings of an expert system project. In this section, we will examine the phases for the implementation of the system on a computer. Our first expert is a plant engineer. In the first phase of a project, the expert's knowledge typically is represented by rules captured almost word for word the way the expert speaks them. Although this format is ultimately not the most efficient or clear representation of the expert's knowledge, we initially wish to minimize the "computerese" in the system. Later we will write these same rules more formally, providing more speed and power (and ultimately more clarity, though first the engineer will need to become familiar with this form of representation).

Phase I

Expert systems are commonly implemented in a series of phases, each phase modifying and refining the work done in the previous phase. In Figure 2-3 we see the components involved in building Phase I of the prototype for a diagnostic system. In this first phase, we start with a single expert— in this example the engineer—whose expertise comprises faults that occur when various plant sensors register abnormal conditions. The outputs of the finished Phase I system are reports identifying faulty components and

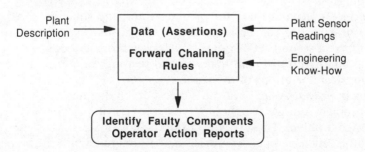

FIGURE 2-3. Phase I of the expert system implementation

recommending corrective actions. When the initial Phase 1 implementation is complete, we will have both a representation of the plant domain and a description of how the expert interprets and manipulates that domain.

In this phase we first implement the engineering knowledge. The knowledge of how to interpret incoming data on potential problems is represented in the expert system by **rules** describing how things work "in the expert's own words." This knowledge is **procedural knowledge**. Procedural knowledge is often accessed subconsciously; when asked how they accomplish a task, experts believe that they "just know how to do it." **Knowledge engineering** is the process of making this knowledge available in a form that can be interpreted by a computer. Thus, when an operator suddenly changes the temperature in a mixing vat, the knowledge engineer must translate this action into rules such as "IF bubbles are forming on the surface of the vat and the pressure in the vat is rising, THEN lower the temperature of the vat."

The information about the domain is implemented after the initial interviews with the expert. Such information about the physical aspects of the world, previously defined as the declarative knowledge: "Stamping machines break down on average every 500 hours"; "automobile accident claims are reported on form number A4407X"; "sensor 43 is directly connected to a thermometer in the switching relay power supply," and so on.

The combination of procedural and declarative knowledge makes up the **knowledge base**. The third component of the system is the changing state of the domain. As conditions change, attributes of the data change, and these changes invoke the expert rules. In the plant, sensor 43 may suddenly indicate a change in temperature, in turn triggering one or more rules. If the temperature has indeed moved to an abnormal state, then more rules will be invoked, leading, it is hoped, to a conclusion similar to the one that the expert would make on the cause and remedy of the problem.

Phase II

As we progress with the knowledge engineering in Phase II (Figure 2-4), we introduce a second expert, the plant operator, and show how this second category of expertise can be integrated into our first expert's information. We now have a second set of rules, which uses the operator's experience in detecting quality problems in the cans and relating these back to problems in the physical operations of the plant.

Our improved system now aids operators in diagnosing the cause of a quality problem, but we also would like to provide advice on how to remedy the detected problem. Thus, we next examine how materials commonly used by operators, such as repair manuals, can be integrated into the system. The changes in this second phase include: the inclusion of an additional expert's

Phase II

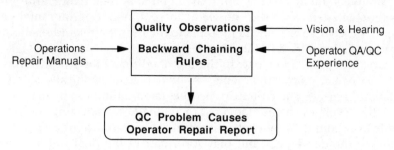

FIGURE 2-4. Phase II of the expert system implementation

knowledge, the expansion of the prototype to include more inputs about the plant's state, and the integration of external reference materials.

Phase III

In Phase III, we examine the development of several sophisticated tools that aid development, testing, and maintenance. We develop an editor to aid in system modification and extension, and simulation capabilities to test the expert rules (Figure 2-5).

Construction of an editor is an inevitable task once a system reaches a certain size. Editors are tools that perform two functions: They maintain consistency when changes must be made to the knowledge base by providing visible constraints and warning messages, and they facilitate the development process by automatically performing many "bookkeeping" tasks when a change is made. For example, take the case of a large system to which the

Phase III

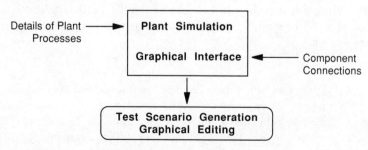

FIGURE 2-5. Phase III of the expert system implementation

user wishes to add a new rule. An editor might check to see that the actor (for example, a pump) and action (having an abnormal temperature) of the rule were both defined in the knowledge base. If not, the editor might either disallow the change or provide prompts to the user that would result in new definitions being added to the knowledge base.

Graphics plays a key part in the use of editors. Flows of materials and relationships between components can be depicted graphically using icons and labeled arrows. The editor can be integrated with these displays in such a way that changes to the domain can be made by selecting and moving graphic icons and their labeled connectors. This graphical interface is useful not just to the developers, but may form part of the final interface. In the plant, a schematic of machines and materials flows can be represented to permit operators to query or update plant components. In a process control environment, schematics can show conceptual models of valves opening, pipes and tanks filling, and temperatures and pressures changing.

These active, graphical models can be made more dynamic with the addition of simulation capabilities. Simulation becomes important when you must test a large expert system, and allows modeling of changes in the domain. Integrating these models with the expert rules and frames provides a capability to automatically generate test scenarios useful for validating the rules.

Such a sophisticated test environment may initially seem to be unnecessary. However, the plant used in this example is relatively simple compared to most processing plants, and the example plant is a greatly simplified version of the actual plant after which it was modeled. Building an expert system representing a very large domain requires sophisticated tools merely to perform consistent testing and validation.

GETTING STARTED

Because of their relative inexperience, the team decided on a two-pronged approach. While one member of the team began the hardware/software evaluation process, other members would initiate preliminary working sessions with the experts.

A great deal of time would be spent with both Nancy and George during the course of the project. We began by thoroughly exploring the plant with Nancy and George, including both the production line as well as the QC laboratory, which is situated adjacent to the line. We had visited the plant on a number of occasions and had even received an official guided tour. Nevertheless, we had never taken the time to gain a detailed understanding of the plant's operation, nor had we ever been able to witness the QC operation for a sustained length of time. More importantly, however, we wanted to get the views of Nancy and George. By going through the plant together, we had a common ground of experience that we could refer back to again and again later, when discussing some particular aspect of the plant's operation.

As we will see later, during the system's development we were forced to devise two different styles for working with our two experts. Broadly speaking, Nancy was much more insistent on seeing immediate results, often wanting to see what we had done with her expertise before we had even decided how to represent it! George, on the other hand, was much more willing to suspend judgment and accept our vaguely worded descriptions of how we were going to capture the information he had given us.

In actual practice, when working with Nancy, we built numerous small prototypes to demonstrate what we were doing. We also concentrated on writing rules and procedures that were easier to read and understand, but somewhat more difficult to program. As the project wore on, we grew to resent Nancy's insistence on being shown prototypes that she could understand. In retrospect, however, we saw it as beneficial, because it focused our attention and forced us to think more carefully about exactly what was being put into the machine.

As it turns out, Nancy had simply believed what she had been told about rapid prototyping and the nature of expert systems in general. In fact, she was basing her expectations on many of the same arguments used to convince top management that an expert system should be built. We could, therefore, hardly afford to disappoint her.

SUMMARY

This chapter establishes a plan for evaluating and implementing the expert system. Using the goals established in the previous chapter, a set of criteria for evaluating alternative approaches to a perceived problem is developed and tested. Using the results of this evaluation, a general approach to the problem is chosen and a set of tools for setting (limiting) the scope of the project is developed. All of this information is then consolidated in a master plan outlining the expert system stages of development, stating major inputs, outputs, and implementation sequences.

3

TRANSLATION OF EXPERTISE INTO THE COMPUTER

How do we make the transition from information in the head of our expert to information stored in the computer? This chapter provides an overview of the process of placing the expert's knowledge into the various software environments currently available for developing expert systems. The process consists of two parts: extracting knowledge from the expert and then capturing that knowledge in the computer.

We begin with an examination of how the knowledge of the expert will be extracted and translated into these development environments. We can then assess the software tools we will need for computerizing the information, examining the desirable—and not so desirable—features to be found in the various expert system development environments.

KNOWLEDGE ACQUISITION

This section addresses the first half of the process—extracting the knowledge from the expert. In the classical description of building an expert system, a single knowledge engineer sits with a single expert, thrashing out the subject matter until it is well understood. The knowledge engineer then builds the system, with the expert acting as a frequent and substantive reviewer.

This description, unfortunately, has very little to do with the real world. First of all, very few real-world systems are so small that they can be designed and built by a single knowledge engineer; software systems are simply too complex to be handled by one individual. Second, it is seldom the case that a single expert can provide all the required information for the system; if nothing else, the political realities of a work situation will prevent this, with each group wishing some representation on the project.

The knowledge acquisition process can proceed in two ways. The most desirable is for the expert to take an interest in the process and actually become somewhat familiar with the computer interface. In this situation, the process of learning each other's terminology will proceed quickly, and the expert can take an active part in debugging the system from the very start. Such an active role has the advantage of quick turnaround; in addition, an expert who is directly involved is more likely to buy into the process of building the system. The other situation is where the expert is either unwilling or unable because of time constraints to take an active role. In this case, there is less need to have an interface he or she can relate to at the start. However, the process will progress more slowly and may get into trouble, because mistakes made in interpreting the expert's statements will be slower to surface.

The knowledge extraction process, once an expert has been identified, is a combination of **interviews**, on-site **observation of the expert at work**, and **evaluation of the materials** used by the expert. At the end of each session, the knowledge engineer must structure the information collected, update the prototype, and then review the result with the expert.

Interviewing

Several techniques and resources are used in the interviewing process. At times, a one-on-one technique can be the most effective, particularly in situations where the primary purpose is review. Also useful is for one person to ask questions while another makes notes and observes the expert's actions. Information may be gathered using **interviews** (asking the expert questions), or using **observations**, observing the expert at work with only occasional (minimal) interruptions to clarify what is happening.

While much of this process is straightforward observation, the knowledge engineer must be careful not to let information gathered in interviews influence observation of how the expert actually works. Most experts when interviewed tend to present a somewhat theoretical or idealized view of the process in which they are engaged. This idealization of the process occurs for two reasons. First, many actions that experts take are at least partially automatic, more reactions to stimuli than the results of explicit plans. Second, most people like to think of their work in a certain light, and this can color how they present information. Particularly in situations where at least one other participant has expertise in the area being discussed, the expert may be inclined to phrase the information in more abstract terms, with the unfortunate consequence that the information gathered is obscure or too general to be transformed into guiding heuristics.

This second point is an important consideration when interviewing multiple experts. Often, separate interviews are advisable, particularly when the two experts are at different levels in the company hierarchy. For example, an engineer with a Ph.D. may be quite intimidating to a line operator, even though the operator's practical experience can be of much greater value than the engineer's theoretical knowledge. Company politics can increase the problem by pairing a theoretician with a self-trained practitioner on the theory that the theoretician will review the practitioner's knowledge for "correctness." In these types of situations, the best solution is to rely heavily on observations of the experts actually performing the tasks they are describing.

In cases where the expert's work is conducted on-site, it will be necessary to conduct interviews at those sites. Having the expert perform a task for the sake of the interview will not work; you must observe the real process. Although a performance is useful, more likely than not it will still be colored by the expert's preconceptions of what the knowledge engineer wishes to see, obscuring the details of how the task is actually performed in a normal work situation.

Initially, the interviews should be purely information gathering, helping the participants to become comfortable with each other's jargon. Very quickly, however, the expert must be focused onto the specific problem being addressed. Otherwise, the project runs the risk of being lost in the black hole of the expert's infinite knowledge, most of which will not be relevant to the project. Too much focusing has one down side: often, information must be gathered that neither the expert nor the knowledge engineer realizes is needed; this provides another good reason for watching the expert at work.

NOTE: We must learn the expert's jargon and become familiar with the domain. But the expert must also learn a little about knowledge representation. A very typical reaction of experts involved in this process occurs in three stages: exhaustion; anger and frustration; and a dawning awareness of their own thought processes. This last stage of the process leaves most experts with a very positive outlook on the experience. Invariably, they come to comprehend knowledge they had never explicitly formulated.

This aspect of the job is probably the most confusing part of the process for the knowledge engineer—quickly learning enough about the domain to recognize when the expert is straying beyond the scope of the project. Prior review of general material on the domain and observation of the expert working are the surest ways to quickly gain this knowledge.

Another method of gaining a handle on how experts work is a detailed examination of the informational materials they use. These are both good indicators of their work style and valuable clues and sources of information about the material that should be included in the expert system. These materials take the form of manuals, textbooks, computer printouts, schematic diagrams, memos, etc.

In George's office we found over a dozen manuals describing the operation of particular pieces of machinery in the plant: pumps, washers, and so forth. Sections of these manuals were obviously well used, with inserts and page corners turned down. George's office also had several schematic diagrams taped onto the walls that depicted the layout of different sections of the production line. These diagrams had been marked up with a bewildering variety of circles, arrows, and hastily scrawled comments. In addition, one entire corner of George's office was devoted to a large stack of computer printouts that were generated every time a major line shutdown occurred.

The contents of Nancy's office were quite different. For one thing, a large bookcase, taking up one entire wall, contained textbooks, research articles, technical memoranda, and computer manuals. A boxed-off section of Nancy's white board contained a set of unreadable equations; otherwise, the board had been neatly erased (as we later found out, for our benefit). Finally, there was a stack of graphical and tabular output that contained the results of a simulation model Nancy had used recently.

The complexity and volume of material that we found was overwhelming. Clearly, we would have to prioritize where to start and what to concentrate on.

The **equipment** used in the interviewing process can include both video and tape recorders. These have the advantage that no single word or action is missed. The problem is, of course, that no single word or action is missed; a tape must be transcribed and a video logged and then the large volumes of material analyzed for useful information. The percentage of useful material additional to what you already have from the interview is small in general compared to the cost in time and money for this process. The exception is situations where the expert is imparting large quantities of detailed information—often at the beginning of the project, when everything is quite unfamiliar to the knowledge engineer. Later interviews seldom make use of this equipment.

After each interview, the knowledge engineer must determine the validity of the information that has been gathered. Three potential problems exist with the expert's information: experts may make a careless mistake while performing a task during observation; say things they didn't mean; and sometimes, even though they are experts, do the wrong thing because their own knowledge is faulty. In addition, the interviewer may misinterpret the expert, for example, because of a misinterpretation of the terminology. Situations such as these illustrate the need for the expert—and one or more peers, if possible—to continually review the work.

> The initial interviews with the experts were intended to provide the team with a feeling for the scope of the project and at the same time provide the experts with an overview of what would be happening over the ensuing weeks. By the end of the initial meetings, both George and Nancy had a good feel for the materials the team would need and the requirements for their time. They were also able to refer the interviewers to supporting material and individuals who could provide basic background knowledge.
>
> While part of the team completed the preliminary interviews with the experts, the investigation of tools that would be used to implement the expert system on the computer was begun.

EXPERT SYSTEMS USER REQUIREMENTS

We begin our assessment of software tools and hardware by evaluating the requirements of two audiences: the developer and the end user. Three questions relating to these audiences come to mind:

1. Does the development environment make it easy to create and modify the expert system?

2. Can the development environment also be used for delivery?

3. Does the delivered system provide an environment that facilitates understanding and access for the end user at the required cost and performance?

In most situations, from a developer's point of view, the more tools and resources the better. For delivery, in situations where the system will be delivered on a single machine (or a very small number or machines), the high-priced hardware and software typically used in development may be appropriate. However, when systems will be used by many users, the development environment's cost and power may be undesirable. None of the large, commercially available shells currently has a low-priced delivery option available—in every case, the hardware requirements (particularly the amount of memory required) exceed the cost reasonable to expect when placing a system on hundreds of desk tops.

We'll explore the preceding questions by briefly describing a shell environment, defining the needs of the three user audiences, and then looking in detail at the available tools and their application to knowledge engineering. This examination will include sets of criteria for judging and choosing among the various development environments.

Expert System Overview

An expert system comprises three parts:

- facts
- rules
- inference engine

The facts describe aspects of the domain, for example, that a wash pump has a temperature of hot or that the wash pump is connected to the washer. Rules describe what an expert might do with these facts, for example, "If the wash pump is hot, then shut down the wash pump." In the same way in which humans infer the solution to a problem based on available facts and previous experience in dealing with a similar problem, the inference engine combines rules and facts in the knowledge base to reach a conclusion (Figure 3-1).

All of the commercial shells supply an inference engine and a facility for building a knowledge base. In the less expensive shells, the facts are usually represented quite simply, whereas the high-end shells all have a structured method for representing facts (Chapter 5 will discuss in detail this mechanism for representing facts and domain objects).

What we will look for in an expert system shell is support for both developers and end users, including: a good mechanism for representing

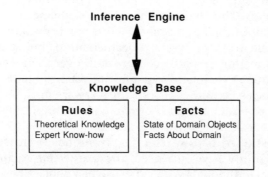

FIGURE 3-1. The components of an expert system

and integrating rules and facts; development support in the form of user interfaces for creating rules and facts; and tools for testing and debugging the developing application.

Developers

Developers range from very experienced programmers, to skilled knowledge engineers with nominal programming skills, to experts with little computer experience wishing to implement their knowledge. While one individual may have all of these skills—expertise in a domain, abstract representation abilities, and programming experience—a more likely scenario is the formation of a team with a combination of these skills. Most of the shells provide facilities for nonprogramming knowledge engineers to build systems, but we have found that sooner or later a programmer will need to be consulted on any large, complex system.

Experienced users include AI R&D groups and line-operations groups that have been working with AI tools for at least a year. All of these users will have within their group individuals with a combined experience in programming, AI knowledge representation, and implementation of at least one AI system.

The requirements of experienced users are for a tool that contains a number of paradigms, what is often called a **hybrid tool**. An important aspect of such a tool is the ability to access, through programming tools, the features that can be accessed through a menu interface. In addition, advanced users should have the facilities to gain low-level access to object structures and inferencing controls.

Typically, experienced developers wonder why they should purchase a high-priced shell when they have the skills within their group to build one themselves. The answer is quite simple, as many such groups have already discovered. The ultimate goal of such research is to produce tools that the company can use. Once the development work is done, most companies would like to see the systems disseminated among the company's operational groups. This in turn requires that someone support the application and maintain the platform on which it has been built. Not only does this mean all the work of system documentation, but it requires adding additional features for less skilled users and, over the long term, supporting the code through each hardware and software upgrade. Finally, as new hardware platforms become available, the software must be ported. None of these is an appropriate task for a development group, but they are exactly the services a tool vendor provides.

As the cost of AI hardware and software has decreased and the ease of use and reliability have increased, the market for AI tools has rapidly expanded. Many individuals with expertise in a domain become (and desire to remain) novice users, with the ability to understand and extend rules—

extending the expert system's domain knowledge—but not to build complete systems (graphic interfaces, links to other programs and machines, etc.). These users have often worked with internal programming groups who now wish to turn the system over to the operational group.

Many users in this group, particularly those with little or no computer training, tend to be wary of learning a programming language and thus evaluate tools on their ability to accomplish tasks through their capabilities for using simple, English-like rules. The choice then becomes whether to buy a "toy" system to learn on, with the eventual aim of switching to a more powerful environment later on, or to find a system that offers low level access but supports a full range of users.

Given the latter case, the tool should provide an environment in which the user can build simple, unstructured production rules, modify these to include variables, and extend this to include objects (e.g., frames, relations). Because no large, sophisticated system can be built entirely without reliance on some lower-level programming, the tool must also provide the ability to interface with a programming language (e.g., Lisp, C, etc.). In addition, there should be some facility for easily constructing a graphical interface for both development and end users, preferably accomplished through a menu interface (no programming).

End Users

End users are individuals who will use the completed system. Their requirements are obviously quite different from those of the developers. The foremost concern is that the user interface must be appropriate. Thus, if graphics is a requirement, a system that supports the required level of graphics must be used. Equally important is speed of execution. If the system does not produce results in the required time, then it will be of little or no use. Finally, with expert systems, you have to remember that the advice being given is often quite sophisticated. Thus, the end-user has to feel confident in using that advice. Building user confidence can only be done by providing features that allow the user to query the system about the logic behind the advice—how the system reached its conclusion. A feature complementary to this is allowing the user to ask why certain requests for information are being made. It is desirable and often necessary, then, that the system have some built-in feature that keeps track of the reasoning, both while it is in progress (why) and when the final conclusions have been reached (how).

Maintainers

A third group sometimes exists separate from the developers: the individuals who will maintain and extend the system once it has been deployed in the field. Their concerns are for a system that contains features that facilitate extensions and testing. Ideally, this would be the original development environment. In the case of a delivered system, the most likely option is to have an automatic conversion facility that transforms the development environment into a deliverable version. In any case, the developers must create clear documentation and a well-developed suite of test scenarios.

Team Stratification

The group at the plant was no exception to the above stratification. George and Nancy had no programming backgrounds and little interest in pursuing that line of endeavor (though as we will later see, the team followed a typical differentiation of interests, and Nancy became quite adept at translating expertise into the more formalized logic required by the computer). It was left to the junior team member to work directly with the consultants on system implementation. The consultants would supply design advice and programming support in the prototyping stage with the team taking over the responsibilities later in the project.

As the project progressed, the end users (the operators) continually made their presence known, both by their constructive comments and also by their often puzzled expressions and dismay at the nascent system's deficiencies.

EXPERT SYSTEM SHELLS

Shells are environments built in a high level language that facilitate building expert systems. When expert system technology was first being used in commercial environments, these shells were adaptations of university research tools, for example, the medical diagnosis expert MYCIN, converted into the domain-independent tool, EMYCIN. The last few years have seen a proliferation of commercial shells available in a wide range of prices, starting at $49.95 for a simple rule-based exploratory system up to powerful tools selling in the $60,000 range.

In this section we'll look at the range of shells available on the market, divided into three sections based on capabilities. The shells in the high range are all hybrid systems, combining rules, object representation, and graphics. The middle and low ranges have these capabilities to varying degrees but do not achieve the high level of integration. Again, we define these three groups not by price but by capabilities. As would be expected, capability and price are fairly highly correlated, but not entirely.

In examining these shells we'll discuss a wide range of features they may contain. Most of these features will be discussed in detail later in the book.

> If you wish to better understand a particular feature, we suggest that you use the Index and Table of Contents to look ahead. We are dealing with one of the most difficult constituents of the expert system process—evaluating tools before you have a good understanding of how to use them or what they are. This section attempts to describe the different features in terms of their use and provide a guideline for evaluating their applicability to a problem.

Environments

Expert system shells should be evaluated as a collection of tools—not only the individual tools themselves, but just as importantly the integration between the tools. The tools provide *facilities* for building a knowledge base, primarily in the form of editors that allow the developer to create and modify representation structures, rules, and graphics and view the resulting changes. The tools also support various AI *paradigms*—techniques that enhance the basic inferencing capabilities of a simple rule system.

Facilities

- editors
- interface building tools
- debuggers
- open architecture

Editors.   Editors allow the developer to build and modify the knowledge base quickly. This includes tools for editing rules and representation structures.

Interface.   A good shell should provide a number of tools for building interfaces to the knowledge base. The developer will need to build these interfaces at all stages of development: for the programmer to test intermediate results, for the knowledge engineer and expert to map graphic images to underlying representations, and for the end user to easily access the completed system.

Ideally, the shell should provide facilities for building simple interfaces without having to resort to programming. These tools either are menu driven or, preferably, allow the user to manipulate graphic objects. The user builds an interface by creating copies of template objects and modifying them by changing predefined attributes. A programmer's interface that provides capabilities for modification and extension should also be available.

Debugging. Debugging is the art of making systems work under all of the conditions they will encounter in normal use. For the rules, having a facility for examining the progress of the inference engine and examining the value of variables set during rule firing can be of immense value. Often, a facility known as a partial matcher may be included. Matching is the process where a variable is matched to a specific value. For rule systems that allow variables to be set as the inference engine runs, a partial matcher will show all the values dependent variables will take on when one independent variable in a rule is set. For example, in a general rule clause that analyses the temperature of a pump, setting the pump variable to a specific pump would cause the partial matcher to show the developer the temperature for that pump.

Graphical debuggers are especially useful. In particular, it is useful to see the dynamic progress of rules firing. In KEE, the debugger will show the rules as the inference engine fires them and place a checkmark next to a true rule and an x next to a failed rule (see Figure 3-2). A facility such as this instantly identifies problems when the course of the reasoning diverges from the expected.

Open architecture. The provision of capabilities that enable the developer to modify and extend various aspects of the shell's operation, including the basic paradigms described in the next section.

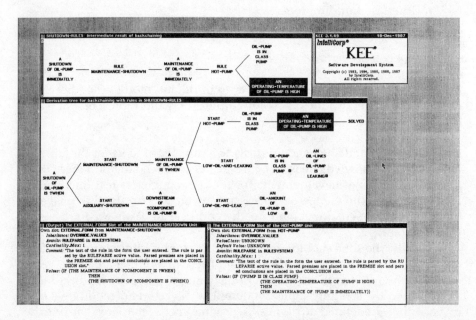

Figure 3-2. Graphic Rule Debugging (KEE)

Paradigms

Most AI shells are now what could be considered hybrid architectures, in that they combine a number of paradigms and capabilities, with varying degrees of integration. These include:

- rules
- frames (classes)
- inheritance
- graphics
- truth maintenance
- alternative views
- external language calls (Lisp, C, etc.)
- external program interface

How much does each feature contribute to implementing a real system? Because users vary in their level of expertise and their requirements of a tool, most AI shells on the market provide, at least superficially, a standard set of features. These include forward- and backward-chaining rules and some type of graphical-interface building facility. With the more expensive shells, a true hybrid environment is provided with the additional features of frames and an interface to a lower-level language such as C or Lisp. Finally, each of the high-end shells offers one or more special features such as truth maintenance, alternative viewpoints, or rule agenda control.

Rules. Rules are English-like sentences used for capturing the knowledge of an expert. The terms "expert system" and "rules" have, for many years, been synonymous for many people, dating back to the original work in expert systems at Stanford. Although many other paradigms are available for building expert systems, rules have maintained their prominent position because of many users' desire to avoid programming. We do not believe that it is possible to entirely build a sophisticated AI system at the current time without using a programming language (e.g., Lisp, C), no matter what system or shell you are in. However, we have been quite impressed with the inferencing capabilities of the high-end shells and believe that they come very close to providing the capability of building a large expert system with almost no programming (we also believe that most of the programming required by a typical user can be reduced to a very small number of concepts and functions).

The inferencing system should provide the following features:

- Rule grouping—any facility that allows creation of rule subsets that can be activated and deactivated independently. The intent is to control which rules are used (fired) when a new fact is introduced (asserted) into the knowledge base. Without grouping, all rules in the system can potentially fire on any new fact—not always a desirable action.

- Priorities—ordering the sequence in which rules are invoked. The effect is to order the firing of two rules that might otherwise fire in a random order. For example, a certain rule might be running a set of procedures. The results of these procedures in turn affect other rules. You would want the procedure rule to run first. Priorities provide a limited amount of procedural control over rule firing.

- Certainty factors—attaching certainty factors, also known as confidence factors, to rules. Given the current debate on certainty, this feature should allow users to implement their own interpretation of how certainty factors should be used. The intent of these factors is to provide advice that is not absolute but rather tempered by the degree to which it might be true.

- Access to a programming language external to the rule system. This access allows special customization of rule language operators, including extensions such as special automated procedures and queries to the end user. This is particularly important for applications that may use changes in external data and device states as a component of the reasoning. This feature enables the system to revise its reasoning based on new knowledge discovered during inferencing (nonmonotonic reasoning).

Frames. Frames (often called classes) are the basic building blocks of an object system, representing the generic classifications of things that make up the domain. A frame consists of a set of attributes, often called "slots." In a factory, these things would be machines, conveyors, tanks, and so on. The slots would be attributes such as temperature, pressure, and operating status. Frames can represent the static description of the domain, while the rules are used to capture the expert's manipulations of that domain.

One of the major evaluation criteria for frames is the degree to which they have been integrated with the rules and graphics. As object-based programming has become more popular, many formerly rule-only shells have added a frame feature. The lack of integration shows up primarily in the way the rules match on the frames and slots. The more flexible the matching between rule clauses and frames, the higher the degree of integration. A good test of this integration is to check the ability to have multiple values in a slot and the way in which the rules take advantage of the frame parent/child relationships (for example, whether a rule can automatically test all of a frame's children).

Inheritance.   Inheritance (often referred to as class hierarchies) is an integral part of a frame system. Inheritance among frames is similar to inheritance among people—traits of the parents are carried down to the children. Inheritance is a critical element of any object-based system because it provides a great deal of flexibility to the frame system. This has implications for development, debugging, and long-term maintenance.

A good inheritance mechanism will allow multiple layers of parent/child relationships. KEE and GoldWorks, for example, both provide unlimited depth to the hierarchy. Figure 3-3 shows a hierarchical frame structure. Apple's HyperCard, on the other hand, limits the inheritance structure to three levels. Limiting the depth of inheritance limits the degree of generality a system can have. Other features to look for are the ability to have multiple parents and the ability to control the way in which conflicting values in the parents are merged.

In general, if you are evaluating an object system and find that is does not contain some type of inheritance mechanism, finding an alternative is most likely the best course.

Truth maintenance.   Many of the high level tools have facilities that store the links between asserted values and the rules that made that assertion. These systems are often called truth maintenance systems because of their ability to enforce those links. Let's take the case of a rule that states "When the oil pump's operating temperature is above normal the pressure is high." When the pump's temperature becomes high, the rule fires and asserts into the knowledge base the fact that the oil pump's pressure is also high. Because the only factor at this point in determining whether or not the pump's pressure is high is the elevated temperature, changing the temperature

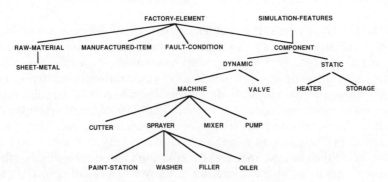

FIGURE 3-3. Hierarchical Frame Structure

to normal implies that the pressure should no longer be high. This is what the truth maintenance system does—it retracts the value it previously asserted for pressure when the temperature changes.

Maintaining the consistency of the knowledge base is obviously a worthwhile task. However, there is overhead associated with using such a facility (compute time in keeping track of changes and memory for storing these histories). Thus, the complexity and nature of the application must justify both its use and certainly any extra cost incurred in purchasing a shell with this feature.

Exploring alternatives.   Known in various shell environments as Worlds, Viewpoints, What-if, and so on, these systems are an attempt to generalize the concept of exploration of alternatives. Such a facility initially sounds extremely useful, but in fact it is more valuable as a concept than as a practical feature. While it is quite true that a large percentage of computer models are built for the purpose of exploring alternatives, it is equally true that built-in generic facilities prove to be inapplicable in all but a handful of cases.

Why aren't these facilities more useful, given the apparent need for controlling the exploration of alternatives? The problem is not the concept—quite a large number of users build their own facilities—but in the assumption that it is possible to build a generalized tool. The problems of a built-in tool are:

- Granularity—the level of detail required for a given problem may not match that implicit in the general system;

- Efficiency—there is inevitably a combinatorial explosion of possibilities, difficult to control and costly in space and execution speed because the generic systems usually lack fine enough filters on what is kept and what discarded; and

- Predefined assumptions—the implicit assumptions as to the nature of the alternatives may not be valid for a given case.

The key issue here is the problem's granularity. When a facility for controlling alternatives is built into a tool, certain assumptions must be made about the level of detail that the system can handle. As a rule, the greater a system's generality the lower its efficiency. In examining alternatives, there is a rapid combinatorial explosion of possibilities, and it is in the requirements for controlling this explosion that the unwieldiness of these systems is truly seen. In other words, anyone can quickly implement an application that uses these facilities to explore all possibilities, but it is very difficult, often impossible, to build the controls that make a solution computationally feasible.

This is not to say that exploration of alternatives is difficult. The general features of most mid- to high-level shells make it easy to build a facility for testing alternatives. The advantage of this custom approach is the ability to tightly focus on the specific problem at hand. Using built-in facilities is almost always as complex as building a custom facility.

External language calls. These come in three types: direct calls to an external language from the rules; indirect calls from a frame system via a mechanism such as **"daemons"** (a term used in the AI literature for computer programs that are linked to slots on a frame—when a change occurs to the slot's value, the daemon is activated); and direct programmer calls using messages (defined using "handlers" written in the programming language).

Performance

This is not a feature but is a very important criterion for selecting among shells. Performance is a complex subject, because a shell's performance is always application-dependent. This dependency results from each shell manufacturer's decisions on which features to optimize. For example, many shell implementors have chosen to make forward chaining more efficient than backward chaining.

Secondary Support

The larger tool vendors often provide after-purchase support for their products in the form of training, technical phone support, and consulting. Assistance of this type can be useful for beginning groups. Support may also be of interest to corporate development groups that will be turning expert systems over to field divisions who will be expected to support the system.

External program interface. An external program interface enables the expert system to interact directly with another software package, for example a database package. Such an interface is critical when the expert system must be integrated with the external environment. Most shells provide a mechanism enabling the user to link the knowledge base to specific external software packages—and provide a facility for advanced users to extend this capability to software of their own choosing.

Matching Requirements to Features

The team at the plant began the assessment of tools by trying to group the various products according to price and functionality. However, they were initially dazzled by the vast array of features and paradigms that the various companies offered. They had to determine what was needed for all projects, what was needed by their particular project, and what actually worked. This last criterion was important, because most of the shells claimed to have, more or less, all the same features as the others. In fact, however, many of these features were add-ons, not well integrated with the core of the shell and consequently buggy, slow, or even improperly implemented (did not operate as advertised) in some instances.

The first step was to group the features into two categories—core features and ancillary features. The core features were:

- frames and slots

- inheritance

- rules integrated with slots

- access to external environments from the shell

Features deemed to be of secondary importance included:

- truth maintenance

- alternatives

- rule confidence factors

The ancillary features were further divided into those features that might aid the team and those that were irrelevant. This was the most difficult step, as many of these features were difficult to evaluate and test. For example, the multiple worlds feature was not easy to use on any of the shells. The problem here was generality: some of the alternative views were very general and thus had many features unneeded by the project, making them much slower and more difficult to use than necessary; others were quite specific, making them quite efficient but requiring that the team go through all sorts of convolutions to make them match the problem at hand. Eventually they decided that features of this type would not be used to pick a product, but only to eliminate a shell in the event that the feature could not be ignored and turned off.

The actual evaluation consisted of visiting each of the high-end vendors and spending a half day working on a small sample of the actual problem. Consultants with experience in building these systems accompanied the team so that a thorough evaluation of advanced features could be conducted. Two of the shells ranked in the final evaluation are shown in Figure 3-4; the shells were ranked using an index from 1 to 10, with 10 being the ideal score. Features were only considered if they provided acceptable performance and appeared to be bug free (a very difficult evaluation to make).

Shell 1 scored the best, but lost points because its integration to external environments was limited to Lisp; no provisions for use of other environments such as spreadsheets had been included. The class hierarchies and frame and slot representations were judged excellent—the open architecture allowed developers

Figure 3-4. Evaluation of commercial expert system shells

Features	Shell 1	Shell 2
frames and slots	10	7
inheritance	10	7
rules integrated with slots •	9	6
pattern matching	8	6
access to external environments from the shell	7	10
editing environment	7	9
open architecture	8	7
delivery	5	8

to modify all aspects of the inheritance structure. The open architecture itself was considered quite strong, but lost points because of the complexity of implementing some of the modifications. The pattern matching capabilities were judged to be slightly weak because of limitations in the types of patterns that could be defined (much of this problem occurred because the shell had originally been designed as a representation engine—rules were added at a later date). Delivery was essentially done in the development environment, ensuring relatively high costs for both software and hardware. However, as this system would not be installed at very many sites, this was judged to be a minor problem.

Shell 2 fared less well because of problems with the object structure. The initial implementation had been purely rule based, and when objects were added, they were perforce juggled around requirements of the inference engine. For example, the slots could not support multiple values. This in turn made for weak integration of the objects with the rules. For example, there were no true variables in the rules with universal bindings; rather, the rule variables were actually globally bound variables. However, because the product had originally been designed to run in a PC environment, integration with external environments was excellent. Delivery options were mixed, good because of the compact delivery module that could be created, but losing points because of the poor support of graphics.

Programming Languages

Programming languages that are typically used in Artificial Intelligence work can be divided into three groups: the object-based languages, new mainstream languages, and the traditional programming languages that have been available for many years. Although the demarcations between these categories have blurred with new modifications in the last couple of years—better interfaces for low-level languages and extended commands for higher-level languages—these designations are still useful as a way of thinking about the different environments and features provided by the languages in each category.

These languages can be used to implement a custom shell or as a complement to an off-the-shelf shell, allowing the developer to add modifications and extensions. Some shells also contain their own custom language, providing developers with a few basic programming capabilities. Usually these can be supplemented or replaced with a standard programming language. This book uses programming languages as a tool for extending and enhancing commercial shells, not as a vehicle for creating a custom shell.

Object/Symbolic Languages

This group, combining symbolic and object programming, includes Lisp, SmallTalk, and newer additions such as the HyperCard scripting language HyperTalk. Traditional computer languages manipulate numbers. While numbers are symbols, they are only a small subset of all symbols, which include words and sentences. The object/symbolic languages excel at manipulating all symbols and thus are ideal for expert-systems work.

Many of the shells provide tools for programming with objects. These include **daemons** (programs that are triggered when a slot value is accessed) and **messages** (programs associated with frame objects). Object-oriented programming combines the frame (defined in the above section on shells) with a procedural element, the programming language. Programming languages are integrated with the frame system through the use of messages and daemons, as well as direct program calls from rules.

Although object-oriented programming is an extremely powerful paradigm, many users shy away because of what are often unfounded fears of delving into a programming language. It is absolutely true that to use object-oriented paradigms one must use a programming language, but for certain types of applications, in particular those with a heavy dependency on procedural operations, avoiding the programming (for example, by using only rules) can be even more difficult. When the rules in a system become harder to understand than the equivalent programming code, it is clearly time to explore solutions other than rules.

Lisp

A great deal of discussion and confusion continues to surround the question of what the underlying implementation language for AI applications should be. This is, of course, an important issue, because the time when large, complex applications can be built with no need to use programming languages is still somewhat in the future.

At present, the debate centers on the benefits of an environment built on top of Lisp versus one built on C. We believe that the ideal development environment is one where Lisp is the primary language but where the system provides facilities either for calling C routines or delivery in C. The major issues of debate are the following:

- speed

- memory allocation

- ease of use

- portability

Speed and memory questions are always difficult, because the only unbiased way to evaluate differences is by comparing similar applications running in the two languages. Ideally, of course, the two applications should be solving the same problem, have been built by users equally skilled in the respective environments, and be running on equivalent hardware. Various benchmarks have been attempted, but with these obvious difficulties, the results offer no clear answers—except that there is no clear-cut winner. In addition, both speed and memory are getting steadily less expensive at about the same rate as human resources get more expensive.

Given the ambiguous nature of performance measures and the relatively high cost of people to implement software, how do Lisp and C compare in programmer productivity? The Lisp language was developed for implementing AI paradigms and thus has several distinct advantages over C for building AI applications. First, Lisp has very good facilities for manipulating list structures, an obvious advantage when your primary paradigm for capturing the expert's knowledge is English-style rules—in essence, words strung together in a list. Second, Lisp is a comparatively easy language to program because of the nature of interpreted and incrementally compiled languages. Without going into great detail, this feature permits the programmer to study intermediate results as the system is implemented and tested.

Still, the concept of using Lisp, with all of those parentheses, is repugnant to many people. However, much of the aversion to using Lisp (or any programming language) is the perceived complexity. Through work with a number of clients, we have developed the concept of "Dick and Jane Lisp," a tiny subset of Lisp (approximately 15 Common Lisp functions plus an equal number of shell-defined functions, see Appendix D). These functions provide the necessary functionality for building 90 percent of the control structures we'll use in later chapters for building custom interfaces and rule control structures.

HyperTalk

HyperTalk is a programming language for Apple's HyperCard software. This is an interesting language because of its highly English-like syntax. HyperCard itself is an object-oriented programming environment that borrows heavily from SmallTalk and Lisp. It combines graphics, cards (frame equivalents), and the HyperTalk programming language.

We use HyperTalk in later chapters in our sample functions because of its clear readability. For real systems this is not a language of choice because of its built-in limitations—it has a very small set of functions and is difficult to extend. However, given that caveat, it is an extremely easy environment in which to program.

New Mainstream Languages

We include in this category Pascal and C. Recent introductions of object C and Pascal make the distinction between this and the first category less clear, but these languages still require the user to do much of the work of allocating memory and other low-level tasks. These languages have become popular in the AI world for four reasons: their perceived speed advantages over Lisp; their ability to run in less memory; their lack of problems with garbage collection (Lisp is optimized for the user, not the machine—unlike C, for example, the user does not have to worry about allocating blocks of memory. The trade-off is that Lisp periodically halts operation to reallocate freed-up memory, i.e., collects the garbage); and a wider installed base of programmers familiar with these languages. Because of these considerations, several of the shells developed originally in Lisp now offer both a Lisp and a C version. Later entries to the field often are implemented only in C or Pascal.

The speed issue was discussed above. Because C and Pascal lack some of the built in facilities and optimizations of Lisp for handling lists, these languages do not always guarantee that the finished AI application will be faster than a similar implementation done in Lisp. Unfortunately, the argument about garbage collection is less tractable. Because of Lisp's dynamic allocation of list structures, working memory is slowly consumed by the application. Periodically, it is necessary to "collect garbage," that is, recover the wasted space. Languages such as C require the programmer to allocate space before running an application; thus, no dynamic space-eating process occurs. The trade-off is in more difficult programming.

As we saw above in the Lisp section, most middle- to large-sized applications require some programming support. This is the other appeal of these more commonly used languages—programmer support for them is more readily available.

Because of these trade-offs, one solution, where programmer resources permit, is to build the prototypes in Lisp and then port the application to a more conventional language such as C. This may result in space/speed efficiencies as well as provide a wider programmer base for system maintenance.

Traditional Languages

These are languages such as Fortran, PL1, and Cobol. While they may in many ways be inappropriate as AI implementation languages, they are still important because of the sheer number of programmers who use only these: something on the order of 85 percent of all programming is done in these languages.

We do not believe that these are very cost-effective environments in which to build AI applications. While a large number of programmers may be available, their training in these languages often makes them unsuitable for building expert systems without extensive retraining. This is because a large measure of what "expert-systems methodology" offers is a new way of looking at representation of knowledge. Use of traditional programming styles often directly conflicts with AI paradigms—not only object programming, but also structuring of knowledge as assertions and rules. Programmers of traditional languages think primarily in terms of structured programming and procedural approaches, both anathema to AI representation.

These languages also do not take advantage of the new programmer productivity environments that more recent languages incorporate. Thus they are more difficult to debug and maintain.

Choosing a Programming Environment

At the plant, the data processing (DP) department had a traditional programming staff familiar with Cobol and Fortran. When we talked to the representative sent to the meetings by the DP department he proudly described the hundreds of thousands of lines of code his department maintained and extended, and quite belligerently matched all of our assertions about the benefits of new programming languages and expert systems with examples of similar Fortran solutions done in his own shop.

This is not an uncommon situation. In fact, it is nearly ubiquitous. Unfortunately, the solution is almost always an end-run around the established programming authorities. At the plant, this was accomplished in two ways. First, the hardware and accompanying software were purchased under a special program for acquiring personal computers, avoiding the central facility. Second, instead of trying to get programming support from the DP department, we found a junior employee from the group we were working with who had received a small amount of programming training in school. We sent her for a refresher course of one week, and with this basic knowledge, combined with the experience of working on the team with the consultants, we now had a programmer capable of writing the simple supporting utilities we would require. For the few areas where more complex programming might be required, we would use the consultants. Before we could finalize on a programming language, we first had to look at the various hardware options for both development and delivery.

HARDWARE

Finally, the hardware that a tool can run on must be examined. Hardware environments are changing so rapidly at present that anything more than a cursory overview of this area would be pointlessly outdated in a few months. The three major hardware categories are personal computers, workstations, and mainframes. The most interesting trend in hardware development is the blurring of the distinction between personal computers and workstations. The low-end workstations are now very competitive in price with the high-end personal computers and performance is also nearly equivalent. One of the major differentiating factors is the type of monitor used—workstations in general have a larger screen with higher resolution.

Personal Computers

What is the appeal of a PC environment? Primarily price and footprint (a PC occupies a relatively small percentage of your desk). Concerns about the PC environment include the perceived lack of a development environment, speed, and the size and resolution of the screen. In fact, these concerns are well founded, but mostly irrelevant.

The screens are, in general, both small and of low resolution. Although larger screens can be purchased, in practice price and the desk space required for the monitor make these purchases relatively infrequent. Apple's Macintosh line of computers is the exception to this rule—these computers have very high resolution monitors and incorporate high-quality graphics as standard features at PC prices.

With the current 386 machines and the Macintosh II series, execution speed becomes a major issue only with systems that are either very large or contain components that are computationally intensive.

One of the big advantages of a PC is its ability to interface to the software available on the PC, for example, Lotus 1-2-3. Most of the shells running in the PC environment provide a basic interface for sharing information through data files and a supported interface for interacting with standard software packages such as spreadsheet and database programs. Use of existing software packages means not having to re-invent standard facilities for every expert system application.

Workstations

Superior screens combined with more horsepower have made workstations the machine of choice for engineers. As these general purpose machines have invaded the market, they have displaced the specialized AI machines (e.g., Symbolics), providing environments only slightly inferior for AI work and vastly more versatile for a wide range of applications. Versatility becomes increasingly important as AI modules become embedded in more traditional systems.

One of the major disadvantages of the current workstation environments is the lack of commercial off-the-shelf software. Supported packages for building databases, spreadsheets, statistical analyses and business graphics are notably absent.

Mainframes and Minicomputers

Large, time-shared systems are still the workhorses of most large companies. They store the corporate databases and provide shared facilities such as large-scale modeling and planning packages. While expert systems have been built in these environments, most expert system solutions that require access to a large machine have been implemented using a hybrid strategy linking stand-alone workstations or PCs to the mainframe. The expert system resides on the PC and accesses/updates data residing on the mainframe.

Two major disadvantages of directly implementing on these shared machines are lack of a good development environment (debugging tools and graphics) and political problems with conservative DP shops. However, the main problem remains computational requirements: Large expert systems tend to require a lot of dedicated compute power and make for objectionable time-sharing partners.

CHOOSING A DEVELOPMENT ENVIRONMENT

At the plant, the team had finally assembled the information available on programming environments, expert system shells, and hardware. Although the initial prototype would be relatively small, unless a major disaster occurred the plan was to build an application that could be fielded. The fielded application would require a full graphical interface and encompass a large number of rules.

Because the application would initially be implemented at only a limited number of locations, the cost of the hardware was not a large factor in the decision. Instead, the team decided to go with a powerful development environment that could also be used as a delivery environment. The use of a workstation environment would provide more flexibility in the interface design where they could experiment with a large screen. Given the fact that the company, like most large organizations, would require at least three to five years to fully field this application at multiple sites, they also made the assumption that delivery environments would be more available at that time.

The expert system for the plant would be medium sized, consisting of more than 20 or 30 rules, containing a complex representation description of the plant, and using a sophisticated interface. The team felt that the implementation of a small system would provide neither a usable end product nor a realistic test of expert system technology. On the other hand, the requirements of a truly large system—in terms of both resources and experience in knowledge engineering and programming—were clearly inappropriate for this initial effort.

The expert system would have **a hybrid architecture**, meaning that it would combine aspects of both object programming and rules. Thus, the criteria for a shell were determined: a powerful development environment integrating rules with object programming support, support of sophisticated graphics, and a long-range potential for delivery on nondevelopment hardware and software.

Summary

This chapter looked at the two aspects of expert system building: extraction of knowledge from the expert and input of that knowledge into the computer. The first half of the chapter looked at the tools and techniques of knowledge engineering, the second half at evaluation measures for software and hardware tools.

The expert system we will develop in the rest of this book is a **hybrid system**. Hybrid systems contain many different integrated paradigms, including rule-based and frame-based paradigms. In our hybrid system, elements of graphics, rules, data structures, and assertions will be combined. All of these will be integrated by a common theme, **object-oriented design**. Each entity in the system, whether it be a rule, a piece of data, or a graphic depiction of a dial, will be assumed to have a base level representation as an object. This common basis will allow the various objects to interact with each other, as well as provide a commonality of design. We will assume the use of a shell that employs an **open architecture**, allowing the developer to modify and extend most features of the shell.

EXPLANATION OF APPENDICES A AND E

In this book we attempt to address the wide range of user needs created by such diverse hardware and software. Because of the wide array of hardware and software that is commercially available on the market, we feel that this text must address developers of expert systems on all forms of platforms. Because the lower-end shells have certain limitations in their capabilities, not all areas covered in the text will be completely applicable to these development environments. However, we have attempted to indicate to the reader how these limitations might be circumvented by clever application of existing capabilities.

Appendix E describes the syntax used in this book, followed by a table showing how this syntax translates into each of the major shell types given in the examples. The shells we will be treating in this manner include: KEE, GoldWorks, Level 5, ADS, KBMS, NEXPERT, and the HyperCard example shell distributed as part of this text.

In those sections that involve programming examples, we will use HyperCard's HyperTalk scripting language (reviewed in Appendix C) for the examples. Comparisions with operators from the other shells are shown in Appendix E. We do this because of the English-like nature of Hyper-Talk—translating HyperTalk into other languages such as C and Lisp is a relatively simple process. In addition, as examples of this process, Appendix D contains a number of HyperText examples translated into Lisp.

READINGS

Dervin, B. 1983. Information as a user construct: The relevance of perceived information needs to synthesis and interpretation. In *Knowledge structure and use: Implications for synthesis and interpretation*, S. A. Ward and L. J. Reed, ed. Philadelphia: Temple University Press.

Harmon, P., R. Maus, and W. Morrissey. 1988. *Expert systems tools and applications*. New York: John Wiley and Sons.

Johnson-Laird, P.H. 1983. *Mental models: Towards a cognitive science of language, inference, and consciousness*. Cambridge, MA: Harvard University Press.

Walters, J.R., and N.R. Nielsen. 1988. *Crafting knowledge-based systems*. New York: John Wiley and Sons.

Winkler, R. L. 1981. Combining probability distributions from dependent information sources. *Management Science*, 27: no. 4.

P A R T

II

BUILDING
THE PROTOTYPE:
FORWARD CHAINING

4

ENGINEERING EXPERTISE: PLANT CONTROL RULES

T his chapter begins our exploration of knowledge representation using forward-chaining rules. The development of these rules will be illustrated by the implementation of an initial prototype expert system of fault diagnosis on the canning line. In this first prototype, programming is avoided. The point is to experiment with different approaches and produce a functioning, but not polished, system.

We'll begin with a short review of rule-based expert systems, covering alternate reasoning strategies and the basic components of a knowledge base: rules and facts. The review ends with a description of how an inference engine interacts with a knowledge base.

Rule development will be illustrated by a series of interviews with our expert plant engineers concerning some common operational problems in the canning line. The experts will explain a set of logic diagrams that we'll use to build an initial set of forward-chaining rules.

Using the information supplied by the experts, we'll look at the details of constructing a knowledge base. First, we'll examine how to represent different types of factual knowledge. Forward-chaining rules will be used to capture the logic of fault analysis diagrams. By exploring the effects of a single mechanical problem on the production line, we'll illustrate how the rules replicate the logic of these diagrams.

FORWARD CHAINING

Let's take a look at how a rule-based system is organized. Rules are made up of English-like sentences or **clauses.** In their simplest form, rules are defined using an if-then syntax that logically connects one or more **antecedent** (or premise) clause with one or more **consequent** (or conclusion) clause:

IF *antecedent* THEN *consequent*

A rule says that if the antecedents are true, then the consequents are also true. The antecedents and consequents of rules refer to specific *facts* that describe the state of the world. Conceptually, each fact may be thought of as a single sentence that describes some particular aspect of the world's state. Taken together, the rules and facts make up the knowledge base.

The rules and facts are analyzed by the **inference engine.** Inferencing begins with an examination of the knowledge base for any rule antecedents that **match** existing facts. The process of matching is finding a rule clause with the same pattern of words (in the same order) as a fact in the knowledge base. When all of the antecedent clauses in a rule have a corresponding fact in the knowledge base, the inference engine can assert the consequent of the corresponding rule into the knowledge base as a new fact. The movement of information in the knowledge base and inference engine is illustrated in Figure 4-1.

The significance of the architecture in Figure 4-1 is the separation of the knowledge base, containing all application-specific information from the program code that interprets the knowledge—the inference engine. The inference engine consists of a generalized computer program that knows about reasoning strategies and various ways to combine rules and facts, but knows nothing about any particular application. The knowledge base of rules and facts—at least in principle—is nonprocedural, while the inference engine is highly procedural. In other words, rules and facts represent *what* the knowledge is, but the inference engine determines *how* that knowledge should be analyzed.

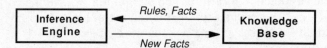

FIGURE 4-1. The interaction of the knowledge base and inference engine

Reasoning Strategies

Most rule-based systems reason using either forward chaining, backward chaining, or a combination of the two. In backward-chaining, the inference engine begins with at least one goal representing hypotheses to be proven. The inference engine then uses the rules to find specific combinations of facts whose presence in the knowledge base will "prove" the hypotheses. In forward-chaining, the inference engine uses one or more new facts combined with the rules to assert further new facts that the rules imply are true.

Forward-chaining systems are sometimes referred to as **data-driven**, while backward-chaining systems are often called **goal-driven**. Data-driven rules are commonly used for monitoring incoming data and making recommendations to the user based on that new data. Goal-driven rules, on the other hand, are typically used for problems where the goals to be proven are specific hypotheses that may or may not apply.

In the canning-line application, we'll use both forward-chaining and backward-chaining strategies to reason about the state of the plant. Forward-chaining rules will be used to represent the shutdown-related decisions of logic diagrams that describe the connection between sensor readings and potential component failures, because such conclusions are driven by changing data. Later on in the project (Chapter 9) we'll use backward-chaining rules to analyze operators' suspicions concerning quality-control problems on the canning line.

Rules and Facts

Our first task as knowledge engineers will be to build a simple knowledge base representing the linkages between abnormal sensor readings and potential machine failures. To do so, we'll use a combination of:

- facts about the canning plant
- facts representing advice for the operator
- rules representing the relationships between those facts

Rules and facts are the basic building blocks of a knowledge base. Facts may be thought of as assertions that certain things are true; stated in English, example facts for the canning plant might include:

The oil-pump is running hot.

The oiler needs to be shut down immediately.

The nozzle on washer-2 is clogged.

Rules logically connect related facts. Stated in English:

> IF the oil-pump is running hot, THEN the oil-pump needs maintenance.

If there were multiple pumps, we could write a separate rule for each pump:

> IF the washer-pump is running hot, THEN the washer-pump needs maintenance.
> IF the paint-pump is running hot, THEN the paint-pump needs maintenance.

However, if there were a large number of pumps, such an approach becomes tedious and error prone. Our real desire is to capture the following statement with a single rule:

> IF any pump is running hot, THEN that pump needs maintenance.

We can capture such a statement about all pumps by using **variables** in our rule. When using variables, each variable acts like a "wild card" that can take on any value. Denoting rule variables as words beginning with a question mark, the pump rule would read:

> IF ?pump is running hot, THEN ?pump needs maintenance.

Given a large number of pumps, our inference engine can set ?pump to each pump in turn. Clearly, the use of variables can greatly reduce the number of required rules. Not only is the resulting single rule more elegant, it is also considerably easier to debug and maintain.

> NOTE: Different expert system shells denote variables differently. Appendix A provides example rule clauses from several popular shells.

The Inference Engine

The inference engine uses rules and available facts to assert additional facts into the knowledge base. When a new fact is placed in the knowledge base, and the inference engine "sees" the new fact, it must check whether that fact matches any antecedents of rules currently in the knowledge base. This process, known as matching, lies at the heart of every inference engine. To match a fact, the pattern of the rule clause must match a pattern in the knowledge base.

Once the inference engine has matched a rule's antecedents, it will **fire** the rule by asserting the rule's consequent into the knowledge base.

We can combine the inference engine's matching and firing of rules as in Figure 4-2. Here we show the inference engine taking in the fact that the oil-pump is hot, matching against the hot-pump rule, and asserting the need for maintenance on the oil-pump.

The interesting part comes when the inference engine fires one rule and asserts a new fact (the rule's consequent), and the new fact matches the antecedent of another rule. This results in a series of related rule firings, often referred to as a **chain of reasoning.**

This is a good place to stop for a moment and look at rule syntax and the behavior of the inference engine. Suppose that the knowledge base already contained the rule we looked at before:

IF ?pump is running hot, THEN ?pump needs maintenance.

Also suppose we inserted into our knowledge base the fact, "The oil-pump is running hot." In this case, the new fact would match the rule's antecedent, with the variable ?pump set to the value "oil-pump." What sort of matching would occur if we chose a similar phrasing for our new fact, with the same overall meaning but slightly different syntax? *Absolutely none.* For example, suppose we forgot to type the word *running*—or didn't even know about it—and asserted instead

The oil-pump is hot.

On the face of it, there's nothing wrong with this observation: The difference between a pump that's *hot* and one that's *running hot* is "merely" one of syntax. This fact, however, would fail to match against the rule's

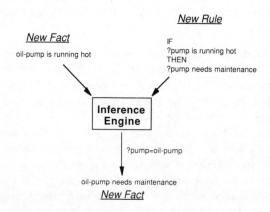

FIGURE 4-2. Generating new facts from rule firings

antecedent. As a matter of fact, the match isn't even close, because without the word *running*, the new version of the fact doesn't have the same number of words as the rule's antecedent. A more subtle error would also cause the match to fail, such as spelling the word *running* with one "n" instead of two.

> NOTE: Not all expert system shells use strict pattern matching. Shells such as Aion's ADS instead maintain tables of names—when a reference is made to a variable name, the inference engine will search for the value;[34] search strategies include facts in the knowledge base, requests for user input, and other rules.[49] This approach makes rules simpler to write but decreases developer control over rule-fire order.

GETTING STARTED ON THE KNOWLEDGE BASE

Let's start the process of building the knowledge base by reviewing, with the expert engineers, a few of the most common problems faced by operators in controlling the canning plant. On the advice of the experts, we'll look at some of the logic diagrams representing standard operating procedure in the plant; these fault trees will later be translated into forward-chaining rules. We'll also describe complications caused by connections between plant components.

Identifying the Most Common Problems

When starting out, the first step is to understand the most common problems faced by the expert system's ultimate users. Ideally, those problems will be directly addressed by the system. Whatever the case, it is always useful to have a good understanding of the day-to-day difficulties faced by the users.

> We spent some time with George and Nancy, our two expert engineers, talking about the most common problems faced by plant operators. Our ideas were deliberately unformed at this point. We knew the operators were going to be involved in helping us diagnose quality-control problems, but first we needed to get a better understanding of their current jobs.
>
> Both George and Nancy agreed that the operators could provide valuable assistance in a QC analysis if they were given guidance in what to look for. They were tracking a large number of systems and, when their board indicated that a machine was out of whack, they had to make rapid decisions on whether to shut it down. The consequences of a false shutdown were expensive and time consuming. Nancy added, "And you should see the operating manuals they have to use. I think they were written for engineers, not operators—the operators only seem to use them for the pictures and diagrams."

Written Documentation for Diagnosis

Nearly every workplace has its thick book of regulations and procedures. Invariably, these books contain vast amounts of information, each piece of which is useful to someone, but only small sections of which are used by a wide range of people. Insurance underwriters, for example, have vast manuals covering the different ways that insurance policies can be assembled. Similarly, automobile mechanics have an array of repair and parts manuals available to them. Even a telephone receptionist often has to deal with formidable documentation describing how to use the latest office telephone system.

For diagnostic problems, written documentation fails in three ways:

1. *Volume of materials:* In complicated systems, involving many different volumes and pages, it can be almost impossible, certainly time-consuming, to track down a solution by working through all this material.

2. *Exceptions to standard behavior:* Many types of "experiential" knowledge are difficult to set down in a manual. A good example of this type of knowledge is "exceptions to the rule." For example, a repair manual for a piece of machinery may state certain conditions under which the machinery will fail. However, an experienced operator might know that in winter, on Monday, when the plant has been idle for two days, cold lubricating oil causes higher stress, causing an "unusual" or undocumented failure.

3. *Timeliness of information:* Large systems are rarely static, and written documentation describing the system becomes obsolete with alarming rapidity. Procedures are altered, people change, equipment is modified—whatever the reason, written documentation often has a short useful lifetime.

Expert systems address these problems (1) by presenting users with only the questions they need to answer, based on previous answers and direct reading of external data, and (2) by incorporating the knowledge of experienced users, including the special cases that make many problems so difficult to solve.

Documenting the Knowledge

Once a set of problems has been identified, the next step is to gather as much documentation as possible describing how to solve those problems. Documentation sources include reference manuals, internal memoranda, and employee training materials. Often, the most useful "documentation" exists as scattered pieces of paper attached to bulletin boards, or notes stuck on the sides of computer terminals. Hand-scrawled notes in the margins of reference materials will often reveal especially frustrating problems. During the canning-line project, the logic diagrams we found provided voluminous documentation concerning plant shutdown.

Figure 4-3 contains one small piece of such a decision tree for over-heating pumps, a common problem in the plant. In this case, the decisions concern shutting down different parts of the washing process.

A decision tree is built step by step, working from an observation or sensor reading to a conclusion about the cause. For example, if a pump is overheating, it may require maintenance. Traversing the decision tree, we see that performing maintenance on a pump requires shutting down the pump, in turn requiring a shut down of all other components that rely on the pump. Thus a decision tree can link a single component (e.g., an over-heating pump) to several different actions that the operator must take. As we quickly discovered, there were many dozens of decision trees (Figure 4-4), each covering a specific problem in the plant. Technically, the diagrams were still part of the plant's standard operating procedure; practically speaking, however, they were unwieldy to use on the plant floor, and difficult to keep up to date.

Documentation in written form contains a great deal of ancillary material that can support the users' decisions. The ability to access this "extra"

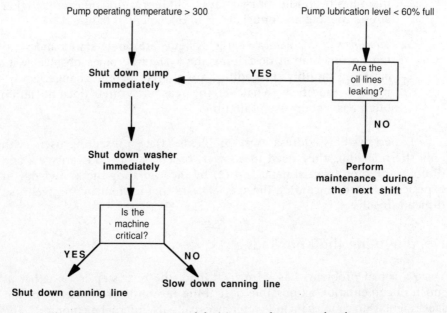

FIGURE 4-3. Fragment of decision tree for pump shutdown

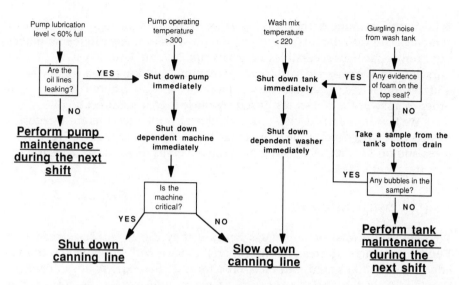

FIGURE 4-4. Some of the shutdown decision trees

information should be available in the expert system, enabling users to supplement—and question—the expert system's decisions.

Building the Knowledge Base Diagrams

Building the initial prototype comprises the following activities:

- representing facts in the knowledge base
- writing rules that refer to those facts
- running the inference engine

A knowledge base is typically built and tested incrementally: few facts are entered, several rules are written that use those facts, then the inference engine is run. Later, some more facts and rules will be defined, and the inference engine will be run again. Mistakes will be found in the way rules were stated, and those rules will have to be modified and retested. Changes made to the syntax of certain facts will necessitate changes in the rules.

REPRESENTING FACTS

For the initial version of the knowledge base, we'll represent our facts as simply as possible using **unstructured facts**—"unstructured" because there is no *a priori* meaning to the ordering of words beyond the logic of an English sentence. Our overall aim is to choose a representation technique that makes our knowledge base accessible and easily understood. Our first step is to put ourselves in the shoes of an operator making shutdown-related decisions and ask ourselves what *facts* this person has to know about the plant in order to answer the questions posed by those logic diagrams.

We'll examine the decision trees and determine the different categories of facts that we'll need in the knowledge base, comparing the relative advantages and disadvantages of using qualitative versus quantitative facts to capture the plant's state.

Using Unstructured Facts

We begin with unstructured facts because they can be made to read like English sentences, decreasing the experts' unease with how his/her knowledge is being translated into electronic form. If the experts are to confirm the validity of the analysis these rules make, and correct the rules when they don't work as expected, they'll have to be able to read them without an interpreter.

For example, suppose we wanted to represent in our knowledge base that the oiler's pump was overheating. We might choose one of the following phrases:

the oil-pump is running hot

the oil pump has overheated

oil-pump hot

temperature oil-pump high

All of these are acceptable unstructured facts, and the choice depends on personal preferences. The first version of this fact is probably preferable because it reads more like natural English than the others.

For the first version of a knowledge base, it is often preferable to use unstructured facts because they are easy to understand. Properly constructed, unstructured facts can be stated to read just like sentences in a natural language. If all facts read like sentences, the need to learn a particular syntax is obviously minimized.

People unskilled in the use of computers are a good audience for unstructured facts. It generally puts people at ease to discover that they can understand what is in the knowledge base without having any special training.

> We take it for granted that the expert's thought processes often seem mysterious. It's easy to forget that what we, the knowledge engineers, are doing may appear even more mysterious to the expert.

Putting the Facts into Categories

It is important to start with a thorough understanding of the different cate-gories of facts going into the knowledge base, because this will help mod-ularize the implementation of those facts. The net result will be a shorter development time, as well as a knowledge base that can be modified and expanded more easily in the future.

Looking at the different kinds of facts needed in our knowledge base, as represented in the logic diagrams in Figure 4-4 above, we see that three basic types of facts are required, representing:

- static plant descriptors—the organization and layout of the plant, which will only occasionally change

- dynamic plant descriptors—current state of the plant, changing con-stantly as sensors, dials, and so on change

- operator recommendations—produced in response to changes in the plant and thus also dynamic

Each of these three types of facts is used at different times in the decision tree's logic. See Figure 4-5 for examples of each category.

Dependencies between Object in the Domain

In most real-world systems, dependencies exist between objects. These dependencies are quite often the focus of the expert system. In medicine, it is the dependencies between symptoms and disease that the rules address; in insurance claim processing, the links between customer claims and ancil-lary facts. In the canning process, symptoms of future failure are directly linked to evidence such as abnormal sensor readings.

FIGURE 4-5. The three types of facts used by decision-tree logic

Fact Type	Examples
Plant description (Static)	Wash-pump provides pressure to washer Stamper is upstream of oiler Oiler is a critical component
Plant description (Dynamic)	Oil pump is running hot Wash-mix temperature is normal
Recommendations	Washer needs shutdown immediately Oil-pump needs shutdown soon

These dependencies are often physical linkages, such as those shown in Figure 4-6, which shows a schematic view of the canning line. If one of the machines fails, it sometimes happens that the entire line must be shut down. For example, one of the first operations performed on the canning line is to cut incoming sheet metal into disks, marked in Figure 4-6 as "Cutting." If the cutter is shut down, the entire line may as well be shut down, because the supply of new cans will quickly be depleted.

In the next section, we will explore the relationship between implied and physical dependencies on the design of the rules.

Qualitative versus Quantitative

In most expert system applications, knowledge can be expressed either quantitatively or qualitatively. On the one hand, there is a need to be precise, and quantitative values are nothing if not precise. On the other hand, there is a need to express knowledge in a form that is easily recognizable by a broad range of users, that is, qualitative terms such as hot or low.

It is quite common for those with a scientific or engineering background to feel uncomfortable with qualitative logic. There is often a feeling that mere words are not sufficiently rigorous for serious work. However, end users' concerns are usually only in knowing relative values, and possibly the degree of that relativity. If the system's logic relies heavily on equations and numerical comparisons, it may be nearly impossible for nontechnical users to understand the results obtained by the system. For example, an operator reading a sensor on a wash tank might not know how to interpret

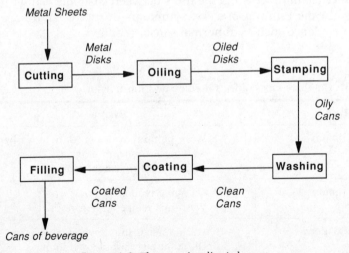

FIGURE 4-6. The canning line's layout

a temperature of 63.4° C but would undoubtedly understand a reading of "normal."

> At the canning plant, we found that the logic diagrams were largely expressed in a quantitative way, as shown in Figure 4-7. The diagrams had been prepared by a group of engineers, who quite naturally thought about the problems in quantitative terms. However, although the diagrams were stated quantitatively, the operators typically discussed the problems in terms of qualitative relationships. Our conversations with the operators and foremen were littered with phrases like "when that thing goes hot" and "the pressure is way down."

The use of qualitative language is quite prevalent in practice because it is easy to understand. Numbers don't explicitly impart a meaning of good or bad, whereas phrases such as "the pressure is way down" are essentially *interpretations* of numerical data. Our approach is to represent the logic diagrams using language that makes the operators feel the most comfortable. This is appropriate, because the operators must be able to explore the decision logic used by the system when it comes up with specific recommendations. To that end, we have represented sensor readings in our knowledge base using qualitative descriptions that correspond as closely as possible to the language of the users of that knowledge base—in this case, the canning-line operators.

In solving any sort of analytical problem, there will always be the danger that qualitative logic is too imprecise. A qualitative approach is not feasible in every case, and the "qualitative versus quantitative" decision must be made on a case-by-case basis.

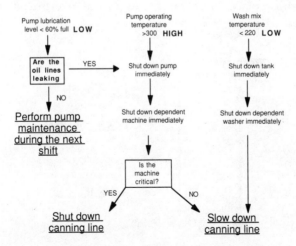

FIGURE 4-7. Quantitative vs Qualitative (bold) representation of a logic diagram

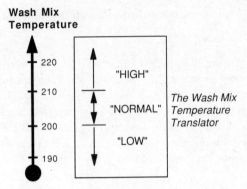

FIGURE 4-8. Translating the temperature of wash-mix into qualitative descriptors

Translating Numbers into Qualitative Facts

Most real world data are quantitative. If rules are going to employ qualitative measures, a translation process must be devised. People often do this translation in their heads, sometimes automatically, but in many cases a mechanized approach must be devised.

When using qualitative measures, time and effort can be saved by defining a small set of terms that are applicable to a wide range of situations. If sensor data are being used, as in the canning plant, a "normal" state and a few abnormal states—such as "low" and "high"—will often suffice. Figure 4-8 illustrates the translation of temperature values into qualitative statements. In a financial situation, we might use "fair market value" instead of "normal", and replace "high" and "low" with "overpriced" and "under-

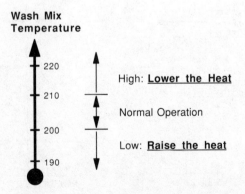

FIGURE 4-9. Set points for the wash-mix temperature

priced." Whatever the case, the actual terms that are used should be chosen to fit the problem, and if at all possible, they should be the same terms used by the eventual users of the expert system.

In many process control applications, the boundaries between "low," "normal," and "high" are defined by set points. The normal range defines the readings indicating normal operation, while low and high are abnormal. Additional categories may need to be defined—for example, correspondingly roughly to "very high" and "very low"—but the basic idea is the same. The implications of such set points for wash-mix temperature is illustrated by Figure 4-9 with the admonitions to raise or lower the heat.

WRITING RULES

The first half of this chapter covered the types of facts that make up our initial knowledge base. To complete the knowledge base, we will add the rules that manipulate those facts.

We'll use *forward-chaining rules* because we wish to discover all possible outcomes (conclusions) from each new piece of information. If we learn that the wash pump is running hot, for example, we will want to know *all* of the ramifications of this fact. Forward-chaining rules are ideal for this purpose. We would use backward-chaining rules if we were beginning with a conclusion (or hypothesis) and wished to know all possible pieces of information that led to that conclusion (or were needed to support that hypothesis).

Our overall aim is to phrase the rules so that they are easily understood by our intended users, the canning-line operators. Ideally, they will be understood by virtually anyone who works at the plant. Therefore, technical engineering language will not be used.

To examine the basic structure of the decision-tree logic, we'll start with the detection of a small mechanical problem. Each step of the shutdown logic contained in the logic diagrams will be represented by a rule.

Breaking Down the Decision Logic

When writing rules, the first action is to break down the logic being represented into a series of discrete steps, each step corresponding to a different stage of the decision-making process. This breakdown is analogous to the categorization of facts described in the previous section. Its purpose is the same: to modularize the building of the knowledge base. The logic in each step of the decision-making process will translate into a set of related rules.

The difficulty of constructing such a breakdown depends on the degree to which the logic has been documented beforehand. In many cases, the knowledge engineer must reconstruct the decision-making process through

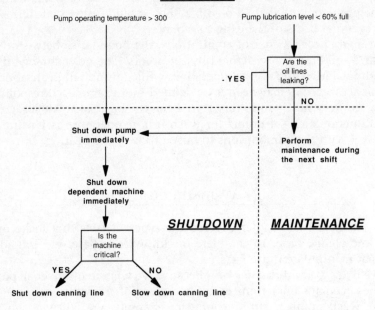

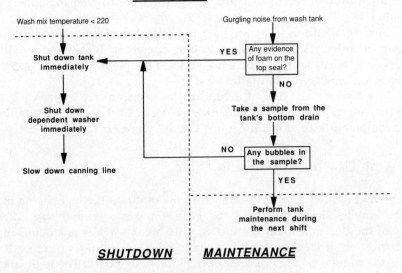

FIGURE 4-10. Example decision trees

observing directly and gathering whatever written documentation is already available. For the canning-line application, we were fortunate to have a set of logic diagrams that thoroughly described the logic of shutting down plant machinery.

As illustrated in Figure 4-10, the decision tree leads an operator through the detection of a component problem and then recommends an action: either maintenance for that component or shut down of the problem component and any others dependent upon it. Each step in the diagram will be represented by one or more linked rules. The order of interpretation of rules is akin to moving down a particular path in the decision tree.

Translating Decision Trees into Rules

When the expert's knowledge is translated into rules, defining a simple grammar or syntax is recommended. Even though we'll be using unstructured facts, the use of a consistent syntax in the rules will make the task of rule building easier. One of the difficulties in writing rules that link together is making sure that the conclusion of one rule matches the premise of a related rule; a consistent syntax will aid in this.

This syntax is implicit. Nowhere in the knowledge base is there a definition of this syntax; its definition exists only outside the knowledge base, as part of the implementation strategy. The syntax we have chosen for the examples in this chapter is

the ‹component› ‹verb› ‹descriptor›

The rules that chain from specific problems to recommendations for maintenance are very simple. Figure 4-11 demonstrates an example of the

English sentence	If the oil-pump is running hot, it needs maintenance immediately.
Rule in the Knowledge Base	IF the oil-pump is running hot THEN the oil-pump needs maintenance immediately
What the rule means to the inference engine	If the fact "the oil-pump is running hot" is found in the knowledge base, assert "the oil-pump needs maintenance immediately" as a new fact.

FIGURE 4-11. Translation of an English sentence into a rule

process of translating from an English sentence to the rule that represents that sentence.

Figure 4-12 shows some examples of rules formed from the logic diagrams. In all of these examples, an abnormal value for a component attribute leads to a requirement for maintenance, asserted in the form

(‹component name› needs maintenance ‹soon or immediately›).

In these rules we see another aspect of our implicit syntax, the convention of using the component name as part of the variable name. For example, there is no reason that we could not have used ?x as our variable—it would match just as well as ?pump.

The trick with unstructured facts is to make sure that you get the expected matches with facts in the knowledge base. There is nothing to stop

---

Rule: **HOT—PUMP**
Documentation: An overheated pump can QUICKLY be
  permanently damaged
IF
  THE ?PUMP IS RUNNING HOT
THEN
  THE ?PUMP NEEDS MAINTENANCE IMMEDIATELY

Rule: **HIGH—TANK—PRESSURE**
Documentation: Usually caused by foaming inside the tank
IF
  THE ?TANK HAS A PRESSURE BUILDUP
THEN
  THE ?TANK NEEDS MAINTENANCE IMMEDIATELY

Rule: **COLD—LIQUID**
Documentation: *ALL* liquid touching the cans is hot
IF
  THE ?TANK PROVIDES LIQUID TO ?MACHINE
  AND
  THE LIQUID IN THE ?TANK IS COLD
THEN
  THE ?TANK NEEDS MAINTENANCE IMMEDIATELY

FIGURE 4-12. Rules for problem detection

us from making the assertion "the cat is running hot"—these rules have no inherent "intelligence" and will happily assert "the cat needs maintenance immediately." In other words, using the word ?pump does not necessarily mean you will get a pump. A more reliable syntax would be "pump ?x is running hot." However, when involved in this earliest stage of prototyping, these types of refinements are not usually important and are easily altered if necessary.

Machine Shutdown

In this section, we'll explore in greater depth the canning plant example. While this section merely provides further examples of the translation process begun in the previous section, many readers may find the information presented here useful background on the canning-line problem used throughout the book.

We've looked at problems that require maintenance of machines. Now let's look at problems that lead to shutdowns:

- A machine is being worked on and thus has to be shut down.

- A machine's operation depends on some other machine, and that other machine has been shut down.

These result in two different types of shutdown rules. The first type is represented by the single MAINTENANCE-SHUTDOWN rule of Figure 4-13. Stated in English, this rule would read something like the following:

Whenever you perform maintenance on a machine, it has to be shut down.

In fact, this sentence *is* the rule's documentation, as shown in Figure 4-13.

```
Rule: MAINTENANCE-SHUTDOWN
Documentation: Whenever you perform maintenance on a
  machine, it has to be shut down
IF
  THE ?COMPONENT NEEDS MAINTENANCE ?TIME
THEN
  THE ?COMPONENT NEEDS SHUTDOWN ?TIME
```

FIGURE 4-13. The MAINTENANCE-SHUTDOWN rule

The second type of shutdown rule reflects dependencies between machines. For example, we want to be able to state that whenever a pump shuts down, the machine that is serviced by that pump must also be shut down. See Figure 4-14 for specific examples. Stated in English, we can summarize this type of shutdown rule by the following sentence:

When a machine shuts down, and there is a second machine that cannot operate without the first one also operating, that second machine must also be shut down.

As can be seen from Figure 4-14, there will be one rule of this type for each kind of connection between machines in the plant.

Finally, as shown in Figure 4-15, there is the LINE-SHUTDOWN rule for shutting down the entire canning line. This rule is similar to the PUMP-SHUTDOWN and TANK-SHUTDOWN rules of Figure 4-14, except that the dependent "machine" is the production line itself.

```
Rule: PUMP-SHUTDOWN
Documentation: When a pump goes down, the machine using
   its pressure goes down, too
IF
   THE ?PUMP PROVIDES PRESSURE TO ?MACHINE
   AND
   THE ?PUMP NEEDS SHUTDOWN ?TIME
THEN
   THE ?MACHINE NEEDS SHUTDOWN ?TIME
```

```
Rule: TANK-SHUTDOWN
Documentation: When a tank is cold, the machine using its
   liquid cannot function properly
IF
   THE ?TANK PROVIDES LIQUID TO ?MACHINE
   AND
   THE ?TANK NEEDS SHUTDOWN ?TIME
THEN
   THE ?MACHINE NEEDS SHUTDOWN ?TIME
```

FIGURE 4-14. Rules describing inter-machine dependency

Rule: **LINE–SHUTDOWN**
Documentation: Shutting down a critical component shuts
   down the line
IF
   THE ?MACHINE IS A CRITICAL COMPONENT
   AND
   THE ?MACHINE NEEDS SHUTDOWN IMMEDIATELY
THEN
   THE CANNING–LINE NEEDS SHUTDOWN IMMEDIATELY

FIGURE 4-15. The LINE-SHUTDOWN rule

The Use of Alternate Representations

Forward-chaining rules are not the only way to represent logic diagrams
like those used in the canning plant.

In principle, all of the decision trees could be turned into a large table
instead of a set of rules. This table would list all the abnormal conditions and
their corresponding actions. Rather than go through the bother of consulting the rules whenever an abnormal condition occurred, the corresponding
action could be consulted immediately. This direct comparison of conditions
and actions is quite easy to do with the simple logic diagram for pump
maintenance, as in Figure 4-16. The corresponding table is shown in Figure
4-17.

There are several advantages of such a table. First, it is simpler to
implement than the other types of representation. Rather than a set of
English-like rules that have to be parsed and interpreted, one simply has a

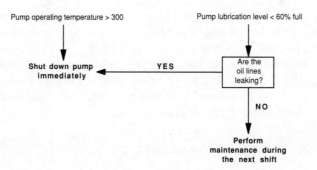

FIGURE 4-16. Logic diagram for pump maintenance

FIGURE 4-17. Decision table for pump maintenance (compare Figure 4-21 above)

Condition	Action
Lubrication low, lines not leaking	Perform maintenance next shift
Lubrication low, lines leaking	Immediate shutdown
Operating temperature high	Immediate shutdown

uniform set of condition–action pairs. Secondly, given a new set of input data that have to be tested, computing new actions is much faster from the table than from the rules.

A table is a good solution for a small, simple system that has few interlinked conditions. However, tables are not practical when there is considerable branching in the logic diagram between the raw observations and the corresponding actions to be taken by the operator. (Consider how the table in Figure 4-17 would grow if extended to include line shutdown.) A table like the one in Figure 4-17 also does not capture the reasoning process that went into the table's creation. The equivalent rules, on the other hand, *do* capture this reasoning process.

FORWARD CHAINING ILLUSTRATED

In this section, we'll look at exactly how our new forward-chaining rules behave when they are triggered by an observation of a specific mechanical problem. We'll follow the actions of the inference engine, step by step, as it runs through the shutdown logic represented by the rules, eventually recommending that the canning line be shut down. We'll then see how to generate an explanation of why that shutdown recommendation was made.

Understanding how the inference engine interprets rules can be important when designing sophisticated applications. For starters, there is no fixed ordering to when rules fire; the inference engine will fire them whenever it can (we'll see in later chapters that this is not completely true—controls can be added on when and how rules fire). Also, even with only a few rules in the knowledge base, the potential combinatorial explosion of rule linkages during chaining can be exceedingly difficult to follow.

Ultimately, there's no substitute for a detailed example when trying to understand how an inference engine works.

The Inference Engine's Agenda

We'll start by asserting the following unstructured fact into our knowledge base:

the oil-pump is running hot

What happens next? Well, first of all, we have to tell the inference engine to notice that our new fact might match the antecedent of some rule in the knowledge base. In our example, we do that by executing the command **ForwardChain.** (Each rule-based software package has a slightly different, but equivalent, mechanism: The important thing is that we have to alert the inference engine that something important may have just happened.)

Our new fact matches the antecedent of the HOT-PUMP rule (this process is shown in Figure 4-18), one of the maintenance rules described in the previous section. Its purpose is to detect overheated pumps and recommend immediate maintenance.

As illustrated in Figure 4-18, when the inference engine matches the fact "the oil-pump is running hot" with the antecedent of the HOT-PUMP rule, the rule is placed on a list of "things to do." What actually happens is an **agenda item** is created and added to a list of things to do, generally known as the **agenda.**

The agenda is a prioritized queue and, as we'll see in later chapters, developers can manipulate aspects of a rule (e.g., its priority) to determine where in the agenda list each rule is placed. Often, users are given choices of how the agenda mechanism works, such as depth-first (last-in–first-out) versus breadth-first (first-in–first-out) ordering. When the inference engine is ready to evaluate a rule, it fires the rule (or, more technically, the agenda item for that rule); when a rule is fired, each antecedent clause is tested to see if it is true or false. If all the antecedent clauses are true, the inference engine then asserts the consequent clauses into the knowledge base.

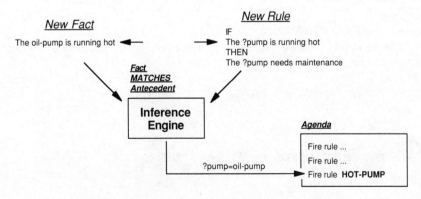

FIGURE 4-18. Creating an agenda item

NOTE: Precisely what happens when a rule is placed on the agenda is somewhat implementation dependent. Some inference engines have no real agenda: Rules are fired immediately whenever their antecedents are satisfied. Other inference engines allow the user to manipulate the agenda (for example, by re-sorting it) after a new item is placed there.

Analyzing Immediate Consequences

When the HOT-PUMP rule was placed on the agenda, the actual component oil-pump was substituted for ?pump in its consequent. When the rule fires, this consequent will be asserted into the knowledge base:

> the oil-pump needs maintenance immediately

Now the inference engine begins a new round of attempted matching, searching to find rule antecedents that match this new fact, and, in fact, a match is found—the antecedent of the rule MAINTENANCE-SHUTDOWN (Figure 4-13). The variable ?component becomes OIL-PUMP and the variable ?time becomes immediately. When this rule fires, the consequent

> the oil-pump needs shutdown immediately

is asserted into the knowledge base.

You may recall that many of the plant components are interrelated. Thus, when one component shuts down, others may also need to be shutdown. In the case of the oil-pump, we also have to shutdown the dependent machine oiler. Figure 4-19 shows the PUMP-SHUTDOWN rule. The

---

```
Rule: PUMP-SHUTDOWN
Documentation: When a pump goes down, the machine using its
  pressure goes down, too
IF
  THE ?PUMP PROVIDES PRESSURE TO ?MACHINE
  AND
  THE ?PUMP NEEDS SHUTDOWN ?TIME
THEN
  THE ?MACHINE NEEDS SHUTDOWN ?TIME
```

FIGURE 4-19. The PUMP-SHUTDOWN rule

Rule: **IMMEDIATE—LINE—SHUTDOWN**
Documentation: When a *CRITICAL* component goes down, the
   entire line goes down, too
IF
   THE ?MACHINE NEEDS SHUTDOWN ?TIME
   AND
   ?MACHINE IS CRITICAL
THEN
   THE CANNING—LINE NEEDS SHUTDOWN ?TIME

FIGURE 4-20. The IMMEDIATE-LINE-SHUTDOWN rule

first antecedent clause "the ?pump provides pressure to ?machine" matches
the static domain knowledge with ?pump set to oil-pump and ?machine set
to oiler and then matches ?time to immediately (from the HOT-PUMP rule
assertion about oil-pump shutdown above).

The new assertion,

   the oiler needs shutdown immediately,

in turn initiates a new round of forward chaining, leading to the rule IMME-
DIATE-LINE-SHUTDOWN (Figure 4-20). The new assertion matches the
first antecedent clause, and the static domain fact that the oiler is a critical
component matches the second clause (the oil-pump is not critical to the
canning line so it's needing shutdown did not cause this rule to fire), causing the final rule in the chain of reasoning to fire, asserting that the canning
line should be shut down immediately.

Explaining Why Rules Fired

As a consequence of the inference engines linking together chains of rules,
expert systems have the ability to explain the chain of reasoning that led
to a final conclusion—the why of what happened, also called the **assertion
derivation**. This explanatory capability is perhaps the most useful feature
for convincing users to trust the advice the system is providing, because
it removes the black-box mystery from the process of converting raw facts
into expert advice. This feature also makes expert systems excellent training
tools, because the novice can examine step by step an expert's thought
process.

In the simplest case, an explanatory facility merely spouts back the
names of the rules in the order they fired, relying on the developers' use of
mnemonic names to make sense of such a report (see Figure 4-21).

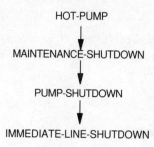

FIGURE 4-21. Explanation of
reasoning using rule names

A more useful, and more common, explanation contains both the rule names and the facts that led to the rule firing and the conclusions. Figure 4-22 shows the progression from the original assertion that the oil-pump is running hot to the conclusion that a line shutdown is necessary. The rule names are in upper case, the knowledge base facts (also known as **axioms**) are in italics, and assertions are in normal type.

Increasingly sophisticated explanations may make use of the rule documentation or a more English text explanation (Figure 4-23).

Another possibility is to construct a graphical tree (Figure 4-24). A graphical display has the advantage that each link in the derivation chain is easy to follow, no matter how long the chain. Checks and crosses can be used

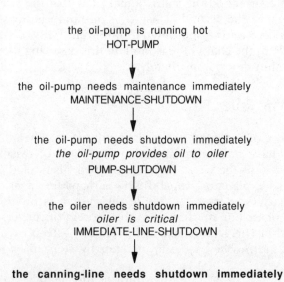

FIGURE 4-22. Explanation of reasoning using rule
names, axioms, and assertions

The fact THE CANNING-LINE NEEDS SHUTDOWN IMMEDIATELY is
  derived from Rule **IMMEDIATE-LINE-SHUTDOWN.**

Rule **IMMEDIATE-LINE-SHUTDOWN** is supported by the facts:
OILER IS CRITICAL (an AXIOM)
THE OILER NEEDS SHUTDOWN IMMEDIATELY

The fact THE OILER NEEDS SHUTDOWN IMMEDIATELY is derived
  from Rule **AUXILIARY-SHUTDOWN.**

Rule **AUXILIARY-SHUTDOWN** is supported by the facts:
THE OIL-PUMP NEEDS SHUTDOWN IMMEDIATELY
THE OIL-PUMP PROVIDES OIL TO THE OILER (an AXIOM)

The fact THE OIL-PUMP NEEDS SHUTDOWN IMMEDIATELY is
  derived from the rule **MAINTENANCE-SHUTDOWN.**

The rule **MAINTENANCE-SHUTDOWN** is supported by the fact:
THE OIL-PUMP NEEDS MAINTENANCE IMMEDIATELY

The fact THE OIL-PUMP NEEDS MAINTENANCE IMMEDIATELY is
  derived from the rule **HOT-PUMP.**

The rule **HOT-PUMP** is supported by the fact:
OPERATING-TEMPERATURE OIL-PUMP HIGH was asserted by the
  operator

FIGURE 4-23. A verbal explanation of why the canning-line needs shutdown immediately

to show successful and unsuccessful reasoning paths. Unfortunately, unless
the screen is very large and/or very small fonts are used, only a few steps
will be visible on the screen at any one time.

There is no way of displaying explanations of rule-based reasoning
that are completely acceptable in all situations. These difficulties become
especially obvious with long and complex reasoning chains. Many applications will require a special-purpose explanation facility that is tailored to
the problem at hand. In the explanation of the line-shutdown recommendation, we could consider using graphics to display a modified plant schematic
(Figure 4-25).

First, we might search through the derivation chain and gather up all
of the axioms. We could then build a list of all plant components mentioned

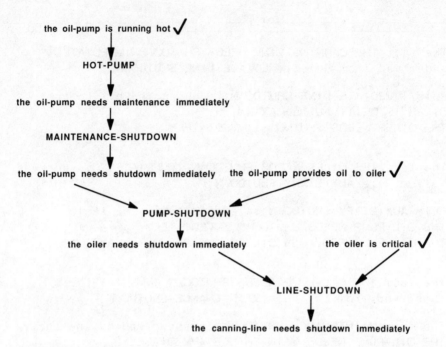

FIGURE 4-24. A graphical explanation of why (the canning-line needs shutdown immediately) is true

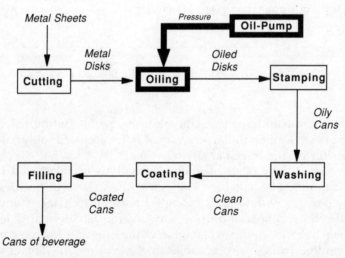

FIGURE 4-25. A graphical explanation of (the canning-line needs shutdown immediately), highlighting only the plant components that are mentioned in axioms

by those axioms and highlight those components on the schematic. Even if it didn't provide a detailed explanation of the reasoning, this would allow the operator to quickly identify where a shutdown originated.

DEBUGGING THE RULES

The developer must work with the expert to ensure that the rules are working properly. Generating explanations of rule behavior is, therefore, also of obvious importance to the developer. In fact, the "explanation" examined here is basically a debugging tool for the developer.

As with programming environments for procedural languages, the amount of debugging support given the developer by expert system shells varies widely from software package to software package. Almost all packages, however, allow the developer to stop the inference engine temporarily at predefined **breakpoints**. Examples of such breakpoints would include:

- just before or after a given rule is going to fire

- just before a fact matching a given pattern is to be asserted from a rule

Breakpoints are useful for seeing if rule fires at all, and for seeing whether the rules are firing in the anticipated order. Once at the breakpoint, however, most inference engines transform the user-defined rules into an internal representation bearing little resemblance to the original rule, making it difficult to interpret the values of rule variables.

The biggest problem when debugging is figuring out why rules do not fire when expected. This is often much more useful than breakpoints, because it not only shows which rules are firing and the order of firing, but also the values for the variables as the rule fires (the problem is, if a variable can take on many different values, you can soon be overwhelmed with data while waiting for that one error for which you are searching.) Advanced environments will display a graphical version of the reasoning chain as it is being constructed during rule firing.

In our experience, there is no substitute for inserting simple print statements within rule antecedents. Such a print statement should be defined to always "succeed"—be found true—whenever encountered by the inference engine, so it doesn't affect the chain of reasoning.

CHAPTER SUMMARY

In this chapter we began by reviewing the fundamentals of an expert system's architecture: the knowledge base and inference engine. The process of finding, documenting, and analyzing expert knowledge led to the translation of that knowledge into a representation using facts and rules. These facts and rules were then used by the inference engine to create chains of reasoning based on the assertion of a single new fact into the knowledge base. Finally, we examined formats for presenting users with the rationale for conclusions reached by the expert system.

READINGS

Brownston, Lee, et al. 1985. *Programming expert systems in OPS5*. Reading, MA: Addison-Wesley.

Buchanan, B. and E. Shortliffe. 1984. *Rule-based expert systems: The MYCIN experiments of the Stanford Heuristic Programming Project*. Reading, MA: Addison-Wesley.

Chandrasekaran, B. 1983. "Towards a taxonomy of problem-solving types," *AI Magazine*, 4, no. 1.

Hayes-Roth, F., D. Watermand, and D. Lenat. 1983. *Building expert systems*. Reading, MA: Addison-Wesley.

Hunt, R. M., and W. B. Rouse. 1984. A fuzzy rule-based model of human problem solving. *IEEE transactions on systems, man, and cybernetics*, 14, no. 1.

Johnson-Laird, Philip N. 1988. *The computer and the mind*. Cambridge, MA: Harvard University Press.

Newell, A. 1973. Production systems: Models of control structures. In *Visual information processing*, ed. W. G. Chase. Orlando, FL: Academic Press.

Newell, A., and H.A. Simon. 1972. *Human problem solving*. Englewood Cliffs, NJ: Prentice-Hall.

5

REPRESENTING KNOWLEDGE WITH FRAMES

In the earlier chapters, we developed a simple expert system that used assertions to represent facts about our canning plant. We also implemented a set of rules that used these facts to advise an operator on the need to shut down all or part of the canning line.

The use of these simple assertions and rules gave us a quick start in interacting with our expert. However, we now require a more robust representation of the plant (a domain model) if we are to extend our system beyond its current simple capacities. All but the most simple of expert systems quickly reach a development stage where combinatorial complexity of the information can be reduced by using a more structured approach to the information representation.

First, without a strong domain model, we cannot begin to write large sets of complex rules, or at any rate write them in a coherent manner. Rules use facts to determine when abnormal conditions occur in the operation of the plant. In a complex domain, such as the can manufacturing plant, a great many facts must be monitored. By clustering these facts in our model, we can manage them more easily. Thus, we increase the likelihood that we can maintain consistency—and the robustness of the application—during application development and later maintenance.

The purpose of this chapter is to explore techniques that will allow us to build a structured representation of the problem domain. To do this we will define a set of objects that represent components of the real world environment and attributes that describe these components. Whereas we have previously described facts about the plant in terms of simple assertions, we will now create an object-based representation containing structures for each component of the canning line.

We must also develop a correspondingly more structured (object-based) version of the maintenance and shutdown logic, which was implemented as rules in the previous chapters. These rules determine maintenance needs and the necessity of shutting down all or part of the canning plant production line.

At this stage in the implementation process, we will also need a user interface, based on object graphics, that allows us to test our revised maintenance and shutdown logic. Up to this point, we have been able to get by in our testing with simply running the rules for a few test cases. As the system expands, however, we'll need to be a lot more organized, structuring the testing around reproducible sets of test scenarios.

Frames

To build the required robust domain model, we will use structures that cluster and organize our facts concerning the canning plant world—structures called **frames**. The replacement of our simple assertions with a representation that uses frames provides:

- the ability to clearly document information about our domain model, for example, the plant's machines and their associated attributes

- the related ability to constrain the allowable values that an attribute can take on

- modularity of information, permitting ease of system expansion and maintenance

- a more readable and consistent syntax for referencing domain objects in the rules

- a platform for building a graphical interface with object graphics

- a mechanism that will allow us to restrict the scope of facts considered during forward or backward chaining

- access to a mechanism that supports the inheritance of information down a class hierarchy

To implement this new representation we will:

- replace the assertions of the previous chapters with frames and the attributes of the frames (slots)

- modify the existing rules to reference these new frames and slots

Let's begin by briefly examining the function and general definition of a frame. Although it is not within the scope of this book to examine the history and variety of representational structures that use frames as their basis, we will take time here to define the way in which we will use frames.

> NOTE: A large number of shells have been built that provide the user with some type of object-based data structuring. Lower-level languages also contain frame-like structures, for example, Object-C and Lisp.

Inheritance

In our new model of the plant, each physical object type will be implemented as a frame. These frames will be organized into a hierarchy that contains all of the canning plant components. We will use the classification techniques developed for all taxonomies used in science—classifications, or **class** structures, that extend from the general down to the very specific. In fact, the parent/child relationship of frames in a hierarchy are often referred to as class/subclass. We prefer the use of the word frame to describe the actual object because of its connotation of a structure. Appendix E contains tables that compare this book's terminology with many of the different commercial shells. We will speak of a class when describing a general category such as all machines; for example, the oil pump is in the class of machines.

In the canning plant, all of the components we will define can be considered to be elements of the factory. Thus, we create a FACTORY-ELEMENT frame as our highest-level class. As the process of class definition continues, we will define frames for all the categories of physical objects making up the plant.

Figure 5-1 shows part of the basic frame hierarchy for the plant. We have defined the following top-level frames (our most general categories):

- FACTORY-ELEMENT (machines such as pumps and stampers)

- RAW-MATERIAL (such as sheet metal used to make the cans)

- MANUFACTURED-ITEM (such as the cans themselves)

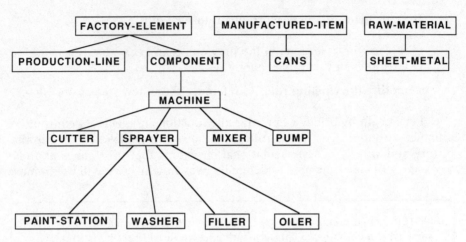

FIGURE 5-1. Defining the frame hierarchy

In a taxonomy, the objects in the classification describe entities that have definitions beyond their relative placement in the hierarchy. A frame is a structure that contains this more detailed information about an entity. The object can exist in the real world or be an abstraction for a type or class of other objects.

Many, though not all, knowledge representation shells contain a mechanism for using the taxonomic classification of the entities to share information between frames. Sharing the information in this manner is known as **inheritance**, because information at the more general level (parent) is passed down to the more specific levels (children).

Frames can inherit attributes from their parents in many ways; thus, many types of inheritance have been defined, and elaborate schemes have been designed to deal with the special cases that always appear when real-world information must be represented. In this book, a very basic scheme (but one which covers most situations actually encountered) is used, as follows:

- Children, the direct descendants of a frame, by default inherit all the attributes of the parent. Thus, attributes specified in the parent will exist in the child.

- The value associated with an attribute can be overridden by the child. Many other types of inheritance are provided in expert system shells, for example, union and intersection, as well as user-defined types. However, overriding the inherited value will be more than adequate for most cases that one encounters.

- A child may have more than one parent. The intersection of attributes define the child. In the case of a conflict, where more than one parent has an attribute with the same name, we have chosen to allow the first parent specified to override the others.

This type of inheritance defines what is often referred to as an **is-a** network, because the links between a parent and child frame represent the fact that the child "is a" type of the parent frame. In essence, we are defining a very simple, one-relation network using the is-a relation.

Most shells, both commercial and academic, have some variation of the basic scheme outlined above. What we have presented here is the most basic and thus most generally available.

Instances

Figure 5-2 shows that portion of the object hierarchy dependent on the frame MACHINE. At the top of the hierarchy is the most general description of the entities, MACHINE, and at the very bottom are the descriptions of the actual physical objects (e.g., wash-pump, oil-pump). The objects in the hierarchy that describe the actual physical objects are **instances**. Frames contain the attribute definitions, and instances contain actual values for those attributes.

In the example of our plant, we might initially define a general structure, starting with MACHINE. We could define several types of machines, such as a pump and a washer (note: use of upper case in the text denotes a knowledge base object rather than the conceptual representation). At the bottom of the hierarchy are the actual components, such as the wash-pump.

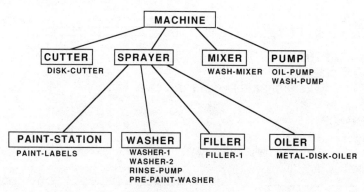

FIGURE 5-2. The frame/instance hierarchy for MACHINE

The different shells have all defined similar, but slightly variant nomenclature to distinguish the generic levels of classification from the lowest level—the representation of the actual physical objects. Examples of these include:

- parent frame, child frame, and instance (GoldWorks)

- class, subclass, and member (KEE)

- class, subclass, and object (NEXPERT)

In this book we will use frame to mean any frame that is a generic definition, and instance to represent any frame structure that describes an actual object with specific local values.

Attributes of a frame are represented as a set of **slots**. These slots in turn can also have attributes, for example VALUE, that we will refer to as **facets**. The facets can, in turn, have values. Some systems, in fact, provide features that let you specify attributes recursively, so that facets have facets "all the way down." For efficiency, most systems stop at one level of facets; we will use this approach in the book.

Let's look at an assertion about a pump:

WASH-PUMP has LOW PRESSURE

In the frame representation, we have created a frame labeled PUMP. One particular pump is represented by the instance WASH-PUMP. This pump has a number of attributes, including PRESSURE. The value of the PRESSURE slot in the above assertion would be LOW.

Figure 5-3 shows the definition of the frame MACHINE; the attributes of MACHINE are defined with slots. The format used in this book to display

---

```
Frame: MACHINE
Parents: COMPONENT
Children: MIXER SPRAYER CUTTER PUMP
-- Slots --
MAINTENANCE:
ON-CRITICAL-PATH:
OPERATING-TEMPERATURE: NORMAL
SHUTDOWN:
```

FIGURE 5-3. The MACHINE frame

```
Frame: SPRAYER
Parents: MACHINE
Children: WASHER PAINT-STATION OILER FILLER
-- Slots --
MAINTENANCE:
NOZZLE: OPEN
ON-CRITICAL-PATH: YES
OPERATING-TEMPERATURE:
PRESSURE: NORMAL
SHUTDOWN:
```

FIGURE 5-4. Frame SPRAYER

a frame is: the frame name, the parent frame(s), the child frame(s), and all slot names followed by the slot's default value when it exists. These default values are inherited by the frame's children and instances, and thus used in the rule inferencing at the instance level. If no value is given, the inferencing treats the value as unknown, and, if a new value is specified further down the hierarchy, that value is the one used.

Now let's examine the frame hierarchy, starting with one of the MACHINE frame's children—SPRAYER (Figure 5-4). MACHINE has defined slots that are attributes of all machines; for example, all machines can be shutdown. For SPRAYER, we add two new slots, NOZZLE and PRESSURE. We also set a default value for all SPRAYER instances: the value for ON-CRITICAL-PATH is YES.

SPRAYER has child frames representing different types of sprayers, such as WASHER and OILER. By observing increasingly fine differences between machines, we can use the hierarchy to categorize types of machines. At each level, new slots and default values will be added.

NOTE: When we show a value in a frame's slot, that value is the slot's default value. For example, the default value for the ON-CRITICAL- PATH slot is YES. All of the child frames and instances of that frame will inherit this value unless it is overridden in the child.

Back at the Plant

The period of time during which the representation began to shift from pure assertions to a frame-based hierarchy was one in which the experts returned to their jobs for a while. This was a typical sequence, with the implementers needing a period of time to systematize the information and clean up the prototype, and the experts needing to take a break and get some work done.

When George and Nancy rejoined the team, their first reaction was mild shock. Said George, "I'm really sorry, but I just don't get it. Why have we gone from a nice clear English style to these things?"

We had expected this reaction, because few experts mentally organize their knowledge in such a structured form. Engineers are probably the group best able to understand these transformations, with people in less structured disciplines having correspondingly greater difficulty.

We needed to show the engineers a clear mapping between the objects they encountered on the plant floor in their work and the objects we were putting into the computer. This initial mapping was the instances. Nancy said, "I can see how the actual objects are represented, what I don't understand is the hierarchy. How do you know how many levels to put in, and how do you decide at which level to place the slots? And for that matter, how do you decide what should be a slot?"

Classification Strategies

Even at this early stage of the system development, the frame structure is several levels deep. In most situations, this is a very desirable design feature, as a deeply nested frame structure allows both a more modular design and a logical grouping of related facts for the inferencing. We derive two immediate major benefits from grouping instances:

- The inference engine will be able to reason more efficiently, and thus more quickly.

- We can write rules that are easier to read and debug.

In later chapters we'll see other benefits of a deeply nested frame structure, such as making it easier to build control structures for the inferencing process.

First, when we construct a knowledge base, deeply nested frames allow specialization of frames at varying levels. For example, pumps have certain unique characteristics that are not applicable to other machines (Figure 5-5). These characteristics, represented as slots of the frame PUMP such as OIL-AMOUNT and OIL-LINES, will be inherited only by frames and instances that are direct descendants of PUMP.

There is a second purpose for deeply nesting a frame structure. In reasoning about facts in the knowledge base, a deep frame structure provides small, logical groupings of information. (This applies whether the "reasoning" in question comes from the expert checking our rules or the inference engine chaining over them.)

```
Frame: PUMP
Parents: MACHINE
Instances: OIL-PUMP WASH-PUMP RINSE-PUMP
-- Slots (not all shown) --
OIL-AMOUNT:
OIL-LINES:
```

FIGURE 5-5. Unique slots of the PUMP frame

Use of the class name—for example, OILER—in a rule clause can limit the instances tested by the rule to instances only of OILER or OILER's child frames; in this case, such a clause would limit the inferencing to the single instance METAL-DISK-OILER. We thus avoid the need for convoluted rules that haltingly grope their way through the entire knowledge base, rules that spend most of their time winnowing out all those objects to which they don't apply. Instead, we have, in one simple stroke, restricted the set of instances to be tested by any one rule.

Revised Shutdown Rules: Matching Rules with Slot Values

So far, we've been examining the implementation of a frame hierarchy and the impact this has on our inferencing. This section expands our knowledge of how to take advantage of these frames to write rules that are both more structured and easier to read.

In the previous chapters, we developed a series of rules to determine whether the canning line should be shut down. Those rules were based on unstructured statements and assertions instead of frames, slots, and slot values. How can we alter that set of rules to reflect our new frame-based structures? One method is to develop a fixed syntax that will allow the inference engine to parse a rule into chunks that match elements of the frame system.

Matching Rules to Frames

Let's start by looking at one of the rules developed earlier (Figure 5-6). This rule states that a pump requires maintenance if it is overheating.

The rule HOT-PUMP (Figure 5-7) illustrates the new frame-based syntax. Let's examine how this new rule makes use of the OPERATING-TEMPERATURE and MAINTENANCE slots of PUMP instances.

Rule: **HOT–PUMP**
Rule Set: **SHUTDOWN–RULE–CLASS**
Documentation: An overheated pump can quickly be
  permanently damaged.
IF
  ?PUMP IS RUNNING HOT
THEN
  ?PUMP NEEDS MAINTENANCE IMMEDIATELY

FIGURE 5-6. The unstructured HOT-PUMP rule (Chapter 4)

The premise of the rule,

?PUMP IS A PUMP
AND
THE OPERATING–TEMPERATURE OF ?PUMP IS HIGH

states that ?PUMP is an instance of the PUMP Frame, and has a slot OPER-
ATING-TEMPERATURE with a value of HIGH. The inference engine parses
the statement in several steps. First, there is a check to see if the frame PUMP
exists and, if so, whether it has any instances. If instances exist, the variable
?pump is set to each instance in turn, and that instance's OPERATING-
TEMPERATURE slot value is tested to see if it equals HIGH. The pump

Rule: **HOT–PUMP**
Rule Set: **SHUTDOWN–RULE–CLASS**
Documentation: An overheated pump can quickly be
  permanently damaged.
IF
  ?PUMP IS A PUMP
  AND
  THE OPERATING–TEMPERATURE OF ?PUMP IS HIGH
THEN
  THE MAINTENANCE OF ?PUMP IS IMMEDIATELY

FIGURE 5-7. Changing rule syntax to use the frame structure: A frame-based rule

Frame: **PUMP**
Parents: **MACHINE**
Instances: **OIL-PUMP WASH-PUMP RINSE-PUMP**
-- Slots (not all shown) --
MAINTENANCE:
OIL-AMOUNT:
OIL-LINES:
OPERATING-TEMPERATURE: NORMAL
SHUTDOWN:

FIGURE 5-8. PUMP frame

frame (Figure 5-8) has three instances. Each will be checked in turn, and
for each that has an OPERATING-TEMPERATURE of HIGH, the premise
will be found true and the conclusion asserted.

The conclusion of the rule,

THE MAINTENANCE OF ?PUMP IS IMMEDIATELY

uses the same value for the variable ?PUMP as was set in the premise.
For example, ?PUMP is set to WASH-PUMP, and, if OPERATING-
TEMPERATURE was found to be HIGH, the rule asserts the value IMME-
DIATELY into WASH-PUMP's MAINTENANCE slot.

> NOTE: Each commercially available shell uses its own syntax for object-rule
> patterns. We have chosen to use our own syntax throughout the book(words
> in italics are constants used to make a more English-style format):
>
> <instance-name> *IS A* <parent-name>
> **AND**
> THE <slot-name> *OF* <instance-name> *IS* <value>
>
> This statement says that the clause will apply only to an instance of the class
> parent-name using the value in the slot slot-name. In GoldWorks, this state-
> ment would appear as:
>
> (*INSTANCE* <instance-name> *IS* <parent-name> *WITH* <slot-name> <value>)
>
> IntelliCorp's shell, KEE, uses a slightly different syntax to achieve the same
> effect:

(<instance-name> *IS IN CLASS* <parent-name>)
(*THE* <slot-name> *OF* <instance-name> *IS* <value>)

Appendix A provides example rule syntaxes from a number of commercial shells.

Let's look at another example. The rule LOW-WASH-PRESSURE (Figure 5-9) has been rewritten to use our new slots. The inference engine will assign the variable ?WASHER in turn to each instance of the frame WASHER, then it will test to see if the PRESSURE slot has a value of LOW. If so, it will assert the value SOON into the MAINTENANCE slot.

Although somewhat implementation dependent, grouping instances into classes and then specifying the class in the rule has two advantages. First, it is usually more efficient to test a rule with a subset of all the objects in the knowledge base, rather than the entire set. Even more importantly, if a rule is meant to apply only to a certain class of objects, not restricting it to that set can result in erroneous conclusions.

Let's look again at how the rule clauses match values in specific slots using the WASHER frame (Figure 5-10). The first WASHER slot, PRESSURE, matches true to the premise (or antecedent) clause:

```
THE PRESSURE OF ?WASHER IS LOW
```

when the value of a WASHER instance's slot is LOW. Another WASHER slot, MAINTENANCE, matches the consequent clause:

```
Rule:  LOW-WASH-PRESSURE
Rule Set:  SHUTDOWN-RULE-CLASS
Documentation: Low pressure can be serious--schedule
   maintenance.
IF
   ?WASHER IS A WASHER
   AND
   THE PRESSURE OF ?WASHER IS LOW
THEN
   THE MAINTENANCE OF ?WASHER IS SOON
```

Figure 5-9. The LOW-WASH-PRESSURE rule

```
Frame: WASHER
Parents: SPRAYER WASHER-2 PRE-PAINT-WASHER
-- Slots (not all shown) --
MAINTENANCE: UNNEEDED
ON-CRITICAL-PATH: YES
OPERATING-TEMPERATURE: NORMAL
PRESSURE: NORMAL
```

FIGURE 5-10. The WASHER frame

THE MAINTENANCE OF ?WASHER IS SOON

such that if an instance of WASHER has a low pressure (tested in the antecedent clause of the rule), then the value SOON will be asserted into that instance's MAINTENANCE slot.

At the Plant

George was the first of the experts to understand our new strategy. He was accustomed to looking at flow charts, and as we began to write the rules he saw that the debugging process would be much easier if sets of rules could be limited to only a few groups of instances. With this in mind, he began to make small changes in the hierarchy, showing us places where certain abstractions could be added.

For example, looking at the washers and the paint machines, he pointed out that both sets of components were in fact sprayers. He had suddenly found a heuristic for grouping: By finding components that had similar attributes, a higher classification could be created that would share slots. In the case of the sprayers, they all had attributes such as nozzles that could become clogged. His confidence increased with the realization that these classifications also allowed for rules that had more general properties. He could now design rules that talked not about washers or paint machines but instead dealt with the more general concept of nozzle problems.

As the team members continued to discuss and dabble with the new representation, they became increasingly excited. By adding comments to each frame and slot they realized that it would be easier to document their work. Generalizing attributes would allow for fewer rules and thus a more testable and maintainable system. And by viewing the plant as a hierarchical arrangement of objects, they could more quickly make changes and test new ideas.

EXAMPLE: WASHER COMPONENT

We'll now take a detailed look at how we can apply the benefits of grouping information within a frame hierarchy to the WASHER frame. The two main constituents of the change in structure are:

- slots of the COMPONENT frame (illustrated with its child frame, WASHER)

- instances of WASHER, one for each washer in the plant

We will also rewrite the earlier relation-based rules to use these instances and slots. See Figure 5-2 for how WASHER fits into the overall frame hierarchy described in this chapter.

Figure 5-11a shows the definition of the WASHER frame; Figure 5-11b shows one of the three specific instances of WASHER, WASHER-1 (the other instances of WASHER are WASHER-2 and PRE-PAINT-WASHER). Note that the default value for ON-CRITICAL-PATH in the class WASHER is YES. However, WASHER-1 has been defined as not being on the critical path, because WASHER-1 and WASHER-2 run in parallel on the canning line. We specify this by giving it's ON-CRITICAL-PATH slot a value of NO.

Levels of Technical Ability

The team was now beginning to differentiate along lines of technical interest. Nancy had a real fascination for the process of translation, and became a diligent

---

Frame: **WASHER**   Instance: **WASHER-1**
Parents: **SPRAYER**   Parents: **WASHER**
Instances: **WASHER-1**
          WASHER-2
          PRE-PAINT-WASHER

-- Slots --   -- Slots --
MAINTENANCE: MAINTENANCE:
ON-CRITICAL-PATH: YES   ON-CRITICAL-PATH: NO
OPERATING-TEMPERATURE:NORMAL   OPERATING-TEMPERATURE:NORMAL
PRESSURE: PRESSURE: NORMAL
SHUTDOWN: SHUTDOWN:

        a   *b*

FIGURE 5-11. (a) WASHER and (b) the instance WASHER-1

explorer of the new techniques. George, on the other hand, was much more interested in learning just enough of the technology so that he could return to his desk and rethink the rules we had been developing.

This split in the team interests was part of the effect for which we, the knowledge engineers, were striving. Just as experts have different levels of expertise, so too do they have different capacities for and interests in acquiring new knowledge. As the system became more complicated, we saw the need for a bridge between our technical expertise and the knowledge of the plant experts. Nancy would be the person who would translate some of our more obscure technical jargon into a form that would be comfortable to George. By a subtle process, Nancy would increasingly take on the role of knowledge engineer, explaining to George the reasons for certain shell-specific techniques that were not necessarily clear in their framework of dealing with plant problems.

SLOT FACETS

Many commercial systems distinguish between **system facets** and **user facets.** System facets are fixed parts of the implementation and are always present. Often, these facets are integrated with other tools in a shell. Figure 5-12 shows a detailed view of a slot with three system facets (most shells have some predefined facets): a default value facet, a documentation facet, and a constraints facet.

The three system facets illustrated in Figure 5-12 all are important aspects of representing knowledge in a frame system. Let's examine these individually before proceeding to user facets.

Default Value Facet and the Unknown Value

When a rule clause matches on a slot value to determine a fact in the knowledge base, one of three things can happen: the value is found, the

---

Slot: **PRESSURE**
Frame: **WASHER**
Default Values: NORMAL
Documentation: This is the apparent pressure at the nozzle head.
Constraints: LOW NORMAL HIGH

FIGURE 5-12. Pressure slot with system facets

value matches the test, and the rule clause is found to be true; the value is found, the value does not satisfy the test, and the rule clause, (and thus the rule) is found to be false; and no value is found (the value is *unknown*).

Default values are used in cases where the developer wishes a slot never to have an unknown value. Sometimes, as is the case in mechanical systems such as the plant, unknown values should not exist; if no problem has been identified, then the system state, and thus the slots representing that state, is assumed to have a value of NORMAL or its equivalent. In this type of situation, a default value is specified at the frame level. Thus, all child frames of that frame and all their instances will have the default value if no new value has been specified locally. Use of default values also provides developers with a handy mechanism for resetting the knowledge base to a default state; by retracting all local values at the instance level, all the instances will then inherit the "normal," default state.

In most programming languages, when a variable value is unknown an error is signaled. In expert systems, however, an unknown value can form an important part of the reasoning process. For example, many situations exist where, at least initially, an expert does not know what the value of some parameter should be. In our rules, we will often test a value to see whether it is unknown. If so, we want to take a specific action, often invoking a new set of rules whose purpose is to discover the missing value using an alternate approach. As a simple example of this, the plant rules might ask an operator if a tank has been foaming over. If the operator has not been watching the tank and answers "unknown," then additional rules might check to see if water is on the floor, the pressure has increased dramatically, and so on.

Documentation Facet

The documentation facet is primarily for developers and later maintainers. It provides a local commentary on the purpose of a slot and other types of maintenance information, such as which rules might depend on it. A documentation facet can, however, serve a second purpose if the developers so desire. When users are queried about a slot value, it is possible for the developer to incorporate a mechanism that will respond to a question from the user as to the purpose of the requested value. For example, if the system requests an operator to identify a foaming tank, the accompanying documentation for the slot might explain that foaming in a tank indicates an improper mixing of wash materials, resulting in a blue foam, all of which provides the user with a frame of reference for the question.

Constraints Facet

The constraints facet restricts the values that the slot is permitted to take on. In the case of the PRESSURE slot, one of three values can be set:

LOW, NORMAL, and HIGH. A number of different constraints are possible, including limiting the value to a type of value (e.g., integer, real number, or character string); a fixed interval of numbers; a fixed set of values (such as our example with the PRESSURE slot); and instances of a certain class (for example, we might wish to indicate that pumps can be linked only to sprayers).

Constraints have a number of uses, primarily for the interface. They give developers a simple, foolproof mechanism for specifying the set of values from which an end user can select. This selection list can then be utilized by graphic images, menus, and so forth. They can also be used by the developer to construct simple truth maintenance systems, mechanisms by which errors are triggered when the user attempts to perform an illegal action. Finally, constraints can be utilized in the rules to help the developer detect errors in rule logic. As we'll see later, rules can be written where a calculated value is inserted into a slot; if this calculated value violates a constraint, the system can indicate a problem to the developer, aiding in the rule-debugging task.

NOTE: Using constraints wherever they are known to exist is an excellent design practice. They can serve as easily maintainable selection sets for user prompts, and they aid the developer in recognizing logical flaws in rules during the development of the expert system.

Several of the commercial shells provide the user with a second type of constraint on a slot's values, cardinality, although in general this is of limited use. Cardinality constrains the number of values that a slot can have. To be useful, of course, the shell must have the capability of a slot taking on multiple values. In practice, we usually only care about two cases: slots with single values and slots with multiple values. In the case of the PRESSURE slot, we want the device to take on only a single pressure. On the other hand, if we are keeping a maintenance history of a washer, then we would like to have multiple values in a HISTORY slot, each value a date when the machine was serviced. Being able to set this type of constraint is useful in that single value slots cannot accidentally be assigned multiple and—as would be the case with the PRESSURE slot—thus meaningless values.

User Facets

User facets enable users to extend slot definitions with their own slot attributes. For example, additional information about the pressure of a pump might be included in a list of facets; we could track both the most recent and the previously-observed values of a pump's pressure. To do so, we might

Slot: **MAINTENANCE**
Frame: **WASHER**
Default Values:
Documentation: "Tells you when a machine needs to be
  worked on"
Constraints: ONE-OF{UNNEEDED SOON IMMEDIATELY}
-- User Facets --
Last-Maintenance-Time:

FIGURE 5-13. The MAINTENANCE slot with user facets

define a Last-Maintenance-Time facet to hold the old reading and use the
slot's value to hold the most recent reading (Figure 5-13).

In shells that provide extended rule patterns that match on slot facets,
user facets make possible a much richer descriptive language for capturing
the expert's heuristics. For example, we might have the rule clause

THE LAST-MAINTENANCE-TIME OF THE MAINTENANCE
OF WASHER-1 WAS IMMEDIATELY

allowing us to reason on the value of the slot in relation to information
about previous values—in this case, checking to see whether this washer
has caused trouble before by requiring immediate maintenance.

USING RELATIONS

Often, we want to define a relationship between objects that:

- defines connectivity between two or more objects

- illustrates a general approach to describing complex interdependen-
  cies between components

Relations allow you to define standard patterns that express relationships between objects (Chapter 8 discusses connectivity in detail with
respect to object programming). In some shells and languages, such as PRO-
LOG, relations are the basic building block for rules. Other environments,
such as GoldWorks, provide easy-to-use mechanisms for defining relations
and including them in rules. And some environments, such as KEE, rely
solely on frames and slot values to define relationships between objects.

As we have seen above, slot values enable us to associate an attribute value with an object—for example, PRESSURE and HIGH for WASHER-PUMP. In environments that use relationships in place of frames and slots, this relationship of a pump to its pressure might be defined as the relation PRESSURE in the form:

PRESSURE WASHER-PUMP HIGH

Although this relation is easily defined using a slot value, situations exist where the value of an instance's slot will not be a simple value but instead a pointer to another instance or a two-part definition. Again, we can use facets to represent the second part of the definition (e.g., our example of a previous maintenance problem stored as a facet value on the MAINTENANCE slot).

Other situations requiring relations include the need to represent a single relationship between a large number of components, and the need for a functional operator that performs some function—for example, a test that involves checking an external state of the system to see whether the relationship holds at a given time.

Let's examine a situation that arose in the plant where a relationship between the plant components required more than two arguments.

An Example Relation: Provides

We wish to describe the fact that different machines provide things to machines to which they are related. For example, a pump provides pressure to a washer. The simplest way to do this is to define a PROVIDES slot whose value is the name of the object being provided with something. Figure 5-14 shows our new slot for WASH-PUMP (the wash-pump provides pressure to washer-1).

Slot: **PROVIDES**
Instance: **WASH-PUMP**
Documentation: This pump instance supplies pressure to
    this slot's instance.
Constraints: ONE-OF{ LOW NORMAL HIGH}
Value: **WASHER-1**

FIGURE 5-14. The PRESSURE Slot

Relation: **PROVIDES**
Arguments: (PROVIDER RECIPIENT)
Description: The PROVIDER provides something to the
  RECIPIENT

FIGURE 5-15. The PROVIDES relation

The relation in Figure 5-15 is *logically equivalent* to using the PROVIDES slot. It is also *functionally equivalent* to using a slot, except that it is difficult to perform several component-specific functions that are possible with slots, such as attaching daemons and documentation.

If we were to define a relation such as PROVIDES in our knowledge base, we would next create assertions that link the components together—the equivalent of adding values to the PROVIDES slot.

Shown in Figure 5-16 are a frame-based definition connecting WASH-PUMP to WASHER-1 and the same connection made via a relation and an unstructured fact.

Some of the PROVIDER-TO assertions for the plant are shown below. Note that this is the syntax used in languages such as Prolog. Assertions matching (PROVIDER-TO ?X ?Y) include:

Representation Type	As It Appears in the Knowledge Base	English Equivalent
Unstructured Fact	the WASH-PUMP provides WASHER-1	The wash-pump is a provider to washer-1.
Relation	"provider-to wash-pump washer-1" provider-to wash-pump → washer-1	The pump and washer are related by the wash-pump being a provider to washer-1.

Object	Instance: WASH-PUMP
	 Slots:
	    temperature: Normal
	    ⋮
	    provides: WASHER-1
		One attribute (among others) of the washer-pump is that it is a provider to the washer-1.

FIGURE 5-16. Table of representation types and their implementation

```
PROVIDER-TO OIL-PUMP METAL-DISK-OILER
PROVIDER-TO WASH-PUMP WASHER-2
PROVIDER-TO WASH-PUMP WASHER-1
```

So far, we have shown no good reason for using a relation in place of a slot—in fact, the lack of facets and other features makes slots the ideal choice for this situation. However, we wish to extend the concept of connectivity to describe the actual materials that flow between components. Although our PROVIDES mechanism works very nicely for expressing the physical connection, situations exist where we must identify the different materials that flow along these connections.

For example, a washer receives pressure from a pump, wash-mix from one tank, and rinse-mix from a second tank. It's difficult to capture these three types of relationships using our simple provides mechanism.

Let's modify our definition of the PROVIDES relation (Figure 5-15) so that we can describe in detail how auxiliary components (such as pumps and tanks) service other components. The new format, containing a third argument to PROVIDES, is:

```
PROVIDES <what> <provider> <recipient>
```

We'll use this relation to assert such facts as:

```
PROVIDES PRESSURE WASH-PUMP WASHER-1
```

establishing that the wash-pump provides pressure to washer-1, and

```
PROVIDES WASH-MIX WASH-TANK WASHER-1
```

establishing that the wash-tank provides wash-mix to WASHER-1.

The advantage of the relation is its ability to become arbitrarily complex. Further arguments might, for example, modify the object being provided. In the case of a process-control application, pipes provide a mixture in which each component is at a distinct concentration. That relationship would appear as:

```
PROVIDES <what> <concentration> <provider> <recipient>
```

Increasingly complex relationships such as these are difficult and awkward to represent using only the frame/slot representation. One alternative to the PROVIDES relation would be to define slots named PROVIDES-PRESSURE, PROVIDES-WASH-MIX, and so forth. For example, PUMP instances would require a PROVIDES-PRESSURE slot, while tank instances would require PROVIDES-WASH-MIX and PROVIDES-RINSE-MIX slots.

Yet another alternative would be to define a PROVIDES slot containing a list of pairs. Using this approach, the PROVIDES slot of WASH-TANK could have a value (WASH-MIX WASHER-1).These approaches work but are unnecessarily convoluted.

In many cases, choosing any one of these three approaches (relation, unique slot names, or paired slot values) is a matter of personal preference or limitations of the implementation shell. Frames and slots can always be designed to meet any of the circumstances described above. We have chosen the PROVIDES relation over either of the frame alternatives just described because, in our opinion, it is clearer and simpler.

RULE BEHAVIOR

In this section, we'll examine, on a rule-by-rule basis, how the inference engine:

- matches rule clauses to frame slot-values
- creates agenda items (a list of rules in the order they will be evaluated)
- fires (evaluates) the rules, asserting new facts and conclusions

This section provides a look inside the inference engine to show how the rules connect together and the order in which events happen. We'll follow the inference engine, step by step, through a single reasoning path. We'll start with a few basic facts (represented by slot values); the inference engine "reasons" from these facts to discover new facts and reach conclusions.

All inference engines have some type of agenda mechanism. The agenda is a list of the rules sequenced in the order in which they will fire. Although agendas are always present, only some of the commercial shells provide access to the agenda. Two types of access can be provided. The most basic lets the user select the mechanism controlling how items are placed on the agenda, for example, between a mechanism that recognizes rule priorities and one that fires rules in a more random order. A second type of access sometimes included provides manipulative access to the agenda, enabling the user to remove or reorder the rules on the agenda. This type of manipulation, needless to say, extremely sophisticated techniques, not required for any but the most esoteric applications.

Forward Chaining Due to an Abnormal Condition

The HOT-PUMP rule (Figure 5-17) requires maintenance when a pump's operating temperature becomes high.

Rule: **HOT—PUMP**
Rule Set: **SHUTDOWN—RULE—CLASS**
Documentation: An overheated pump can quickly be
  permanently damaged.
IF
  ?PUMP IS A PUMP
  AND
  THE OPERATING—TEMPERATURE OF ?PUMP IS HIGH
THEN
  THE MAINTENANCE OF ?PUMP IS IMMEDIATELY

FIGURE 5-17. HOT-PUMP rule

Let's start by inserting the value HIGH into the OPERATING-TEMPERATURE slot of OIL-PUMP (Figure 5-18). We assume that a sensor or a human operator has somehow kicked off this process.

With the insertion of the value HIGH into the OPERATING-TEMPERATURE slot of OIL-PUMP, the antecedent of the HOT-PUMP rule (Figure 5-17) becomes true. The inference engine now places the rule HOT-PUMP on the agenda, ready to fire the consequent (its THEN clause).

When the agenda item for the HOT-PUMP rule fires, the need for pump maintenance is asserted. This in turn matches the antecedent of the rule MAINTENANCE-SHUTDOWN (Figure 5-19). The process is as follows:

- When HOT-PUMP fired, it inserted the value IMMEDIATELY into the MAINTENANCE slot of OIL-PUMP.

- Next, the antecedent of MAINTENANCE-SHUTDOWN (Figure 5-16) was matched, setting the rule variable ?COMPONENT to OIL-PUMP and ?WHEN to IMMEDIATELY.

Instance: **OIL—PUMP**
Parents: **PUMP**
—— Slots (not all shown) ——
OPERATING—TEMPERATURE: HIGH

FIGURE 5-18. Getting Things Started: The Pump Overheats

Rule: **MAINTENANCE–SHUTDOWN**
Rule Set: **SHUTDOWN–RULE–CLASS**
Documentation: A component must be shut down during
  maintenance.
IF
  ?COMPONENT IS A COMPONENT
  AND
  THE MAINTENANCE OF ?COMPONENT IS ?WHEN
THEN
  THE SHUTDOWN OF ?COMPONENT IS ?WHEN

FIGURE 5-19. Rule relating the need for maintenance to the need to shutdown

When the agenda item for the MAINTENANCE-SHUTDOWN rule
fires, advice is given that the oil-pump is to be shut down. The rule AUXI-
LIARY-SHUTDOWN (Figure 5-20) links a component to other components
that depend upon it.

NOTE: The rule checks all components in turn. We have not, at this point,
created a frame such as AUXILIARY-COMPONENT—this rule, however, provides a great deal of incentive to add a second frame to the knowledge base to
indentify all auxiliary components.

?AUXILIARY-COMPONENT IS A COMPONENT

could then be changed to read

?AUXILIARY-COMPONENT IS AN AUXILIARY- COMPONENT

and only components defined as auxiliary by the new parent could be checked,
greatly reducing the rule search space.

After setting the variable ?WHEN to IMMEDIATELY (the SHUT-
DOWN slot value for OIL-PUMP), we test to make sure the value is not
UNNEEDED. The rule states that the metal-disk-oiler must now be shut
down also, since it is linked to the oil-pump. This linkage was earlier
defined by the assertion

PROVIDES PRESSURE OIL–PUMP METAL–DISK–OILER

Rule: **AUXILIARY-SHUTDOWN**
Rule Set: **SHUTDOWN-RULE-CLASS**
Documentation: If a supporting secondary machine shuts
  down, the primary machine shuts down also.
IF
   ?AUXILIARY-COMPONENT IS A COMPONENT
   AND
   THE SHUTDOWN OF ?AUXILIARY-COMPONENT IS ?WHEN
   AND
   NOT ?WHEN IS UNNEEDED
   AND
   PROVIDES ?SUBSTANCE ?AUXILIARY-COMPONENT ?SUPPORTED-
   MACHINE
THEN
   THE SHUTDOWN OF ?SUPPORTED-MACHINE IS ?WHEN

FIGURE 5-20. The AUXILIARY-SHUTDOWN Rule

which now matches the rule clause

PROVIDES ?SUBSTANCE ?AUXILIARY-COMPONENT ?SUPPORTED-
MACHINE

in the AUXILIARY-SHUTDOWN rule. When the agenda item AUXILIARY-
SHUTDOWN fires, it calls for a shutdown of the oiler by asserting

THE SHUTDOWN *OF* OILER *IS* IMMEDIATELY

This assertion in turn matches the antecedent of the rule LINE- SHUT-
DOWN (Figure 5-21).

THE SHUTDOWN OF ?COMPONENT IS ?WHEN

This rule in turn asserts that the entire line must now be shut down, because
METAL-DISK-OILER has an ON-CRITICAL-PATH slot value of YES.
   We have been prefacing our rules with an is-a clause such as

?COMPONENT IS A PUMP

because we wish to limit the instances that will match in the rule. However,
in LINE-SHUTDOWN, we do not need to use this format for the CANNING-

```
Rule: LINE-SHUTDOWN
Rule Set: SHUTDOWN-RULE-CLASS
Documentation: The shutdown of a critical machine forces
   the entire line to shut down.
IF
   ?COMPONENT IS A COMPONENT
   AND
   THE SHUTDOWN OF ?COMPONENT IS ?WHEN
   AND
   NOT ?WHEN IS UNNEEDED
   AND
   THE ON-CRITICAL-PATH OF ?COMPONENT IS YES
THEN
   THE SHUTDOWN OF CANNING-LINE IS ?WHEN
```

FIGURE 5-21. The LINE-SHUTDOWN rule

LINE instance because we use the actual name of the instance, not a variable. Specifying an instance's class (frame parent) is only necessary when a rule variable is used, not a specific instance.

INTERFACE

Even though we have built only the most rudimentary system at this point, it is nonetheless quite complex in the interrelatedness of the parts. An important constituent of the development process is creating tools that permit consistent testing and analysis of the developing system. With the introduction of frames and slots, and their associated default values and user facets, we have the first building block necessary to creating repeatable test conditions.

As we add more rules and domain information into the system, it will be important to have a **consistent** basis for examining the impact of these changes on already working systems. Because of the combinatorial effect of rules, unexpected side effects often crop up. Note the stress on the word consistent—we want to test the new additions, but we also need to keep testing old parts of the working system to make sure we have not introduced confounding interactions.

The ideal test interface consists of two parts: a set of queries to the system, exercising the problem-solving logic; and a graphical interface that allows us to easily extend the test scenarios, alter domain parameters, and observe the functioning of the system as it runs.

From this point on in the book, we will describe interfaces that can be implemented without graphics, but we will assume graphics exist and use illustrations and descriptions that utilize this more facile form of user interaction. With the recent advances in hardware and software, it is hard to imagine that any shells will be offered that have no built-in graphics capabilities.

Rule Firing

The actual process of rule firing may be either **automatic** or **manual**, though at this stage of development it is unlikely that we will want anything other than a manual interface. For example, we might have sensors directly linked to the computer and thus to our expert system. In this case, as data values change, the rules might be fired automatically.

Another possibility is to provide the user with a manual control, allowing a number of values to be changed and then, at the user's discretion, invoking inferencing. For example, if the canning line prototype is being tested on the factory floor, the operator might update several values in the knowledge base and only then invoke the inferencing.

SUMMARY

In this chapter we examined the use of **frames** (classes) for representing objects in the problem domain. The attributes of these objects are represented in the frames as **slots**. The slots in turn may have attributes of their own (**facets**). The diagnostic rules of earlier chapters were modified to interface to the frames and slots using fixed patterns in the rule clauses.

The process of creating frames, slots, and rules is an ongoing one. As rules are added to the knowledge base, we will occasionally find it beneficial to add corresponding new slots and new frames. These extensions will gradually increase our descriptive mastery of the domain. The more accurately (and succinctly) we can describe the domain, the better we'll be able to model it with an expert system.

READINGS

Brachman, R.J. 1979. On the epistemological status of semantic networks. In *Associative networks: Representation and use of knowledge by computers*, ed. N. V. Findler. Orlando, FL: Academic Press.

Minsky, M. 1975. A framework for representing knowledge. In *The psychology of computer vision*, ed. P. Winston. New York: McGraw-Hill.

Negoita, C. V. 1985. *Expert systems and fuzzy systems.* Menlo Park, CA: The Benjamin-Cummings Publishing Company.

Norman, D.A., D.E. Rumelhart, and LNR Research Group. 1975. *Explorations in cognition.* Freeman.

Quillian, M.R. 1968. Semantic Memory. In *Semantic information processing,* ed. M.L. Minsky. Boston, MA: MIT Press.

Woods, W. A. 1986. Important issues in knowledge representation. *Proceedings of the IEEE 74,* no. 10: 1322–1334.

Woods, W. A. 1975. What's in a link: Foundations for semantic networks. In *Representation and understanding: Studies in cognitive science,* ed. D. Bobrow. Orlando, FL: Academic Press.

6

BUILDING A
GRAPHICAL INTERFACE

At this point in the development process of an expert system, a better interface than that provided by the development environment is required. Having gone through several cycles of revision and expansion, the expert system is ready for the first field test with end users, and if they have to work with an interface that is difficult to use, the evaluation will fail to produce meaningful feedback. At the same time, the knowledge base is becoming sufficiently complex to require a graphical interface that will allow observation of both the state of the knowledge base and changes that occur in the state and provide controls to allow rapid setup of test scenarios.

The overall development time for the knowledge base can be greatly reduced by the use of simple graphical test interfaces. The user interface will make or break the final system—users willingly adopt these new systems only when they have an interface that is straightforward and easy to use. The user interface of an expert system is particularly important, because it reflects both the state of the world that is being used in the reasoning and the process and rationale for that reasoning. Only by clearly viewing this information will the users feel confident of the advice they are being asked to follow.

> The combination of object-based graphics with the expertise encoded in the knowledge base is what sells expert systems to management and the end users.

At the canning plant, the team had completed the overall assessment of the quality-control problem, chosen a working environment (hardware and software), and completed the initial knowledge acquisition and prototype implementation. The working prototype now contained enough information to present to the future users. The evaluation would consist of a visit to the factory floor where the operators would work with the system as if it were actually on line, entering plant states and noting down any problems they were having with the system. This assessment would include logging the advice the system gave, the procedures it requested they follow, and the actual problem and the solution. However, before the evaluation could begin, one last thing remained to be done—the design and implementation of a graphical interface enabling the testers to easily access the system.

WHY OBJECT-BASED GRAPHICS ARE NECESSARY

Good interfaces are required in computer systems because they reduce the learning time required to get started, as well as the number of mistakes users make using a system. Graphical interfaces are superior to textual interfaces because they can be made to more closely resemble the environment to which a user is accustomed. Cognitive psychologists say that people make errors when they have the wrong mental model of how a mechanism operates. Graphical interfaces, which can combine realistic pictures, color, and animation, provide clear illustrations of how a system operates. And all computer hardware now available, from the least expensive PCs to the high-end workstations, provides high-quality graphic capabilities.

The knowledge base that we are designing is oriented around objects (the frames). These objects have attributes, which are described using slots. Ideally, we would like to extend this object paradigm to our graphics, because this will provide the highest level of integration between the graphics and the expert system. Also, as we have seen from the previous chapter on frames, object-based systems are easy to build and maintain because of their modular nature.

Let's start with our objective: to be able to build developer and end user interfaces for the initial prototype. We would like to accomplish this without resorting to a programming language. In the rest of this chapter, we'll describe the components of an object-based graphical interface tool and the manner in which such a tool would be applied to building interfaces.

NOTE: From this point on in the book, we'll be using examples of graphical interfaces that assume the availability of a graphics package with features similar to the one described here. More advanced users may wish to use this chapter as a starting point for implementing their own object-graphics system.

A graphical interface should enable developers and end users to:

- observe changes in the knowledge base as they occur, e.g.
    slot values changed by the user
    slot values changed as a result of rules firing
    slot values changed by external sensors

- interact with the knowledge base, e.g.
    change slot values
    execute handlers and commands

- emulate interfaces the expert is used to seeing, e.g.
    end user control panels
    schematic diagrams

Observations of changes in the knowledge base are important to both developers and end users, though for slightly different reasons. The developer requires an easy way of simultaneously viewing a large number of slot values while the rules are running, in order to check for proper rule logic and sequencing of rule firing. The end user needs to confirm that before inferencing occurs, the correct plant state is reflected in the knowledge base.

Developers must constantly interact with the knowledge base to set up different test scenarios. End users must set plant states and initiate requests for information and advice.

The developer needs to develop an interface that the end user will be comfortable with, but that is still easy to maintain as the knowledge base changes and expands.

Terms for Graphical Objects

The following terms are used in this book and in most of the commercially available software:

- **Active Region** (also referred to as hotspots, hyper regions, etc.): An area of the screen that will respond to a user action. In an object-based system, an active region will often correspond to an object or an object's attributes.

- **Point**: To point at an active region, move the mouse until the cursor is positioned over the region. When the cursor is positioned over an active region on the screen, the region is usually indicated by being highlighted or boxed. In some environments, a key must be pressed to highlight the active region.

- **Mouse button**: A mouse pointing device will have from one to three buttons (left, middle, and right). On systems that don't support a mouse, combining the enter or return key with another key such as shift, command, or control can simulate the different mouse buttons. In systems that have heavy usage, industrial-quality track balls with a similar button replace the mouse.

- **Click:** To click a mouse button, press and release the button quickly. Clicking on an object or region means to point at the object and then click a mouse button.

- **Select:** To select an object or region, point the cursor at the object or region and click a mouse button. In systems that do not have a mouse, you can move to a selectable object or region using the tab or arrow keys on the keyboard. These keys move the cursor from one selectable object or region to the next.

- **Touch Screens:** An increasing number of systems use touch screens; in this case, the action of pointing and clicking is replaced by the user touching the active region with a finger or other solid object.

GRAPHICAL INTERFACE ARCHITECTURE

To design and lay out our interface, we would like to use an arbitrarily large drawing space on which we can place graphical images. This region, a **canvas**, is a conceptual object represented by a frame. We are, of course, limited to the size of the screen in what we can see at any one time, but our infinite canvas can be scrolled about to show control panels and the like that are larger than our display screen. A canvas is displayed in a **viewport**, a rectangular region defined on the screen by a solid border and, possibly, scroll bars. The viewport is most often implemented as a **window**.

Knowledge base objects are presented on the canvas using **images**, which are also represented as frames. Images are made active by associating them with **active regions** on the viewport. When you place the mouse cursor over an image and click, the active region is recognized by the software that implements the window mechanism, causing the image to respond. Figure 6-1 illustrates a simple canvas that contains two images.

The kinds of images we might expect to see in a graphical interface include those that display text or numbers stored in the knowledge base, allow manipulation of these values, and present displays along more than one dimension. In Figure 6-1, we are displaying information on the pump's temperature. The value is currently NORMAL but can also take on the values LOW and HIGH.

Because we are building interfaces for the end user, we need images that correspond to real world objects, for example dials and gauges. These basic images can be combined to build up complex visual displays, for example an operator's control panel. An ideal system will enable users to

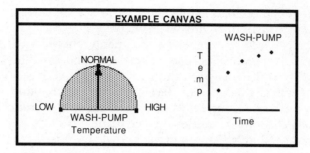

FIGURE 6-1. Canvas with two images

define their own images, providing more accurate emulation of the end user's environment.

> The team at the plant wished to design an interface that would give the operators many graphic clues as to the expert system's operation. One idea they had was to show a picture of the plant, with graphical depictions of each machine. Clicking on a machine would inform the operator of that machine's current status, reassuring them that the computer was working with an up-to-date set of data. Another idea was to have the components be highlighted as the inference engine ran. This would provide the operator a quick overview of the information that was being used in creating advice. And there was an obvious need for a simple interface that would let the operators rapidly update the knowledge base (since at this point in the system's development no direct sensor input would be used).

In Figure 6-2, we see the beginnings of a simple schematic diagram, a canvas containing images of the wash-pump and the washer. Note the two different images for the wash-pump, one a schematic representation, the

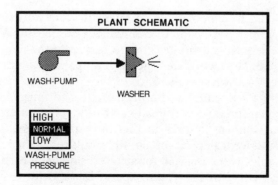

FIGURE 6-2. Plant schematic canvas

other a menu of choices that allows the user to set the current state of the pump's pressure to HIGH, NORMAL, or LOW.

The user can select a value in the menu image with the mouse. Selecting the value places the chosen value in the slot and also might change the color of the image. In the figure, NORMAL has been selected. Using images such as this one, the developer can quickly build an interface enabling users to inspect current knowledge base values and change those values to reflect changing conditions in the plant.

This interface shows changes in the knowledge base as they occur. For the developer, it provides a way to debug the dynamic elements; for an end user, a similar interface might provide a way of ensuring that the knowledge base representation of the state of the plant accurately reflects the current state of the plant when inferencing takes place.

Building a Developer Interface

An interface that is to be used solely by a developer does not need to emulate something familiar, but has only to efficiently utilize available screen space to show the most information. Developers need to test the environment, so they require images that show changing values and enable rapid changes to knowledge-base values. Additionally, they should provide facilities for quickly building a command interface (e.g., a command to reset the knowledge base to the default values).

Figure 6-3 shows an example control panel taken from work done for NASA (the example is taken from the Albathion Expert System Learning Environment (AXLE) version 1.0 on the IBM PC). The NASA expert system, FIXER, was designed to explore computer controls as part of automating a space station. The expert system underlying the diagram diagnoses problems in the oxygen recovery mechanism in the space station's life support system. In this case, we see the values of selected slots that were set after a fault occurred. As the rules run, the slot values change as the rules assert intermediate results. The final diagnosis is shown in the lower left and right of this canvas.

Of course, the development team often includes an expert, who may require a different perspective on the knowledge base, using a more familiar interface. Figure 6-4 shows another graphical view of the NASA knowledge base. This interface closely mirrors the original paper schematic of the system used by the NASA designers. Each of the component names shown in the schematic is an active region, implemented as an image on a canvas.

This particular interface was designed to allow the expert on the development team to simulate failures in the life support system. Clicking on a component produced a menu of possible failures. When a failure was selected, fault values were asserted for selected slots, and then the inference engine was activated. In this way, the expert could quickly assess the impact of new rules as they were added to the knowledge base.

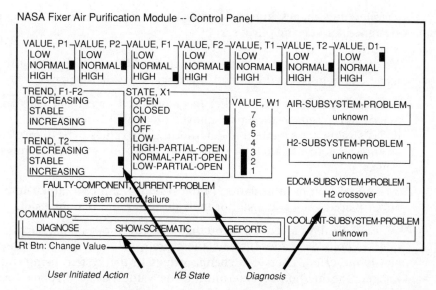

FIGURE 6-3. Developer canvas showing slot values in NASA application(AXLE)

Types of Images

Images are used to represent the value of object attributes. Graphical objects provide a mechanism for monitoring changes as the expert system runs, as well as for entering information about the outside world or changing the progress of the inferencing. As an interface building tool, images can also be used to instigate actions in the system.

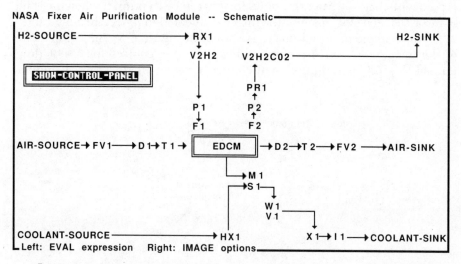

FIGURE 6-4. Engineers' schematic for space station life support module (AXLE)

The following images are basic types, modifiable to create custom images designed for specific purposes:

Value displays the value of a slot associated with the image. The user may be able to select the image to change the value displayed.

Dial/gauge displays the values that the monitored object can take on. Selecting a point on the image moves the dial pointer and sets the object's value. One method of determining the values to be displayed as choices is to use the slot constraints (e.g., one of a set, number ranges, etc).

Plot is a depiction of information in the system along two dimensions, either paired values in a slot or the values in more than one slot.

Fixed menu displays a vertical menu that is fixed—it does not disappear once a choice is made. Instead, the current value of the associated slot is indicated. Users can change values in the system using this image. One method of determining the values to be displayed as choices is to use a slot constraint; each of the constraining values becomes a choice.

Actuator displays the name of a handler. Selecting the image activates the handler or function.

Bitmap is a graphic picture depicting an object (e.g., a pump). This image responds in a fashion similar to the actuator.

The value that an image displays can be the value of any slot (or variable) in the knowledge base. An image that displays the value of a slot is **associated** with that slot. Many graphics images can be **dynamic**: when the value of the associated slot changes, the image is updated to reflect the new value.

An example of a dial image is shown in Figure 6-5. The components of the image are: active regions indicating value choices for a slot (low, normal, high); an indicator of the current value, in this case a pointer;

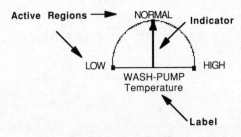

FIGURE 6-5. Dial image

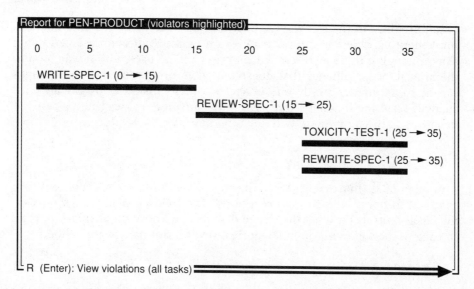

FIGURE 6-6. Gantt chart showing project start and end times (AXLE)

a label identifying the instance and slot this dial is monitoring (WASH-PUMP's TEMPERATURE slot).

Many applications require images that show relationships among multiple slot values in the knowledge base. For example, in a planning application, it is desirable to show tasks to be done in a display known as a Gantt chart (Figure 6-6). Here, each image represents two slot values, the start and end times for the task, shown as a bar. The left end of the bar, positioned with respect to a horizontal axis—here the number of days from the project's start—represents the start time and the right end represents the end time. Thus, the length of the bar shows the duration of the task. Placing the bars relative to one another provides the user with an overview of the total schedule.

In this example, the value image was modified to show a bar instead of a numeric value. When the user clicked on a bar, he/she was queried for new start and end times. Changing the times resulted in changes to the image's location and length, causing the image to "slide" along the time scale (seen at the top of the image). In this modified image, the image not only changed shape but also location in response to value changes in the knowledge base. However, the image is still only displaying the value of a single object's attributes.

CANVAS AND IMAGE OBJECT REPRESENTATION

Each canvas and image has a set of related attributes, represented as slots in a frame system or variable values. Because of the many benefits of frame-based graphics in the knowledge base and the increasing number of shells implementing object graphics, we'll examine attributes represented using slots. Changing these attribute values provides the user with a way to alter the appearance of images that doesn't involve programming. The changes can be local, affecting only one image or canvas instance, or global, with changes resulting in a new frame with new attribute values (in this case, all instances of the new frame will have the new attribute values).

Canvas and Image Slots

A number of attributes exist for both canvases and images. Most of these are common to both, with a few exceptions. The following attributes provide the basic controls on what the image displays and how the display appears. In each of the following four categories, several slot names are defined:

- Value

    Images (canvas only)—a list of all the images that are attached to the canvas.

    Displayed object (image only)—when the image is associated with an object's slot, this attribute tells the image where to find that slot when the mouse is clicked on the image. The slot being displayed must have a corresponding reference back to the image—for example, an IMAGE facet. This cross-referencing provides the mechanism that maintains a one-to-one correspondence between the value the image is displaying and the value in the displayed slot.

    Value (image only)—the actual value that the image is currently displaying. For example, on a dial this would be the value indicated by the pointer.

- Size and Location

    Top—for a canvas, the top of the viewport with respect to the top of the physical screen; for an image, the top of the image with respect to the top of the canvas.

    Left—the left side of the canvas and the image (see *top*).

    Width—the width of the canvas and image (see *top*).

    Height—the height of the canvas and image (see *top*).

- Border and Color

    Border—the thickness of the border surrounding the canvas or image. Choices might be either none or the width in characters or pixels.

Border-color—on systems supporting color, the color of the border line.

Text-color—the color of text in the images. Color often has meaning in real-world systems, and some shells provide facilities for linking color to different values. For example, many control panels display NORMAL in green and abnormal conditions such as HIGH or LOW in red. A SELECTED-ITEM-COLOR slot enables mapping of slot value to color, for example (NORMAL green)(HIGH red).

• Label and Documentation String

Label (or *title*)—text associated with the image, for example the name of the instance and slot the image is monitoring.

Documentation—on systems that support mouse documentation, text that appears when the user enters the image's active region, indicating what will happen if the mouse is clicked.

Figure 6-7 shows an example of a CANVAS instance, illustrating values for the slots of a CANVAS frame. This example contains one image, WASH-PUMP-TEMP-IMAGE, that is monitoring the wash-pump's temperature.

Figure 6-8 shows the image for the wash pump's temperature, illustrating the slots for the image frame. This image, being part of EXAMPLE-CANVAS, references that canvas in its CANVAS slot.

```
Instance: EXAMPLE-CANVAS
Parents: CANVAS
-- Slots --
BORDER : SINGLE
BORDER-COLOR : LIGHT-BLUE
DOCUMENTATION : "Mouse Click: Add Image"
HEIGHT : 200
IMAGES : WASH-PUMP-TEMP-IMAGE
LEFT : 0
TITLE : "Example Control Panel"
TOP : 1
WIDTH : 300
```

FIGURE 6-7. The CANVAS frame

```
Instance: WASH-PUMP-TEMP-IMAGE
Parents: FIXED-MENU-IMAGE
-- Slots --
BORDER : NONE
CANVAS : EXAMPLE-CANVAS
DOCUMENTATION : "Click on new value to update plant status"
DISPLAYED-OBJECT : WASH-PUMP TEMPERATURE
HEIGHT : 40
LEFT : 1
SELECTED-ITEM-COLOR : (NORMAL green)(HIGH red)
TEXT-COLOR : WHITE
TITLE : "WASH-PUMP TEMPERATURE"
TOP : 1
VALUE : NORMAL
WIDTH : 40
```

FIGURE 6-8. Example of FIXED-MENU image frame

Mechanism Linking Graphics to the Knowledge Base

Two methods of changing a slot value are possible: by inserting the value into the knowledge base using a keyboard command and by interacting with a graphical image. In either case, the slot value is changed, in turn causing the graphical image display to change. This process is illustrated in Figure 6-9, showing the steps that occur when the value of WASH-PUMP's PRESSURE slot is changed by either assertion or image selection.

In the section above describing the attributes of images, we discussed the mechanism by which the system can find a slot's image and vice versa—the IMAGE facet on the imaged slot and the corresponding DISPLAYED-OBJECT slot on the image. Figure 6-10 illustrates the relationship between image instances and the slots they are displaying.

Entering and Exiting

When a user is moving a pointing device over the canvas, it is often desirable to provide a visual indication that an image's active region has been entered. **Highlighting** occurs when the image region is marked on entering by a reverse video of the region (popular with bitmaps), or by drawing a rectangle around the region (useful with text). On exiting, the highlighting is reversed or removed.

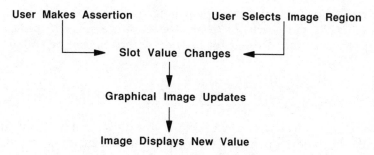

FIGURE 6-9. Changing a slot value, causing an image to update

Another possibility when entering an image region is to **document** the entry with a line of informative text. Use of the documentation slot mentioned above provides a visual cue by displaying the documentation. The difficulty with this type of indicator is deciding where to place the text information on the screen. Some hardware operating systems actually reserve a documentation region; others leave it up to the user to find a convenient place for the text output.

When the documentation describes what will happen if the object is selected, it is often referred to as "**mouse documentation.**" For obvious reasons, mouse documentation is particularly useful when a multiple-button mouse is being used, because clicking different buttons can invoke different actions not obvious before they are attempted. As with highlighting, upon exiting the documentation is removed from the screen and replaced with whatever is now appropriate for the position of the mouse.

Yet another possibility is to **change the mouse cursor's appearance** on entering an image region. This convention usually maps a set of standard

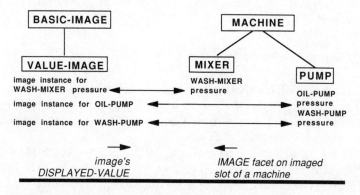

FIGURE 6-10. One-to-one correspondence between graphic instances and component instances

actions to a set of cursor icons. For example, editable text is often identified by changing the mouse cursor to an I-beam appearance; if the user then clicks the mouse while this cursor is evident, the text can be edited.

CUSTOMIZING GRAPHICAL OBJECTS

One of the great advantages of working with a object graphics system is the ease with which developers, and even end users, can customize an interface. Instead of the image definition being encoded in a programming language, the salient aspects of the definition are defined as slots. Changing a canvas or image's look can be as simple as changing the slot value.

There are five levels of customization available in most systems, the first two of which we have covered in this chapter, the last three of which are covered more in the object-programming chapter (Chapter 8): 1) changing attribute values, 2) alteration of the active region of an image, 3) minor modifications to existing mouse actions, 4) modification of functions controlling how images are drawn on the screen and behave, and 5) building an image from scratch using the basic building blocks of a basic image frame. We'll look only at the first level, which requires no programming knowledge—all changes can be made through changes to slots of the basic images and canvas.

We can change attribute values in two ways:

- We can create an instance of an image or canvas and then change the instance's attribute values.

- We can create a copy of an existing (or new) canvas or image object, setting new default values. In this case, all images we create of this new type will have the new default characteristics. This is the route to follow if more than one canvas or image is desired that has the new characteristics.

User-Defined Text Image

A quick example will clarify customization process. We'll modify an existing value image, such that all of the new value image instances will default to a width of 300 and red text with no border (we'll assume that the standard defaults are width 200 and black text).

We start by defining a new frame, WIDE-RED-VALUE-IMAGE, as a child of VALUE-IMAGE, and then change the slot value for WIDTH to 300, BORDER to NONE, and TEXT-COLOR to RED. All instances of our new image will have red text and a width of 300.

Frame: **VALUE–IMAGE**
Parents: **TOOLKIT–IMAGE**
Children: **WIDE–RED–VALUE–IMAGE**
––– Slots (not all shown) –––
BORDER : SINGLE
WIDTH : 200
TEXT–COLOR : BLACK
(a)

Frame: **WIDE–RED–VALUE–IMAGE**
Parents: **VALUE–IMAGE**
Instances: **EXAMPLE–2 EXAMPLE–1**
––– Slots (not all shown) –––
BORDER : NONE
WIDTH : 300
TEXT–COLOR : RED
(b)

FIGURE 6-11. Customizing images

Shown in Figure 6-11 are the original frame VALUE-IMAGE (Figure 6-11[a]) and our new frame, WIDE-RED-VALUE-IMAGE (Figure 6-11[b]).

User-Defined Fixed-Menu Image

Let's look at a second example. Suppose that we wish to use color to differentiate various component states. If we define the STATE slot with constraints (Figure 6-12), we can use another type of image, the FIXED-MENU image.

We can now build a custom image to attach to all of our components' STATE slots—a customized version of the FIXED-MENU image. We can set the SELECTED-ITEM-COLOR slot value to encompass pairs of values. Each pair consists of (1) a value representing the state of the component and (2) the color to use when the component is in that particular state. In this customization, as with the VALUE-IMAGE above, we first create a new child frame (Figure 6-13) of the image we wish to customize, FIXED-

---

Slot: **STATE**
Frame: **COMPONENT**
DEFAULT–VALUES : OK
CONSTRAINTS: OK SHUTDOWN FAULT
DOC–STRING: "The current state of a component"

FIGURE 6-12. The STATE slot

```
Frame: COMPONENT-FIXED-MENU
Parents: FIXED-MENU
Instances: EXAMPLE-3
-- Slots (not all shown) --
SELECTED-ITEM-COLOR : (OK GREEN) (FAULT RED)
                      (SHUTDOWN WHITE)
```

FIGURE 6-13. The COMPONENT-FIXED-MENU frame

MENU. Then we change the value of one or more slots—in this case, the
SELECTED-ITEM-COLOR slot.

What happens when a new image of type COMPONENT-FIXED-
MENU is associated with a component's STATE slot? As the value of the
slot changes, the color of the image will change correspondingly.

> NOTE: If you are going to use expert systems with color displays, it is important
> that the colors convey the meanings that the end users expect. Many situations
> have standard meanings defined by convention; for example, it would probably
> never make sense to show an abnormal condition as green. In other situations,
> the use of color should be designed in consultation with the end users.

DESIGNING AN END-USER INTERFACE

We've now finished our examination of the components of a graphics system that will permit us to build interfaces linked to the knowledge base.
Let's return to the canning line, where the team is now ready to make a
preliminary field test of the prototype. Before testing, however, they'll need
an interface that is graphical enough for the operator to use easily—an operator control panel from which observations can be entered, consultation and
resulting advice initiated, and explanations requested detailing why recommendations were made.

At the end of a typical first prototype effort, we should have a working
set of rules and related domain state information in the knowledge base.
For the canning plant, the following items have now been built:

- a set of rules that tell us if and when a component needs maintenance, based on sensor data read directly or, as is the case here,
  entered by the operator

- a set of rules that determine the linkage between a need for component maintenance and a need for component shutdown

- rules that determine the need for shutting down components that are related to other components being shut down and, for critical components, determine whether the entire line must be shut down

- a set of instances representing plant components, with slots that represent attributes of these components

Using these definitions, we will now begin implementing an interface that will enable the plant operators to try out the expert system.

Control Panel Definition

Our goal is to build a control panel from which a user can enter information on the current state of a problem and then request advice from the expert system. The request for advice will trigger forward chaining of the rules.

This control panel is intended to provide a mock-up of the final interface for the expert system. Although we want the end users to get a chance to see what some of the system's capabilities might look like, everyone involved must realize that this is still an early test situation—as likely as not, most of what they are seeing in the interface will remain in a functional sense, but will be significantly changed in the final design.

From this stage of development on, a typical expert system development effort will continue to evolve graphical interfaces that give the end users a sense of how the system is shaping up and also provide an opportunity to obtain their feedback.

NOTE: The user of the diagnostic system in our example is the end user. However, in the early testing phases, the term "user" may also refer to the expert.

A control panel also helps with system development. Even the simplest expert system will be quite complex at this stage of development. While we'll continue to add features in the next round of prototyping, the current prototype already has a full set of working capabilities. In many systems developed to this point, simply revising and expanding the existing rules to cover more cases would be enough to provide the end users with an effective tool, adding more details about the plant (both components and the sensors that monitor them) and building a more sophisticated graphical interface. In other, more complex systems, this initial prototype and its interface would go through several major and minor revisions and extensions.

Control Panel Layout

The first step to designing a user interface is to determine the overall layout. In the plant, the most important information concerned the description of canning-line components and the display of the conclusions of rule-based inferencing. The following layout was used for the prototype's user interface:

OPERATOR COMMANDS

WASH UNITS   PUMP UNITS   TANK UNITS

PRIMARY SENSOR DATA

SECONDARY SENSOR DATA

Next, issues such as the desire to avoid typing on the part of users must be considered. In the plant, typing was avoided by displaying the sensor data using a fixed-menu style of image—an image that portrays the current state and allows for state modifications, but requires no typing by the end user.

NOTE: Avoiding typing by the user is always an important design consideration—there is no requirement that users of systems be good typists, and many are not. More to the point, providing a complete set of options, when possible, avoids erroneous entries.

Next, implementation details must be worked out. For the operator panel, a customized fixed-menu image was required. We'll call our new image OP-PANEL-GAUGE. It is a child-frame of FIXED-MENU. We'll change the SELECTED-ITEM-COLOR slot (Figure 6-14). The default color for a selected item is white; however, wherever possible in graphical interfaces, color should have meaning (other than making something look pretty). Remember, this slot contains pairs of values, namely, the value of the sensor followed by the gauge color when that value is current. Our slot value covers normal (green) and abnormal (red) conditions.

```
Frame: OP-PANEL-GAUGE
Parents: FIXED-MENU
Instances: EXAMPLE-3
-- Slots (not all shown) --
SELECTED-ITEM-COLOR : (OK GREEN) (FAULT RED)
                      (SHUTDOWN WHITE)
```

FIGURE 6-14. The COMPONENT-FIXED-MENU frame

Now, when an operator selects an image, not only will the value change in the knowledge base but the color of the gauge on the control panel would reflect that change. With the basic tools built, further refinements can be undertaken.

Data Filtering

A major contribution of expert systems to diagnostics is in the area of data filtering—providing users with only the information that is important for the job being done. Our basic FIXED-MENU image can do this only to a certain extent for an object attribute defined with a constraint, using the set of constraint values to build the image.

However, from our knowledge engineering work at the plant we know that the operator is concerned with only two values for any given component: either NORMAL and HIGH or NORMAL and LOW. For example, experienced operators have found that if the temperature of the rinse in the rinse-tank is low, the fluid will congeal and cause spraying problems; on the other hand, if it's hotter than it should be, no spraying-related problems occur. Consequently, we would like to limit the display options to only those relevant to actual plant operations.

Image instances contain a slot we haven't yet mentioned, POSSI-BILITIES. We can use this slot to define a subset of the actual values that a component can have, displaying only those important for the operator to track. In Figure 6-15 we see that for the wash-pump's oil-amount, only the values of normal and low are considered.

Use of filters has several advantages. In the daily plant operation, less experienced operators can quickly learn what information represents significant abnormalities in each component. Limiting the choices also reduces the amount of information displayed on the control panel, providing a less confusing presentation of the overall plant state. Figure 6-16 shows the control panel with all sensors added.

```
Instance: WASH-PUMP-OIL-AMOUNT22
Parents: OP-PANEL-GAUGE
—— Slots ——
POSSIBILITIES : NORMAL LOW      <-------
TEXT-COLOR : GRAY
HEIGHT : 4
VALUE : NORMAL
WIDTH : 20
LEFT : 0
TOP : 4
TITLE : "OIL-AMT,WASH-PUMP"
DISPLAYED-OBJECT : (WASH-PUMP OIL-AMOUNT)
PLANE : STG4-OPERATOR-PANEL
BORDER : SINGLE
SELECTED-ITEM-COLOR : (NORMAL GREEN) (LOW RED) (HIGH RED)
```

FIGURE 6-15. Data filtering in operator interface using POSSIBILITIES slot

Control Panel Commands and Labels

Let's assume we've finished adding our sensors. Two tasks remain: adding the commands and placing labels above the various groups of gauges. Both of these tasks are quite simple.

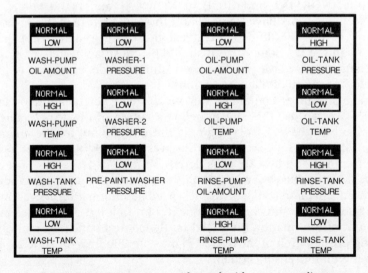

FIGURE 6-16. Operator control panel with sensor readings

To add a command, we create actuator images. An actuator image is not connected to a frame or slot, but rather to an action to be taken (although in some object-programming systems the actuator may be associated with a frame and its handler). These images display the name of the action to be taken and, when selected, execute a function (this could either be a user-created function or the assertion of a value and the invocation of the forward chainer). We will create four commands: a "diagnose" command that starts the forward chainer, a reset command that returns all slots to their default values, a documentation command that provides the user with help on using the control panel, and an explanation command that provides the user with an explanation of the reasoning leading up to the advice given by the expert system.

Our last task is to build the labels; this is the simplest task of all. We create a label by creating an image that has *no* action when selected (and also, as with the actuator image, no associated frame or slot; we do not fill in the DISPLAYED-OBJECT slot of the image instance).

Not filling in the DISPLAYED-OBJECT slot gave us a basic image that will display only the value stored in the VALUE slot of the image. Once the images are placed, we can set the VALUE slot to the text we wish displayed, for example, "PUMP UNITS." Figure 6-17 shows the completed control panel.

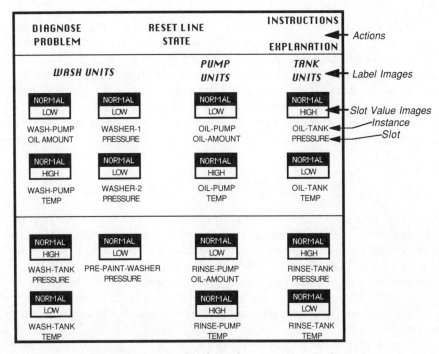

Figure 6-17. Completed Level I operator control panel

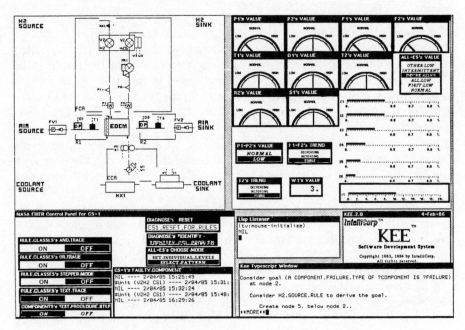

FIGURE 6-18. Life support system control panel (NASA)

Early graphical interfaces should echo the existing working conditions of the domain as realistically as possible. Innovations can always be added later, but it is important at first to minimize the new ideas the evaluators must cope with. The interface may consist of a simple set of choices for each object that the user can set or may require graphic images emulating dials, gauges, or even complex diagrams. Figure 6-18 illustrates an interface taken from an implementation of work done for NASA in IntelliCorp's KEE on the Symbolics machine.

ASSESSMENT OF THE LEVEL I PROTOTYPE

One of the most difficult decisions is to call an end to all the "fine tuning." At some point, the decision must be made that the prototype contains all the necessary information, is working at a satisfactory level, and is thus ready for presentation. Often, an assessment of completion is done when time or resources have begun to run low. If the decision is that more work is required before an evaluation can be made, often a partial evaluation can be done to determine whether consuming more resources is going to produce the desired prototype.

Once a prototype has been produced, it must then be evaluated to see whether the original goals were met and whether further work should be undertaken. Two typical results of such an evaluation are a decision to undertake a second phase, or the decision to transfer the acquired knowledge and system-building experience into a related but new project.

Criteria for Evaluating When the Prototype is Finished

Three sets of criteria, one for each set of reviewers, must be evaluated.

The *development team* checks for *implementation stability*. The team must make the initial evaluation of what has been produced to determine whether the system is technically sound: Does the system run without breaking, are the answers produced those that the expert specified for a given situation, does the interface reflect the end-user environment? Once these criteria have been met, the system is ready for review by the experts and end users.

Experts and *end users* check the *validity* of the information in the knowledge base: domain facts, rules, and inferencing conclusions. They must also be comfortable with the interface: Does it supply the required information and enable the user to inspect and update facts? The expert must approve of the answers and advice produced; the expert and end users must try the system for usability, have their comments folded in and retested, and have had a chance to provide suggestions for improvements. Finally, the experts and the end users must judge the performance of the system to be satisfactory (this does not mean that the system must be fully optimized, but the prototype should run at an acceptable speed to allow testing).

Finally, *management* should review the completed prototype to evaluate whether projected *goals* have been met. More than the other two groups, management must assess how well the initial projections concerning the project were met: resource requirements, schedule, performance of the expert system, and acceptance of the expert system by the user community. The management group will be the biggest beneficiary of a clear, understandable graphic interface, because their evaluation of the technical accuracy of the prototype must rest primarily on the recommendations of the experts.

Assessing Future Benefits

To continue with the project, there must be clear future benefits. The initial prototype indicates feasibility, but also provides a clearer picture as to whether such a system will be used and if it will be cost effective. Benefits of the completed system will ultimately be in terms of dollars saved by its use, measured by one or more of the following criteria: reduced personnel (seldom the case), increased performance, increased consistency of results by the end users, addition of new capabilities, and training of less skilled employees.

The implementation team must develop a new set of goals for the next phase and then assess whether they are feasible using criteria such as cost, speed, user acceptance, maintenance, and delivery options—the same basic steps that were followed in Chapter 2, but with more available information.

The major pitfall to planning later phases of expert system projects (in general, this is true for most software projects) is allocating enough time for later phases. The fully working initial prototype usually appears much more complete than it actually is. Thus, the time required to complete future phases is consistently underestimated. Expanding an expert system proceeds progressively more slowly—not more quickly—for the following reasons: all the easy domain knowledge is already in; the developers have inevitably chosen to postpone confronting those difficult paradoxical situations that trouble even the expert; additional experts may be added to the team, leading to contradictory information and disputes; the system is getting larger, and thus much more complicated, because of the interactions between existing and new rules and frames; and finally, the requirements for stability and interface are increasingly strict, as focus shifts from experimentation to hardening of design.

> At the plant, the big day had arrived. The finished Level I prototype had been tested extensively with the operators, and the working system was finally demonstrated to management. The prototype showed that building an expert system to support the operators was indeed feasible. More than that, the system solved a real problem, the lack of consistency in operator training and thus problem response. The preliminary tests on the factory floor had shown that the result of using a complete system would be reduced downtime on the line (resulting in higher through-put) and more consistent quality in the final product. The system also appeared to offer an indirect benefit—less experienced personnel were extending their knowledge, because the system could explain a diagnostic process in the same way as the expert, but with much greater patience and unlimited repetition.
>
> To no one's great surprise, management gave approval for a second phase of the project. In this phase, the team would have access to the operators themselves, and the goal would be to extend the system to incorporate knowledge about sounds, sights, and smells on the canning line. There was also a desire to provide operators with more information on how to detect problems and how to fix them.

SUMMARY

The purpose of this chapter was to explore mechanisms with which the developer can build a graphical interface for an initial prototype without resorting to a programming language. This initial interface provides prototyping and debugging displays to support the developers and the experts.

The interface enables the developers to:

- *observe* changes in the knowledge base as they occur
- *interact* with the knowledge base
- *emulate* interfaces the expert is used to seeing

After examining the general design principles of using object graphics, we defined the following standard image types:

value—displays the value of a slot

actuator—selecting the image executes a command

dial—displays values a monitored object can take on

plot—displays two-dimensional data

fixed-menu—displays a set of user options and their associated attributes

This chapter defines a graphics system composed of frames representing graphical interface building blocks. There are two types of graphical objects, **canvases** and **images**; images reside within a **viewport**, the portion of the canvas being displayed on the screen. An application interface is built by creating instances of these graphics frames. The slot values of each graphic instance determine the appearance of the graphical objects.

With the material covered in these first six chapters, we now have the capability to develop a good-sized expert system application, complete with test interface. Although our paradigm has been a manufacturing model, these same techniques and approaches can be applied to a wide variety of domains from insurance to aerospace, as we'll see in the next chapter.

READINGS

Holan, J. D., E. L. Hutchins, and L. Weitzman. 1984. STEAMER: An interactive inspectable simulation-based training system. *AI Magazine* 5, no. 2: 15-27.

Hutchins, E. L., J. D. Hollan, and D. A. Norman. 1985. Direct manipulation interfaces. *Technical Report* 8503. San Diego, CA: Institute for Cognitive Science, University of California.

Rauch-Hindin, W. B. 1985. *Artificial intelligence in business, science, and industry.* Englewood Cliffs, NJ: Prentice-Hall.

7

APPLYING THE
ANALYTIC PARADIGM

U p to this point, we have been looking in detail at the analysis of problems in a manufacturing environment. However, the expert-systems approach being used is a generic one for solving most **analytic** problems; it is not limited to a specific problem domain. What are some other applications to which the approach in this book can be applied? We will briefly describe four different application domains in this chapter—insurance, finance, aerospace, and communications—mapping the paradigms we have described in the manufacturing environment onto the equivalent elements in these other domains. In order to provide a complete mapping between the manufacturing example and these other domains, we'll begin with an overview of all aspects of the canning-line expert system described in this book. This will include both the material we've covered so far and a look ahead to parts of the application that will be discussed in later chapters.

As illustrated in Figure 7-1, the canning factory can be thought of as a process that takes in a raw material and produces a product. The process consists of a series of well-defined steps (the production line). The materials (metal sheets) are transformed by the process into a product (finished cans).

Using this framework, we can draw analogies between the canning-line application and other applications taken from totally different domains. These analogies will describe the parallels in both the structuring of domain knowledge (objects in the knowledge base) and the problem-solving logic

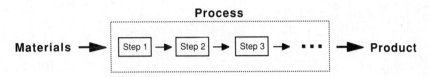

FIGURE 7-1. Generic processing of materials—each step in the process corresponds to a single component of the canning line.

used for solving problems in different domains (the rules). The canning-line expert system is composed of three major knowledge categories, as summarized in Figure 7-2. The first knowledge category (monitoring) has been discussed in the previous chapters and corresponds to the shutdown rules first introduced in Chapter 4. The second and third knowledge categories (diagnosis and repair) will be introduced in Chapters 9 and 10. Diagnosis knowledge concerns finding the causes of quality problems on the canning line. Repair knowledge revolves around isolating and fixing specific problems in the plant's machinery.

Let's look at each knowledge category in a little more depth. The individual steps in the manufacturing process (as performed by the canning-line machinery) occasionally develop serious problems. The shutdown rules, which are forward chaining, monitor the plant's machinery and watch for the development of these problems. The rules then provide an alert to the line operators whenever a problem occurs that is sufficiently serious to require the shutdown of a particular machine.

The items being processed (that is, the cans) are subject to a variety of quality-control problems during the manufacturing process. To uncover the

FIGURE 7-2. The breakdown of knowledge categories for the canning-line application described in this book

Knowledge Category	Application Module	Direction of Chaining
Monitoring	Abnormal sensor reading leads to component shutdown	Forward
Diagnosis	Determine faulty component from quality-control observation	Backward
Repair	Fault correction	Forward

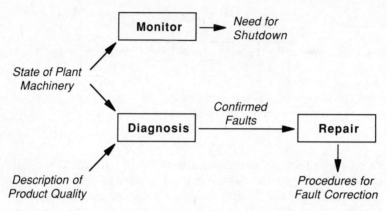

FIGURE 7-3. Interaction between knowledge categories of the canning-line application described in this book

cause of those problems, backward-chaining diagnosis rules will be used. These backward-chaining rules will examine the individual processing steps (that is, the plant components) to determine whether any of those steps could be the cause of the observed problem. During the diagnosis, the rules will query the operator for further information that might confirm or reject specific plant components as the origin of the quality-control problem.

Once a problem has been isolated as coming from a specific plant component, the problem must be corrected. Generally speaking, the plant operators will then go through a fixed procedure for repairing the machine in question. In later chapters, we'll see the development of forward-chaining correction rules that act on confirmation (by the operator) that some plant component is faulty. Once a problem has been confirmed, these rules invoke repair procedures, then recheck the original problem to see whether the repair procedure was effective.

The three knowledge categories work together as illustrated schematically in Figure 7-3. The state of the plant's machinery is used when monitoring the need for machinery shutdown, as well as when diagnosing problems with can quality. If successful, the diagnosis will confirm the presence of a mechanical fault in some plant component. Given a confirmed fault, the operator is advised on repair procedures for correcting the faulty plant component.

INSURANCE: CLAIMS PROCESSING

One of the most time-consuming activities in the insurance industry is the processing of claims. In the simplest cases, processing a single claim requires only that standard clerical procedures be followed. In difficult cases, a claim might involve a complex decision process on the part of experienced adjusters. Using our diagnostic paradigm, we might capture the experience of these expert adjusters in their process of "diagnosing" a claims form to see if it is valid.

As many of us know from personal experience, the details of specific insurance policies are under constant revision by most insurance companies. These revisions, while necessary for actuarial purposes, make claims processing more difficult and error-prone than it might otherwise be. In addition, the processing of insurance claims is a tedious and often boring task, causing heavy turnover among claims-processing personnel. The training of new staff is therefore a major problem, and experienced adjusters are considered by virtually all insurance companies to be a highly valuable resource.

Many claims are quite straightforward, and there is little doubt that the claimant is entitled to full reimbursement for the claim. At other times it is equally clear that the claimant is not entitled to any reimbursement whatsoever. Detecting these simple cases and recommending the appropriate action to the adjuster are valuable services that a knowledge-based system can provide. The more difficult cases would still be handled by expert adjusters in any event, but a knowledge-based system could sort incoming claims into those that are obvious and those that are not.

In building a knowledge base for claims processing, there are two types of objects of interest: the claim itself and the details of the insurance policy under which the claim is being made. In the canning plant, as mentioned previously, sheet metal is transformed into cans; in processing insurance claims, a claim is transformed into a settlement. As with cans going down a production line, the settlement may or may not be rejected as invalid.

In an insurance application, the individual policy descriptions (life, medical, and so forth) take the place of canning-line component descriptions. The different policy types can then be combined into a customer policy. In the canning plant, we first defined component types and then strung them together into a specific canning line; here, instead, we start with general descriptions of insurance policies (as formulated by the insurance company) and then string them together to form an individual policy (the claimant's policy). Figure 7-4 illustrates how the inheritance hierarchy would be modified in going from a canning-line application to a claims-processing application.

There are three major types of analysis we might consider performing on an insurance claim that are analogous to our analysis of the canning line. These three analysis types correspond closely to the three knowledge categories described earlier in this chapter, as summarized in Figure 7-5.

First, we could monitor all incoming claims in a uniform fashion, looking for claims that were obviously either invalid or incomplete—this monitoring is similar in principle to the shutdown rules for the canning

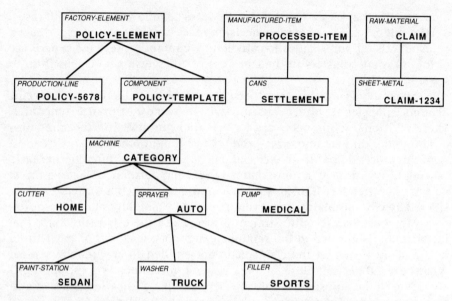

FIGURE 7-4. The modified inheritance hierarchy for a claims-processing system (The corresponding objects for the canning plant are shown in smaller print.)

FIGURE 7-5. The breakdown of knowledge categories for the processing of insurance claims (The categories for the canning plant application are included for comparison.)

Knowledge Category	Insurance Claims	Canning Plant
Monitoring	Identify incomplete or erroneous claim information	Abnormal sensor reading leads to component shutdown
Diagnosis	Determine what additional information is needed	Determine faulty component from quality-control observation
Repair	Follow standard procedure for requesting more documentation	Fault correction

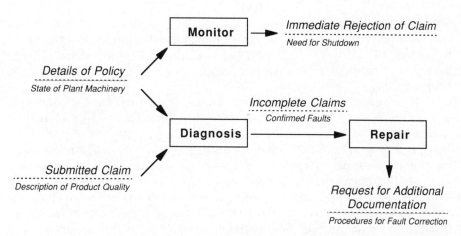

FIGURE 7-6. Interaction between knowledge categories in a claims-processing system (For comparison, the corresponding items from the canning-line application are shown in smaller print.)

line (Chapter 4). Second, given a claim that was incomplete, we could determine what additional information was needed to resolve the validity of the claim. This search for causes is analogous to our QC diagnosis in the canning factory (Chapter 9). Finally, once a problem with the claim had been isolated, that problem would have to be resolved with a request to the claimant for additional information—perhaps additional documentation on the claim or even, if it was a medical claim, a request for additional tests (Chapters 10 and 11). This request for more information is analogous to our fault-correction rules in the canning-line application; the essential idea is to fix some problem that has already been isolated by the backward-chaining diagnostic rules. Figure 7-6 illustrates the analytic flow for both the canning plant and the claims-processing system.

A variety of knowledge-based systems for claims processing have been built, and several have been successfully fielded. The references for Lockheed MEDCHEC (Davis 87; Newquist 87) provide further examples of applying these same ideas to the processing of insurance claims.

FINANCE: LOAN APPLICATIONS

The analysis of loan applications is another area that can benefit from applying the methodology described in this book. Most institutions find it quite difficult to keep up with the number of requests received by their credit departments. This is particularly true of banks, of course, but is also true of other organizations that provide credit, such as department stores and oil companies. We discuss the approval of a loan application by a hypothetical bank, but the same ideas will apply to any situation in which credit is being extended, including credit card purchases, commercial lines of credit, and home mortgages.

There are two basic types of loans: individual and commercial. Generally speaking, individual loans are smaller and simpler to analyze than commercial loans. Moreover, banks often use firm, quantitative guidelines when deciding whether to issue a loan to a specific individual, based on income, fixed assets, past history in repaying loans, and so on. Commercial loans, on the other hand, are much less likely to have such guidelines—there is simply too much financial variability in the commercial world to allow the use of rigid, quantitative criteria. In both cases, however, expert judgment is required for making the final decision whether to issue a specific loan.

In the canning-line application, sheet metal is transformed by the canning process into finished cans. In a bank, a loan application is transformed by the loan-review process into a loan. Just as cans may or may not be rejected on the production line for quality-control reasons, a bank may or may not reject a specific loan application. In representing the canning line, plant components were strung together to form a production process. In a bank, on the other hand, different areas of an applicant's financial background are combined to form a financial statement. For an individual, these would include shelter, transportation, retirement, and so forth. The categories are different for a corporation, of course, but the principles are the same. The main point is that, like the components on the canning line, each financial area is a potential source of quality problems. Figure 7-7 illustrates a modified frame hierarchy showing the objects required for a knowledge-based system that analyzes loan applications.

In the canning plant application, we captured three separate knowledge categories: monitor, diagnosis, and repair. As we saw above, the processing of insurance claims has a similar set of knowledge categories. The loan-review process in a bank also may be characterized in this fashion, as summarized in Figure 7-8.

In the canning factory, we monitored for the need to shut down the production process. In a bank, we can prescreen all loan applications to categorize loans into those that are difficult to resolve and those that are easy. This would be a typical monitoring application using forward-chaining rules similar in form to those used in the shutdown rules of the canning-line application. On the canning line, we found some quality problem, then used backward-chaining diagnosis rules to isolate the cause of a problem. Similarly, in processing a loan application, there is a clear need to diagnose an applicant's financial health if there seem to be problems with issuing a loan of the requested size and terms. Once specific problems have been

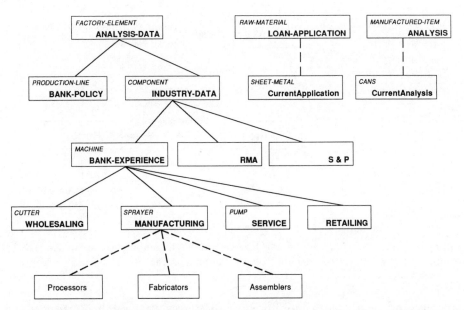

FIGURE 7-7. The modified inheritance hierarchy for a loan- application system. The corresponding objects for the canning plant are shown in smaller print.

FIGURE 7-8. The breakdown of knowledge categories for the processing of insurance claims (The categories for the canning plant application and claims processing are included for comparison.)

Knowledge Category	Loan Applications	Canning Plant	Insurance Claims
Monitoring	Prescreen loan requests	Abnormal sensor reading leads to component shutdown	Identify incomplete claims
Diagnosis	For marginal applicants, find the cause of financial difficulties	Determine faulty component from quality-control observation	Determine what additional information is needed
Repair	Suggest terms to make the loan acceptable	Fault correction	Follow standard procedure for requesting more documentation

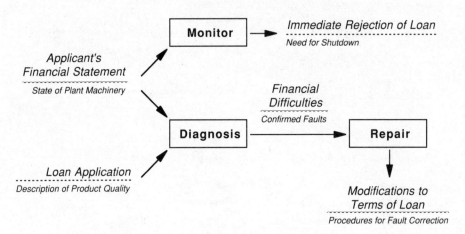

FIGURE 7-9. Interaction between knowledge categories in a loan-application system (For comparison, the corresponding items from the canning line are shown in smaller print.)

isolated, the next step is to invoke procedures that might correct the problem. On the canning line, this logic took the form of forward-chaining production rules that entailed repair procedures for fixing faulty components. In a banking situation, there is analogous logic for suggesting ways to make a marginal loan acceptable to the bank, either by reducing the loan's size, attaching specific assets to the loan, or modifying the terms of the loan. The flow of information in both cases is illustrated in Figure 7-9.

Several knowledge-based systems are currently in use that assist financial institutions in the processing of loan applications. Most of these systems are used for analyzing loans to individuals, although some are used for commercial-sector credit as well. In general, because of the complexity of corporate credit, most commercially-oriented systems are designed to provide only general guidance to the decision maker, rather than detailed recommendations. For those interested in knowing more about these applications, one obvious problem is that most financial institutions are loath to say anything publicly concerning how they evaluate loan requests. One well-documented exception is a consumer-credit application developed for American Express, the Authorizer's Assistant.

COMMUNICATIONS: NETWORK ANALYSIS

A network consists of a set of objects (**nodes**) connected by **arcs**. Communications systems are complex networks of interconnected equipment. The nodes in a communications network are transmission points. These transmission points may be **sources** and **destinations** or, as is found in a telephone system, **switches.** Switches route information from one node to the next, enabling many source/destination pairs to be made within the network. The arcs in the network are **channels,** carrying voice or other data over long distances. Information is routed from a source to a destination by selecting a path through the nodes and channels. In a large network, a path connecting a single source and destination may pass through many nodes and arcs. In this example, we'll look at the issues surrounding the analysis of switching problems, that is, the failure of information to be properly routed through the network from a source to a destination.

A switch in a large network generates diagnostic messages each time a connection fails; a central office telephone switch can make interconnections between tens of thousands of telephone lines each day and in the process generate hundreds of messages. In order to maintain a large network, experts analyze the diagnostic messages from all switches in the network, identifying problems and recommending maintenance actions.

A communications network is actually composed of multiple layers, similar to the canning line. In the canning line, the first layer of information comes from the machines themselves; when a pump overheats (Chapter 4), for example, an alarm may register or a red light appear on a control panel. In a communications network, the lowest information layer is the remote monitoring of the physical equipment; when a relay fails because of a short circuit, for example, the failure may be indicated on monitoring equipment as a change in potential. At a higher level, problems may be indicated by the switching software's inability to make a connection between two nodes. And at the highest level, similar to an operator noticing a problem in a finished product such as a can (Chapter 9), a call may fail to go through and be reported by a user at the call's source.

An expert system to analyze a communications network must have at least three components (Figure 7-10): the ability to assess the state of the system by monitoring information to determine whether a problem is occurring (Chapter 10), the ability to diagnose the particular component failure (Chapter 4), and the ability to offer advice to the operator on repairing the problem (Chapter 11).

An early version of a communications network analysis expert system was Automated Cable Expertise (ACE), Bell Laboratories' system for analyzing intermittent problems in communications cables. We'll examine a more recent system in detail, GTE's COMPASS system, on which one of the authors (Payne) provided design review.

The purpose of COMPASS (Central Office Maintenance Printout Analysis and Suggestion System) is to analyze data collected by GTE's No. 2 Electronic Automatic Exchange (EAX), which contains information on failed connections routed through a switching office. When a failure is detected, EAX produces a printout of the entire path along which the call was being routed. Unfortunately, EAX does not contain the capability to identify the

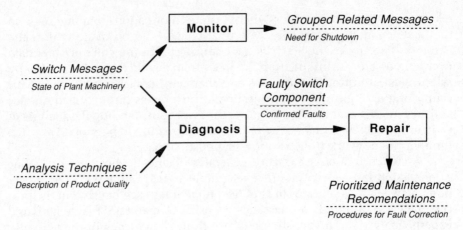

FIGURE 7-10. Flow of analysis in a communication network analysis expert system

exact location of the failure; only through the analysis by an expert of many such failure notifications can the particular faulty location be identified. The COMPASS expert system performs this analysis and produces a list of suggested maintenance actions.

The analysis of a switch consists of several actions (summarized and compared to the canning line in Figure 7-11), including:

- collecting related messages that are likely to have been generated by the same switch fault

FIGURE 7-11. Knowledge categories for network analysis and repair

Knowledge Category	Network Analysis	Canning Plant
Monitoring	Group messages generated by switch faults	Abnormal sensor reading leads to component shutdown
Diagnosis	Analyze messages for faults	Determine faulty component from quality-control observation
Repair	Determine maintenance actions	Fault correction

- analyzing messages within a collection for faults that could have generated the errors

- determining maintenance actions

- prioritizing the list of actions

- presenting recommendations to user

COMPASS makes extensive use of object-oriented programming techniques (see message passing, Chapter 8) to integrate and group similar diagnostic messages. In a manner similar to the representation of observed canning-line quality-control problems presented in Chapter 10, COMPASS contains a frame for each message generated by the switch monitor. An instance of one of these generic message types is created for each error message that occurs in the communications network.

In Figure 7-12 we see a hypothetical knowledge structure for a switch diagnosis expert system. The three top-level frames from the manufacturing knowledge base have become SWITCH, CALL-PATH, and MESSAGES (representing the error messages generated when a call cannot be completed). In the SWITCH hierarchy, we have two major elements: each node (SWITCH-SITE) where switching equipment can fail (each site would be represented by instances of this frame) and the actual components that make up a switch (SWITCH-STRUCTURE); slots represent the status of the nodes and switch components. Slots on each instance of a switch-site frame would contain sets of switch component frame instances that represent the unique makeup of each individual site.

CALL-PATH represents information on each failure to complete a path between a source and a destination. Attributes of this frame might include a slot for all messages generated by the failed call and a slot containing all of the switch sites that composed the failed call path. Finally, the message

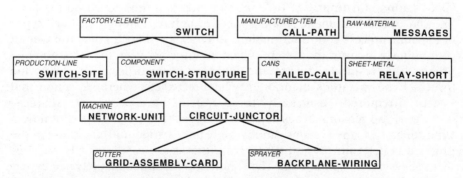

FIGURE 7-12. Frame hierarchy for communications network problem detection

frames each represent a generic type of message. For a particular failed call, each generated message could be represented in the knowledge base as a new message instance.

The diagnosis rules would then try to group failed calls (the COM-PASS system uses a procedure similar to the downstream/upstream message-passing scheme described in Chapter 8). Another set of rules would take this information and identify potential faulty components (Chapter 4 rules). Finally, another set of rules would determine maintenance procedures (Chapter 10) and present a checklist of repairs to the user (Chapter 11).

AEROSPACE: CONTINUOUS SYSTEM ANALYSIS

At NASA, numerous expert system prototypes have been built to explore automation of space exploration. Some of these systems are designed to aid in the planning of space missions, others aid in detecting favorable conditions for launch, and still others provide ground-based support for problems that occur in space. For this example, we'll examine a continuous process system designed to work on-board a projected space station.

A continuous system is one in which material—typically liquids and gases—is measured not in discrete amounts or sets (e.g., move a sheet of metal from the oiler to the stamper) but rather in amounts per unit of time (e.g., 10 gallons per minute from unit 1 to unit 2). These systems are found in areas as diverse as large process facilities (e.g., refineries), discrete entities (e.g., jets and rockets), and government activities (e.g., waste water treatment). The "process" in continuous systems is similar to manufacturing—the conversion of materials (gases and liquids in this case) into new forms. In a commercial facility such as an oil refinery, these conversions may be used to create new products or convert waste products back into usable forms.

Our sample problem will be limited to a single module of the NASA space station, **automatic failure management** in the life-support system. The concept of "automatic" management of failure is important to all types of dynamic process control. Situations often exist where an operator cannot continuously monitor the system; when the time between the inception of a problem and resulting catastrophic outcomes is small (less than the period for which the operator's attention may be directed elsewhere), an automated system is required. Historically, these systems have been quite simple—when a critical sensor reaches a hazardous level, the operation is shut down. Unfortunately, many systems cannot safely be restarted until the cause of the problem is determined, and discovering that cause easily usually requires that the system be operational. The solution to this dilemma: have an expert system automatically perform analysis procedures, interpret the results, run new procedures, and so on, accumulating information on the failure before the shutdown occurs. This automatic diagnosis before shutdown is the focus of the NASA expert system.

The life-support module is composed of components to recover waste and regenerate the cabin air. Regeneration uses a catalytic conversion process to remove carbon dioxide from the cabin air; the rules in the NASA expert system analyze the sensors that monitor the conversion process, including sensors for pressure and temperature. When combinations of sensors yield readings outside of their setpoints, the expert system is triggered and begins analysis to discover the failure cause. Finally, repair actions are taken and recommendations made to the astronauts. Figure 7-13 compares the three major analytic components of the expert system to the equivalent canning plant modules.

Figure 7-14 illustrates how, with minor modifications, the canning plant frame structure can be modified for use with the NASA application. In the diagram, factory elements are replaced with elements of the life-support system. The two major diagnostic elements are the components, such as pumps and valves, and the orbital replacement units (ORUS). Similar to a production line, which might be thought of as a collection of components (represented using a slot containing the component names), the ORUS system groups life-support components together into subsystems (for example, circulation and gas recovery). In the canning plant, a line can be shut down; on the space station an ORU can be replaced as a single unit by the astronauts.

In the knowledge base, the manufactured items from the canning plant (cans) become the substances of the recovery system (oxygen, hydrogen,

FIGURE 7-13. Knowledge categories for continuous process analysis

Knowledge Category	Network Analysis	Canning Plant
Monitoring	Identify sensors with abnormal readings	Abnormal sensor reading leads to component shutdown
Diagnosis	Run procedures to determine faulty component	Determine faulty component from quality-control observation
Repair	Override controller and present action list	Fault correction

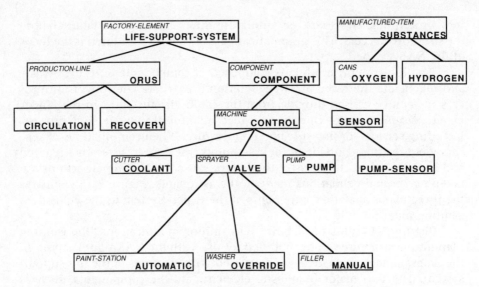

FIGURE 7-14. Frame hierarchy for life-support system problem detection

coolant, etc.). The frame hierarchy maintains the same depth as was required for the canning line, showing three levels of detail below component: component categories of operation, component types, and specializations of each type.

The example knowledge base represented in Figure 7-14 is taken from the expert system FIXER (Fault Isolation eXpert to Enhance Reliability), a diagnosis and repair system implemented with the author's (Payne) assistance at NASA's Johnson Space Center. FIXER monitors the space station life-support system and, when a sensor reading indicates a problem, FIXER's diagnosis rules chain to isolate the cause, using the same rule strategy employed by the Chapter 4 rules. For example, the HOT-PUMP rule (Figure 7-15) for the canning plant translates into NASA rules that analyze the coolant motor pump when a coolant pressure drop is indicated by sensors. These rules may make recommendations for shutdown of the life-support recovery system and maintenance of the coolant system.

FIXER makes extensive use of operator procedures imbedded in rules, very similar to those integrated into the canning line in the Chapter 10 rules (see the section on Nonmonotonic Reasoning). When a problem is confirmed, additional rules make recommendations to the user about possible repair strategies (Chapter 11 rules). FIXER can also, in certain circumstances, communicate directly with the space station controller, readjusting set points and making other minor changes, allowing the system to remain in operation (Chapter 15). Figure 7-16 illustrates the parallels between FIXER and the canning-line application.

Rule: **HOT–PUMP**
Documentation: An overheated pump can QUICKLY be
  permanently damaged.
IF
  THE ?PUMP IS RUNNING HOT
THEN
  THE ?PUMP NEEDS MAINTENANCE IMMEDIATELY

FIGURE 7-15. Rule to determine a need for maintenance

The canning plant rules and FIXER's rules deliberately, and for the same reasons, use qualitative rather than quantitative measures (e.g., hot instead of 46°C). Use of qualitative terminology was an important aspect of the expert system, because the astronauts who will ultimately use the system typically have no knowledge of the exact values indicating that a component is abnormal; however, they often need to know if a reading is above or below a normal range.

To get a better appreciation of the close match between the canning line example and the work at NASA, we particularly recommend reading Malin (87), which provides a detailed review of the FIXER expert system. More recent work on FIXER includes integration with discrete simulation models to generate complex fault occurrences for testing the expert system (Chapter 14).

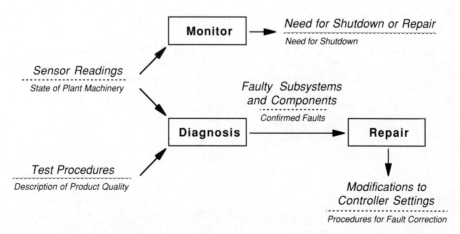

FIGURE 7-16. Parallels between FIXER and the canning-line expert system

READINGS

Bartee, T. C., ed. 1988. *Expert systems and artificial intelligence*. Indianapolis, IN: Howard W. Sams & Company.

Davis, D. 1987. Artificial intelligence goes to work. *High Technology*. April: 16–25.

Goyal, S., D. Prerau, A. V. Lemmon, and R. E. Reinke. 1985. COMPASS: An expert system for telephone switching maintenance. *Expert Systems* 2, no. 3: 112–126.

Malin, J. T., and N. Lance. 1985. An expert system for fault management and automatic shutdown avoidance in a regenerative life support system. *ISA Proceedings*, 1985. ISA 1985—paper #85-0333.

Malin, J. T., and N. Lance. 1987. Processes in construction of failure management expert systems from device design information. *IEEE Transactions on Systems, Man, and Cybernetics* SMC-17: 956–967.

Mantelman, L. 1986. AI carves inroads: Network design, testing, and management. *Data Communications* 15, no. 8.

Newquist, H. 1987. American Express and AI: Don't leave home without them. *AI Expert* 2, no. 4: 63–65.

Piketty, L., et al. 1987. The authorizer's assistant: A large commercial expert system application. *Proceedings of the AI and Advanced Computer Technology Conference*. April, Long Beach, CA.

Prereau, D. S. 1985. Selection of an appropriate domain for an expert system. *AI Magazine* 6, no. 2 (Summer).

Prereau, D. S., A. V. Lemmon, A. S. Gunderson, and R. E. Reinke. 1985. A multi-paradigm expert system for maintenance of an electronic telephone exchange. *Proceedings of the Ninth Annual International Computer Software and Applications Conference*, October.

Vesonder, G. T., S. J. Stolfo, J. E. Zielinski, F. D. Miller, and D. H. Copp. 1983. ACE: An expert system for telephone cable maintenance. *Proceedings of the Eighth International Joint Conference on Artificial Intelligence*, vol. 1. Karlsruhe, W. Germany.

PART III

EXTENDING THE PROTOTYPE: BACKWARD CHAINING

8

PROCESS FLOWS: OBJECT-ORIENTED MODELING

This chapter explains how object-oriented programming is similar to and different from rules, when each technique is appropriate, and how object-oriented programming is implemented. We'll start with a brief overview of object programming, then take an example problem, look at how we can solve it with rules, and explore how and why that same problem could be solved using object programming.

Usually, no programming is required (or desired) while developing the initial prototype. First, prototyping in a shell is much faster than trying to do the equivalent work with programming. Second, avoidance of programming provides a wider range of individuals access to the development environment. Most important, however, avoiding programming keeps the initial focus of development on exploration and away from long, detailed implementations of approaches that ultimately may not be useful. For example, to date our expert system has not included any procedural control over rule firings, nor have we used programming to customize the graphics environment.

As we begin to develop a second-level prototype, however, we must face some facts. Each successive prototype requires more effort to build and test than the preceding version, and the increasing complexity of the expert system will most likely require some procedural-language programming for application-specific needs, including:

- procedurally controlling the order of inferencing
- increasing the run-time efficiency of the application
- building customized graphical interfaces
- interfacing to other languages, external software, or hardware

All of these tasks contain a requirement for some procedural programming. Because our application is primarily object-based, before we can seriously begin to extend our expert system, we need to look at the issues involved in programming with objects.

> At the canning plant, the Phase I prototype was finished. After a review by the experts, the operators, and management, a decision was made to continue with the next phase of the project.
>
> No custom programming had been undertaken in the first phase, as it was felt that rapidly capturing the experts' knowledge and turning this into a working system was more important than any particular refinements. In the next phase, however, the team had a number of programming areas they wished to explore. Much of this desire was spurred on by requests from the operators for a better interface and more integration in the system of special procedures that they performed as part of certain diagnoses. The team also realized that because the system was going to become increasingly complex they would require a systematic approach to testing additions to it.
>
> One of the design possibilities that the team felt they should assess was whether object programming techniques should be used, reducing or eliminating the use of rules. The increasing need for a robust model of the plant, both for testing and also as an aid to getting operator input and providing explanations of results to the operators, indicated a corresponding need for more object modeling. Several members of the team were also interested in exploring the integration of simulation techniques into the knowledge base to aid in test problem generation.

STRENGTHENING THE DOMAIN MODEL: CONNECTIVITY

As we begin expanding an initial prototype, we often need to make the representation of the domain—in this case, the canning plant—more robust and complete. A robust representation will provide a stable base for later expansions. One way to increase representational power is to establish **connectivity** between knowledge-base objects.

We'd like to define connections between objects in the knowledge base that represent physical connections between the corresponding components in the real world. Connectivity is fundamental to any object programming design because one of the basic precepts of object programming is communication between objects. For example, suppose a problem has been detected at a canning plant machine, and the model of the factory requires investigating all nearby machines for related problems. To define a generally applicable procedure for responding to this situation, each object must have a standard way of finding the related objects that need to be identified.

We define the links between objects by defining slots on the object containing the names of related objects in the knowledge base (defining relationships was briefly discussed in Chapter 5). In the canning-line application, we can represent physical links between machines in the plant by two slots, UPSTREAM and DOWNSTREAM . These two slots are defined at the COMPONENT frame, as shown in Figure 8-1. Thus, they are inherited by all objects representing the various pieces of equipment in the plant. A relationship exists between components of the canning line when a DOWNSTREAM slot of some component contains a reference to another component in the line. Using this technique, we can describe the flow of materials through the plant.

Two aspects of these slots bear special attention. First, DOWNSTREAM and UPSTREAM are multivalued slots; placing more than one value in a slot enables the developer to indicate that a component is linked to more than one other component. Second, these two slots demonstrate another application of constraints. Because the slot can only contain instances of COMPONENT, a component can only be linked to another component, maintaining the consistency or "truth" of the knowledge base. We

```
Frame: COMPONENT
Parents: FACTORY—ELEMENT
Children: MACHINE
——Slots (not all shown)——
UPSTREAM :
  Constraints: INSTANCE—OF COMPONENT
  Documentation: Materials flow to this component from
    UPSTREAM
DOWNSTREAM :
  Constraints: INSTANCE—OF COMPONENT
  Documentation: Materials flow from this component to
    DOWNSTREAM.
```

FIGURE 8-1. The DOWNSTREAM and UPSTREAM slots

may further constrain particular components; for example, we might further limit pumps so that they can only be connected to sprayers by replacing INSTANCE-OF COMPONENT on the PUMP frame's DOWNSTREAM slot with INSTANCE-OF SPRAYER. Thus, object definitions can take the place of rules in constraining and checking how new information is added into the knowledge base.

> NOTE: The choice of slot names and their specific meanings is highly application dependent. For example, a DOWNSTREAM slot might also be used in a model of a communications network or to represent the ordering in a set of tasks. Alternatively, different slot names could be used to denote different relationships. For example, slots AFTER and BEFORE could be defined to denote time ordering between objects in a project planning application, in the same way that we've used DOWNSTREAM and UPSTREAM to denote the flow of materials in the canning plant. Extensions to the concept of relations between objects is discussed in greater detail in Chapter 13.

In Figure 8-2, CAN-COATER is the value of WASHER-1's DOWNSTREAM slot, indicating that material flows directly from washer-1 to the can coater. The UPSTREAM slot of CAN-COATER, in turn, references WASHER-1, implying that the can coater receives material directly from washer-1. The can coater also receives material from washer-2.

By linking several knowledge-base objects together with slot values, we have represented in the knowledge base the simple network—the canning

---

Instance: **WASHER-1**
Parents: **WASHER**
--Slots (not all shown)--
DOWNSTREAM : **CAN-COATER**

Instance: **CAN-COATER**
Parents: **COATER**
--Slots (not all shown)--
DOWNSTREAM : **PRE-PAINT-WASHER**
UPSTREAM : **WASHER-1 WASHER-2**

FIGURE 8-2. The links between WASHER-1 and CAN-COATER

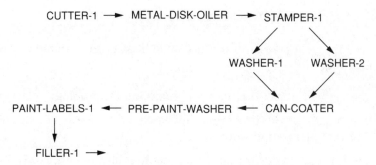

FIGURE 8-3. Canning line representation using DOWNSTREAM slot

plant production line—shown in Figure 8-3. The bold-faced items are names of knowledge-base objects, and the arrows indicate links represented by values in the DOWNSTREAM slot.

Figure 8-3 shows only one small part of the total canning-line network. If we "zoom in" on the WASHER-1 component (Figure 8-4), we see a much more detailed set of objects showing all of the auxiliary components upstream of WASHER-1. This view illustrates a complete set of connections for a small section of the canning plant. The thicker arrows indicate the flow of cans through the plant. Other types of material flow, such as washer mix, are indicated by the thinner arrows. In Chapter 13, we'll discuss in depth different methods of defining multiple types of links between objects.

By defining an upstream/downstream network, we get a feel for the full configuration of this section of the canning line. We've also now laid the groundwork for the fault diagnosis of the following section.

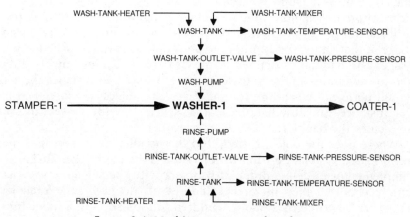

FIGURE 8-4. Machines upstream of washer-1

OBJECT-ORIENTED FAULT DIAGNOSIS

In this section, we'll take an introductory look at object-oriented programming, including:

- a review of object-oriented programming terminology
- a synopsis of the programming functions necessary to extend our canning plant application
- an approach to using object-oriented techniques in expert system applications

We'll start by defining the elements of which an object system is composed.

Messages

The essential paradigm of object-oriented programming is that an object contains within its definition all of the information required for it to function as an independent entity. The object definition includes not only attributes of the object but also actions that the object can perform. These actions enable the user to communicate directly with the object or to allow two such objects to communicate with one another. In traditional procedural programming languages, you have data structures and programs that manipulate those data. In object programming, the procedural programs are directly associated with the data structures. In the terminology of object programming, procedures associated with objects are called **messages**. You **send** a message to an object (or between two objects) in much the same way as a person might communicate by calling a friend and leaving a phone message.

In most facilities that support object programming, messages are defined by **handlers** (some environments, such as SmallTalk, call these handlers **methods**). A handler ties a message name to a programming procedure for some group of objects. Whenever one of those objects is sent a message of that name, the appropriate procedure is invoked to "handle" the message. The handler is defined as an element of a frame and is directly linked to each frame in the knowledge base. You tell an instance the action it should perform by sending it a message. The object language then goes to that instance, finds the handler that is associated with the sent message, and executes the handler.

Where does the object system find the handler for a message? In an object-oriented system, **handler inheritance** is the mechanism that enables the implementor to define different handlers with the same message name at each level of the object hierarchy. Handlers are defined at the frame level, and they are inherited by a frame's children. All instances of a frame inherit the same set of message names. Thus, any instance of a given frame can safely receive any message defined for that frame. If no handler has been defined for the child, then a message sent to that child will use the parent's handler. However, if a new handler for that message name has been defined lower in the inheritance hierarchy, then the instance will use that handler instead.

Let's start with a very simple example of why we might want to define a message for a frame. We first define an EMPLOYEE frame with the attributes START-DATE and VACATION-DAYS. VACATION-DAYS has an initial value of 10. We next define a rule that states "When the employee has been at the company more than 5 years, number of vacation days is 15." We could define a TIME-AT-COMPANY slot, of course, but it will be awkward to maintain a database of employees whose length of tenure at the company must be constantly recalculated and placed in a slot. Instead we can define a message for (sometimes referred to as attaching a method to) the EMPLOYEE frame that we'll call TIME-AT-COMPANY. The handler (program code) for this message will take the current date, calculate the difference from each employee's start date, and provide the rule with the length of time the employee has been at the company. The nice thing about a message is the definition flexibility. For example, we could extend our frame hierarchy with a subclass of EMPLOYEE, HALF-TIME-EMPLOYEE. For this special case, we would modify the handler so that the number of days at the company only counted half of that for a full time employee; because the employee works only half time, the calendar time employed at the company required to get an extra week's vacation doubles. Now, no matter which type of employee is evaluated by the rule, a consistent measure of time employed will be used.

Procedural Languages

Just because a developer is not an experienced programmer does not mean that he or she should be limited in customizing an application. True, all programming languages are composed of dozens of functions. However, the majority of these functions are not required for the types of customization work we will describe in this book.

Required functions fall into six groups:

- procedure definition—getting the computer to recognize that a new function has been defined

- program control—controlling the flow of control, for example, iteration over a list

- list manipulation—controlling addition, removal, and indexing of items in a list (e.g., first, second, sort)

- logical (boolean) operators—logical comparisons, such as equal to and less than, that return true or false

- input/output—requesting information from users/printing or otherwise displaying information

- arithmetic functions—plus, minus, and so on

Within each of these groups are numerous functions that allow the programmer to fully control the environment. As a general rule, a small set of programming functions, two or three from each group, or approximately 20 for each language, is adequate for 95 percent of the programming that must be done (this is true for all of the common programming languages). Although a good programmer will use the exact function that yields the most efficient results in a given situation, this does not mean that the more generic choice necessarily differs in any significant manner.

All of the examples in the book will be written using an English-style programming language—HyperTalk, the scripting language used to program Apple's HyperCard. HyperTalk is close enough to English to provide a very legible "pseudo-code" suitable for quick translation into other languages. HyperTalk is certainly not as sophisticated or flexible a programming language as Lisp or C. Even with considerable extensions, HyperCard does not compare to the more sophisticated shells as an environment for building large, complex expert system applications. As a learning environment, however, HyperCard has a number of advantages, including:

- simple programming syntax

- extremely easy-to-use graphics

- facilities for rapidly building linked objects (HyperText concepts)

The HyperTalk operators used in this book's programming examples can be found in Appendix C. Examples of the Lisp function subset and programming are provided in Appendix D.

Shell Accessors

Each commercial expert system shell on the market has a set of procedures that enable programmers to access and modify values in the knowledge base, invoke the inference engine, and manipulate aspects of the inference engine such as the agenda. For the moment, we'll define the three basic procedures:

- `getValue`: Return the value in an object's slot, for example, `getValue("WASH-PUMP", "TEMPERATURE")`

- putValue: Install a new value in an object's slot, for example, putValue "WASH-PUMP", "TEMPERATURE", "NORMAL"

- forwardChain: Invoke the forward chainer.

A full list of the shell-accessor functions for several different shells can be found in Appendix A.

Using Messages

To illustrate the principles of object-oriented programming, we'll implement a set of object messages that can perform a simple diagnosis of faults at the canning plant. The idea is that mechanical problems propagate down the canning line. If an operator sees a can with soap suds on it, for example, it implies that the rinsing process is not working correctly. On checking the rinsing sprayer, perhaps a clogged nozzle will be found. Further checking upstream might indicate that the wash mixture was not properly stirred, creating undissolved powder clots. Continuing up the chain of components, we might find that the stirring motor was not working correctly. Thus, we could infer, not by using rules but by following this chain of physical links between components, the origin of the problem.

We'll solve the diagnosis problem by defining a handler, called diagnose, that, starting with a component in a fault state, successively iterates through linked components, working its way upstream from component to component until it finds one that is in an OK state. In other words, we're making the assumption that the effects of faults ripple down through the line. If A is connected to B, and B is connected to C, we can thus find the cause of a fault at C by working up toward A. If B shows a fault also, but A does not, then our simple diagnosis heuristic will assume that the original fault occurred at B.

To represent the status of each plant component, we'll use a new slot called STATE, defined at the COMPONENT frame. As shown in Figure 8-5,

---

```
Slot: STATE
Frame: COMPONENT
Values: OK
CONSTRAINTS: OK SHUTDOWN FAULT
DOC-STRING: "The current state of a component"
DEFAULT-OBSERVATION: OK
```

FIGURE 8-5. The STATE slot of the COMPONENT frame

the STATE slot is constrained to have only three values: FAULT, SHUT-
DOWN, and OK. The default observation is OK. Values for the abnormal
conditions are placed in the STATE slot when a problem occurs or an operator performs some action.

Using inheritance, we'll define the diagnose handler for the COMPO-
NENT frame, thus allowing any COMPONENT instance to receive a diagnose message. Diagnosis begins with the suspicion of a fault at a particular
component. The operator tests that component with diagnose. We're assuming in this early example that the state of the plant components in the
knowledge base has somehow been set, perhaps using automatic sensors.
Figure 8-6A details the process of checking the suspected component, its
upstream components, their upstream components, and so on as long as
faults are detected; the resulting reports to the operator indicate the causal
chain of the original component's fault.

The diagnose handler is shown in Figure 8-6B. Before we start examining the code, we'll provide just a brief review of HyperTalk programming;
for a more detailed explanation, go to Appendix C. To define a HyperTalk
handler, the first line of the handler begins with ON followed by the message name. Comments in the code are indicated by two dashes, as in the
second line of the diagnose handler. In order to store information in temporary variables, PUT is used in conjunction with the place to put it (INTO
replaces contents, AFTER and BEFORE insert the new value), for example,
PUT 43 INTO state (PUT *a value* INTO *a variable*). Conditional tests begin
with an IF followed by a logical test (equal to, not equal to, less than, etc.),
the word THEN, the action(s) to take (similar to the rules), and close with an

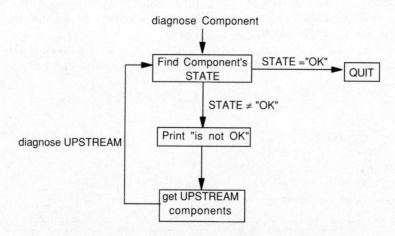

FIGURE 8-6A. Flow chart of diagnose handler

```
on diagnose component
  put component into componentsToCheck

  repeat until componentsToCheck is empty
    put item 1 of componentsToCheck into testingComp
    --get first on list
    delete item 1 of componentsToCheck

    --CHECK IF THE COMPONENT IS IN AN ABNORMAL STATE
    sendMsg testingComp, "checkForAbnormalState"
    if the result is true then
      answer component & "is not ok"

      --add all of this faulty component's upstreams to
      --test list
      put getValue(testingComp, "upstream") after
        componentsToCheck

    end if
  end repeat
end diagnose
```

FIGURE 8-6B. The diagnose handler

END IF; for example, IF state = "OK" THEN...END IF. ANSWER followed by text is used to pop up a message (the text) to the user. Finally, to iterate through a number of items in a list, use: REPEAT WITH *variable* UNTIL *test-condition actions-to-take* END REPEAT. To pick a particular value from a list, HyperTalk uses ITEM i OF *variable* and to remove it DELETE ITEM i OF *variable*.

The diagnose handler begins by setting up a list of all components to be tested (the componentsToTest variable)—initially, this is the only component that the user wants to investigate. Now, using repeat we begin iterating through all of the components in componentsToTest by placing the first element of the list into the variable testingComp. Each time we start to test a variable, we use delete to remove it from the list; thus, next time through the loop, the new first element is the next component to be tested. We'll continue repeating this loop until no more elements remain in the list.

Now we invoke a second handler, checkForAbnormalState. Handlers can return values—if the state is abnormal, then checkForAbnormalState returns true. The test *if the result is true* signals the need for a report on the problem, using the answer function, and then adds the upstream components (UPSTREAM slot) for that component to the end of the components-to-be-checked list (using the command PUT . . . AFTER). Each upstream component is in turn diagnosed by adding the component to the end of the list of upstream components being tested until no more faults are discovered.

NOTE: The arguments to **sendMsg** are the object being sent the message and the message name. In the definition of the handler, the first argument ("component" in Figure 8-6B) is automatically supplied by the object system to be the object to which the message was sent. In the example, we see the object name the handler is defined on following the message name as the first argument. To initiate using this handler, for example, to test the can-coater, we would type:

sendMsg "CAN-COATER", "diagnose"

In Lisp, this might appear as (defhandler (component diagnose) (Program-Code)), and in the handler code the special word SELF would be set to the object to which the message was sent.

The second handler, checkForAbnormalState (Figure 8-7A), returns true if the state slot is in an abnormal state. We use the slot accessor function getValue to get the STATE slot value of the component being tested. The handler then compares the STATE slot's value to the default, "OK." If the state is not ok (state ≠ "ok"), then the handler returns TRUE for use by the diagnose handler.

A separate handler is defined for this relatively simple test because of the many exceptions to the "ideal" component that exist in the real world. In the next chapter, we'll see the importance of exact translation of terminology usage from the expert into the expert system. As an example, we'll take the case where the state of a mixer is thought of not as "ok" but rather as "running"; thus, if the state is not "running," the mixer is in an abnormal state. In a traditional programming language, we would deal with this situation by placing tests in diagnose to see whether component referred to a particular type of component—if it did, we would use a different test. Of course, each time a new component was added to the system, someone would have to remember to update this function, a maintenance nightmare.

```
on checkForAbnormalState component
   put getValue(component, "state") into state
   if state ≠ "ok" then return TRUE
   else return FALSE
end checkForAbnormalState
```

FIGURE 8-7A. The checkForAbnormalState handler

However, handlers can be specialized for specific child frames. If we redefine a handler for a particular frame, the new definition will override the definition inherited from the frame's parents. We've customized the diagnose handler for MIXER instances. The new version, Figure 8-7B, uses as the test "running" instead of "ok" (changes from the original are marked in bold). Although the *message name* (CheckForAbnormalState) is the same, the frame that the handler is defined for (MIXER instead of COMPONENT) and thus the component-name argument part of the *handler name* (mixer instead of component) has changed.

Without the specialized checkForAbnormalState handler, all COMPONENT instances would inherit the standard handler, which for the case of MIXER performs the wrong test. Now, whenever an instance of MIXER is tested in the repeat loop in diagnose, the system will automatically find the handler shown in Figure 8-7B, not that shown in Figure 8-7A.

We've now implemented a primitive diagnosis scheme that begins with a detected problem at some component and works its way upstream, reporting the existence of all abnormal components. We've implemented this scheme by passing messages between plant components and shown how inheritance can be used for handlers as well as slot definitions.

```
on checkForAbnormalState mixer
   put getValue(mixer, "state") into state
   if state ≠ "running" then return TRUE
   else return FALSE
end checkForAbnormalState
```

FIGURE 8-7B. Customization of MIXER's checkForAbnormalState handler

ADDING A DYNAMIC ELEMENT

In this section we'll look at how rules and object programs can be used to add a **dynamic element** to interrelated objects in the knowledge base. We'll use an example from the canning plant, propagating state changes from machine to machine (**state-change propagation**). This propagation of changes is a simple type of simulation in which a chain reaction effect is simulated. A perturbation is introduced at some point in the canning line, and the effect of that perturbation is then communicated to other parts of the plant by traversing relations (using the DOWNSTREAM slot) between the machines.

A change of state at one machine will cause downstream components to change their states in response. In the propagation problem, a small (local) effect has a large (global) impact; a single change in state causes a "domino effect" in the components downstream of the fault.

We'll start by implementing this simulation of state-change propagation using forward-chaining rules. We'll then look at an equivalent set of handlers that produce the same effect as the rules. Finally, we'll discuss daemons, a mechanism that uses object concepts to automate processes in the knowledge base (daemons work with both handlers or rules).

NOTE: Sometimes the decision between using rules and handlers is a matter of personal taste. In other cases, the requirement for stringent procedural controls dictates the use of handlers. For applications that require simulation or other procedural techniques, the use of message passing will eventually become necessary. Building a simulation or other highly procedural process using rules alone, although theoretically possible, turns out to be both impractical and inefficient. We'll look at this issue in greater depth when we build a simulation model in Chapter 14.

In both versions (handler-based and rule-based) we'll use a STATE slot to represent the status of each component. Connectivity between components will be represented by the DOWNSTREAM slot. Figure 8-8 illustrates the three possible event sequences that can occur when a machine changes state. The table explains the logical progression in English, then translates the English into a procedural description. Assume initially that both components' STATE slot values are OK.

Case 3 is used for the case where the component's fault status does not result from a propagated state change, but rather reflects a fault in this

FIGURE 8-8. The three fault-propagation event sequences

Case	English	Implementation
1	When a fault occurs, shut down the machines immediately downstream. When the fault is fixed, turn the downstream machines back on.	If UPSTREAMS's STATE gets set to FAULT, DOWNSTREAM's STATE is then set to SHUTDOWN. When UPSTREAM's STATE is reset to OK, DOWNSTREAM's STATE is also set to OK.
2	When a machine is shut down, the machines immediately downstream must also be shut down. When the original machine is back on, start up the downstream machines, also.	If UPSTREAM's STATE is set to SHUTDOWN, DOWNSTREAM's STATE is set to SHUTDOWN. If UPSTREAM's STATE is reset to OK, DOWNSTREAM's STATE is also set to OK.
3	When a fault has occurred at some machine, its state is unaffected by changes in the state of the machines immediately upstream of it.	If UPSTREAM's STATE is SHUT-DOWN but DOWNSTREAM's STATE has been set to FAULT: when UPSTREAM's STATE is reset to OK, then DOWNSTREAM's STATE will remain set at FAULT.

specific component. The only way to change the component's **STATE** slot once it has been set to fault is to fix the component.

Fault-State Propagation Using Rules

We have chosen forward-chaining rules to implement state propagation. Forward chaining is ideal for this situation because we wish to know *all* the implications of a fault condition. In forward chaining, we start with a change in information (some new assertion, in this case a state to be propagated downstream) and infer all consequences (the new states of successive downstream components). Backward chaining, where you begin with a hypothesis and work back to a cause, would be difficult to implement with this fact-driven heuristic (Chapter 9 discusses situations where backward chaining is appropriate).

Let's take a look at the rules that implement the three event cases shown in Figure 8-8 above. The rule FAULT-MEANS-DOWNSTREAM-SHUTDOWN (Figure 8-9) handles the first part of case 1:

Rule: **FAULT–MEANS–DOWNSTREAM–SHUTDOWN**
Rule Set: **PROPAGATE**
Documentation: If a component has a state of fault, then
   find all its downstream components and set their state
   to SHUTDOWN.
IF
   ?COMPONENT IS A COMPONENT
   AND
   THE STATE OF ?COMPONENT IS "FAULT"
   AND
   THE DOWNSTREAM OF ?COMPONENT IS ?DOWNSTREAM
THEN
   THE STATE OF ?DOWNSTREAM IS "SHUTDOWN"

FIGURE 8-9. The FAULT-MEANS-DOWNSTREAM-SHUTDOWN rule

  1. If UPSTREAM's STATE gets set to FAULT, DOWNSTREAM's
     STATE is then set to SHUTDOWN.

The rule DOWNSTREAM-SHUTDOWN (Figure 8-10) handles state-propagation case 2:

  2. If UPSTREAM's STATE is set to SHUTDOWN, DOWNSTREAM's
     STATE must be set to SHUTDOWN

In this way, a STATE of FAULT can propagate a STATE of SHUT-DOWN to all machines downstream of the component where the fault occurred.

A separate rule, DOWNSTREAM-OK (Figure 8-11), restores the STATE of all machines to OK once the original STATE of FAULT has been corrected:

  1, 2, 3. When UPSTREAM's STATE is reset to OK, then DOWN-
            STREAM's STATE is set to OK, but do nothing to DOWN-
            STREAM's STATE if it's already in a fault condition.

Note that the DOWNSTREAM-OK rule first ensures that the down-stream machine is *not* in a FAULT state before it tries to reset the machine's STATE slot. We have used the syntax NOT to take care of this case—

Rule: **DOWNSTREAM–SHUTDOWN**
Rule Set: **PROPAGATE**
Documentation: If a component has a state of SHUTDOWN,
then find all its downstream components and set their
state to SHUTDOWN also.
IF
  ?COMPONENT IS A COMPONENT
  AND
  THE STATE OF ?COMPONENT IS "SHUTDOWN"
  AND
  THE DOWNSTREAM OF ?COMPONENT IS ?DOWNSTREAM
THEN
  THE STATE OF ?DOWNSTREAM IS "SHUTDOWN"

FIGURE 8-10. The DOWNSTREAM-SHUTDOWN rule

Rule: **DOWNSTREAM–OK**
Rule Set: **PROPAGATE**
Documentation: If a component STATE changes to OK, then
find all its downstream components and, if their state
is not FAULT, then set their state to OK also.
IF
  ?COMPONENT IS A COMPONENT
  AND
  THE STATE OF ?COMPONENT IS "OK"
  AND
  THE DOWNSTREAM OF ?COMPONENT IS ?DOWNSTREAM
  AND
  NOT THE ?COMPONENT STATE IS "FAULT"
THEN
  THE STATE OF ?DOWNSTREAM IS "OK"

FIGURE 8-11. DOWNSTREAM-OK rule

different shells use similar methods for testing the negative of a proposition. This covers case 3 as well as the second part of cases 1 and 2. Once the downstream machine is reset, it can then take care of the next component(s) downstream.

To get things going after inserting a new value into some component's STATE slot, these three propagation rules have to be activated by invoking the forward chainer. This can be done either explicitly through a direct, top-level invocation (in our HyperCard example, we do this by running the procedure forwardChain) or implicitly with daemons (as described in a following section).

Fault-State Propagation Using Object Programming

Situations will occur when we will start implementing a heuristic with rules, then suddenly decide to switch to object programming. Why might we want to implement this propagation heuristic using object programming, when this small set of rules certainly seems straightforward enough? Let's take a situation where we have multiple links emanating from a single object, and we want to make two tests on the downstream components—first to see if any one of them contains a batch of cans, then to see what their state is.

Rules are notoriously uncooperative for situations where a test must be made on a number of components and then a second test, also run on all the same components, must follow if the first test fails. Rules are not designed to fire in a procedural order for complete sets of objects (in Chapter 11 we'll see how rules can be coerced into an awkward semblance of procedural ordering). Rather, they evaluate a single object for all cases, then proceed to the next object. However, procedural order is exactly what the object-programming paradigm can provide us. As a general rule, rules are quite adequate for completely evaluating a set of objects one by one, but become convoluted when the entire set must be evaluated for multiple sets of criteria one by one. Chapter 13 provides an in-depth look at a case in which the use of rules in a procedural setting completely breaks down.

Implementing Messages

To propagate faults with handlers, the architecture is very simple. We'll again address the situation of propagating faults as discussed above for rules (Figure 8-8).

Whenever we want to change a component's state and cause that new state to be propagated down the production line, we'll send the component a propagateState message. The component will then test each of its downstream components with calculateComponentState to determine its

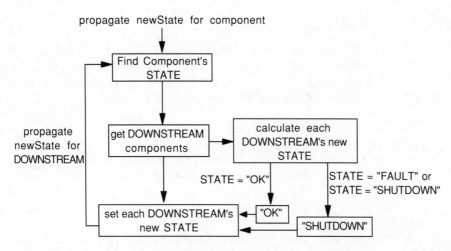

FIGURE 8-12A. Flow of control in propagateState handler

new state. In turn, each of these components will have a propagateState
message sent to its downstream components, and so on, till a component is
reached with no downstream components (Figure 8-12A).

We'll use the handlers propagateState and calculateComponent-
State to implement the three cases. Figure 8-12B shows the order in which
the handlers are called, with the looped arrow representing a **recursive** call
to propagateState.

NOTE: a **recursive function** is one that repeatedly invokes itself. Recursive
functions are useful for situations where an iterative loop is difficult to implement, typically a case where the iterations occur at several levels. In the plant
example, when we look at the upstream slot of CAN-COATER, we find two
components. However, those components in turn have their own upstream
components, and so on. A recursive function can successively look at these
levels, quitting only when no more levels are found.

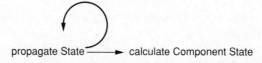

FIGURE 8-12B. The calling sequence for the fault-
propagation handlers

```
on PropagateState instance,newVal
  --First install the value of STATE slot if new
  if newVal is not empty then putValue instance,state,newVal
  else put getValue(instance,state) into newVal

  --Now loop through all downstreams...
  put getValue(instance,downStream) into downStreams
  repeat with i = 1 to the number of items in downStreams
    put item i of downStreams into downStream

    --Ask the downstream component to calculate its new
    --state
    sendMsg downstream, "calculateNewState",instance,newVal
    put the result into newLocalState
    --** 1 ** Tell downstream component to propagate
    --state
    sendMsg downstream, "propagateState",newLocalState
  end repeat
end PropagateState
```

FIGURE 8-13. The propagateState handler

The source code for propagateState is shown in Figure 8-13. Each time that a new downstream component is found, propagateState is invoked on it (see line ** 1 **); this is what is known as a recursive call, where the handler (or function) is invoked from within itself.

The sendMsg to calculateNewState handler takes care of the three different combinations of shutdown and faults, as described above. It has been implemented as a handler to facilitate possible differences in state calculations from one type of plant component to another. The first argument, downstream, is the component receiving the calculateNewState message; instance is the component upstream of the downstream component; newVal is the new state. CalculateNewState is shown in Figure 8-14.

To illustrate what actually happens, consider the connections shown in Figure 8-15(a) between object components WASH-TANK, WASH-PUMP, RINSE-PUMP and WASHER-1 (each arrow shows a connection between components via the DOWNSTREAM slot). We begin with all components having a state of OK, and start things off by setting a fault at WASH-TANK with the following command:

```
on calculateNewState component,upstreamComponent,newState
  --Return the value which the state slot of a component
  --will be set to, decide based on upstreamState.
  put getValue(component, "state") into currentState

  --Case 3: If component is already in fault state,
  --no change
  if currentState = "fault" then return "fault"

  --Cases 1,2 for newState (the following 2 ELSE clauses)
  else if newState = "fault" OR newState = "shutdown" then
    return "shutdown"

  --Upstream's OK so this one's OK (We know it's not in
  --fault state because case #3 came first)
  else
    if newState = "OK" then return "OK"
  end if
end calculateNewState
```

FIGURE 8-14. The calculateNewState handler

```
sendMsg "wash-tank","propagateState","FAULT"
```

The following sequence then occurs:

- The STATE of WASH-TANK is set to FAULT in propagateState.

- calculateNewState determines a new STATE of SHUTDOWN for WASH-PUMP (WASH-TANK's downstream).

- WASH-TANK sends a propagateState message to WASH-PUMP with a newState of SHUTDOWN.

- calculateNewState determines a new STATE of SHUTDOWN for WASHER-1 (WASH-PUMP's downstream).

- WASH-PUMP sends a propagateState message to WASHER-1 with a newState of SHUTDOWN.

The new situation is shown in Figure 8-15(b). Notice that RINSE-PUMP remains unaffected, because it is not downstream of any of the other

WASH-TANK ——→ WASH-PUMP ——→ WASHER-1 ◄—— RINSE-PUMP
OK   *OK*   *OK*   *OK*
a) Initial state

WASH-TANK ——→ WASH-PUMP ——→ WASHER-1 ◄—— RINSE-PUMP
FAULT   *SHUTDOWN*   *SHUTDOWN*   *OK*
b) After sendMsg "WASH-TANK", "propagateState", "FAULT"

WASH-TANK ——→ WASH-PUMP ——→ WASHER-1 ◄—— RINSE-PUMP
FAULT   *OK*   *OK*   *OK*
c) After sendMsg "WASH-PUMP", "propagateState", "OK"

WASH-TANK ——→ WASH-PUMP ——→ WASHER-1 ◄—— RINSE-PUMP
FAULT   *SHUTDOWN*   *SHUTDOWN*   *OK*
d) After sendMsg "WASH-PUMP", "propagateState", "SHUTDOWN"

WASH-TANK ——→ WASH-PUMP ——→ WASHER-1 ◄—— RINSE-PUMP
OK   *OK*   *OK*   *OK*
e) After sendMsg "WASH-TANK", "propagateState", "OK"

FIGURE 8-15. Value of STATE slot after sending `propagateState`
messages

three components. Now suppose we see that the wash-pump is really ok,
and we execute the following command:

`sendMsg "WASH–PUMP","propagateState","OK"`

The new situation after the calls to `propagateState` and
`calculateNewState` is shown in Figure 8-15(*c*). WASH-TANK and RINSE-
PUMP remain unaffected, of course, because they are upstream of the altered
components WASH-PUMP and WASHER-1. So let's again shut down the
two altered components by executing

`sendMsg "WASH–PUMP","propagateState","SHUTDOWN"`

The new situation is shown in Figure 8-15(*d*) (that is, we've restored
the states as they were in Figure 8-15(b)). Now let's "fix" the wash-tank by
executing the following command:

`sendMsg "WASH–PUMP","propagateState","OK"`

We've finally got all four components up and running again! The new
states are illustrated in Figure 8-15(*e*).

Automatic Updating: Daemons

So far, we've seen how to initiate state propagation between objects in the knowledge base using either handlers or rules. In both cases we had to explicitly run a procedure that caused the propagation to start, given a new slot value—in the preceding case, the STATE slot. Using object programming, we had to send a propagateState message; with rules we had to invoke the inference engine by executing the forwardChain procedure. There are times, however, when we need a mechanism that can automatically take some action when a slot value changes. This automatic behavior can be implemented with a daemon.

A **daemon** (demon) is a function that is triggered when the value of a monitored slot is affected—for this reason they are often referred to as when-**modified** and **when-accessed**. Some shell implementations also refer to daemons as "pre-defined" message handlers such as when-modified, etc.; we distinguish daemons from message handlers by the fact that daemons are automatically invoked by the system, not the user. Because daemon functions are invoked by the shell, they are usually defined to take a standard set of arguments: commonly, the instance and slot name that are being modified, the new slot value, and (in some implementations) the old slot value. Daemons can be quite useful in situations where you always want to take the same action whenever a slot's value is accessed, including:

- collecting historical data

- updating a graphical image

- printing a warning message when the new value exceeds some set of parameters

In most expert system shells, daemons are installed by placing a function name in a system-supplied slot facet.

In our case, let's say that we wanted to make sure that the fault-propagation logic described previously was invoked every time the value of a STATE slot changed. If we wanted to propagate state changes through *all* components in the plant, we would attach the daemon to the STATE slot in the COMPONENT frame; this would cause the daemon to be inherited by all of COMPONENT's children frames and their instances. Alternatively, if there were only a few problem components, we could install the daemon only on those particular instances.

The propagateStateChange daemon shown in Figure 8-16 sends a propagateState message (described earlier in this chapter) whenever the value of the slot slotName changes. Care must be exercised with the function as shown, because it makes sense only when attached to a STATE slot.

```
on propagateStateChange instance,slotName,oldVal,newVal
  --a when-modified: when a value in the state slot
  --changes, send a message
  if oldVal <> newVal then
    sendMsg instance, "propagateState",newVal
  end if
end propagateStateChange
```

FIGURE 8-16. The `propagateStateChange` daemon

Alternatively, the `propagateWithRules` function shown in Figure 8-17 invokes the forward chainer rather than sending a `propagateState` message.

Because daemons can automatically trigger additional modifications in the knowledge base in response to a changing slot value, daemons are somewhat similar in effect to rules' forward chaining in response to a slot value changing. Figure 8-18 provides a comparison between using rules and daemons.

Daemons, which are located on the object, provide the developer with a clear causal link between changes in a slot and the side effects produced by the daemon. Rules, on the other hand, are not physically connected to the objects they affect. However, unlike rules, there is no one place to look and find all of the daemons currently in the system. This lack of a central organization makes the use of daemons in a large system prone to unexpected and hard-to-detect effects.

```
on propagateWithRules instance,slotName,oldVal,newVal
  --a when-modified: when a value in the state slot
  --changes, run the forward chainer
  if oldVal <> newVal then
    forwardChain
  end if
end propagateWithRules
```

FIGURE 8-17. The `propagateWithRules` daemon

FIGURE 8-18. Automatic updating—rules vs. daemons

Rules	Daemons
Don't require programming	Require some programming
Are relatively difficult to install and retract	Are easy to install and retract
Aren't located on the object, sometimes obscuring causality	Are located on the object, resulting in clearer causality

OBJECT-ORIENTED GRAPHICS

Having looked at object programming in more depth than was covered in Chapter 6, we can now complete the overview of object graphics to include a programming-driven interface: the messages that manipulate canvases and images. Remember that the fundamental principle of object-oriented programming is that an object contains within its definition all of the information required for it to function as an independent entity. The object definition includes not only attributes of the object (the height and width, for example) but also actions that the object can perform. These actions enable the user to communicate directly with the object (instance) or to allow two such objects to communicate with one another. Examples of graphics messages include:

- action commands (for example, a message to a canvas telling it to open and display its images)

- information transfer (for example, a message to a graphical gauge that a value has been changed in the knowledge base)

All implementations of object graphics provide at least a few simple messages for manipulating the graphics (you might think of these as a simple command language). Examples of graphics languages useful to expert systems include Gold Hill's Dynamic Graphics, IntelliCorp's Active Images, and SmallTalk.

Once you have defined instances of canvases and images for your application, you need a mechanism for controlling them. For example, you might want to attach an image to a canvas, display a canvas and the images attached to it, move the canvas to a different area on the screen, remove one of the images or attach another image, and so on. Messages, described at the beginning of the chapter, are the mechanism for manipulating the canvas and image instances.

The messages for an image are summarized below:

- *Redisplay Image* redisplays the image.

- *Move Image* displays a pop-up menu prompting you for new top and left coordinates for the image. The coordinates are measured in number of characters.

- *Close Image* closes the image but does not detach the image from the canvas or delete the image instance.

- *Reshape Image* displays a pop-up menu prompting you for new top, left, width, and height coordinates for the image. The coordinates are measured in number of characters.

- *Display Image Instance* displays the slot values and handlers for the selected image instance.

- *Change Border* displays a menu from which you can select the type of border you want around the image (single, double, or no border).

- *Delete Image* closes the image and deletes the image instance.

- *Draw* draws the lines of the image on the screen.

The messages for a canvas are:

- *Exit Canvas* closes the canvas, returning you to the top level interface.

- *Redisplay Canvas* redisplays all the images on the canvas.

- *Add Image* attaches an image instance to the canvas. Further choices are possible:

  · the object to be displayed on the image (You can specify the name of an instance in your application, an external programming-language function name, or no displayed object.)

  · the name of a slot on the instance specified, or the name of a function

  · the type of image to attach to the canvas

  · the top, left, width, and height coordinates for the image (These coordinates are measured in number of characters.)

- *Display Canvas Instance* displays the slot values and handlers for the current canvas instance.

- *Open All Images* opens and displays all closed images on the canvas.

- *Reshape* changes the top, left, width, and height coordinates of the canvas. A menu is displayed prompting you for the new coordinates, measured in number of characters.

- *Delete Canvas* closes the canvas and deletes the canvas instance.

SUMMARY

This chapter took an introductory look at object programming. We went through a brief review of object-oriented terminology, showing examples — based on state-change propagation — of how object-programming techniques can be used in a diagnostic application. We also illustrated the differences between object-oriented and rule-based approaches, by showing how identical fault-propagation logic translates first into handlers and then into rules. Finally, we looked at adding a dynamic element to the knowledge base through the addition of daemons.

This chapter was in some ways a slight divergence from the main path of application building, although we'll make use of this material in the remaining stages of the application. We've added in this chapter another weapon to our bag of implementation tricks — the procedural-programming techniques of message passing and daemons. These techniques give us access to a variety of tools for making automatic changes to the knowledge base.

Overall, the team members felt their experimental foray into object programming was a success. They were surprised to discover the relative ease of writing simple procedures and integrating them into the knowledge base. Compared with writing rules, object programming had advantages and disadvantages. The handlers were considerably easier to debug and certainly allowed for more complex procedural reasoning strategies. On the other hand, the handlers were accessible only to the programmers and might be more difficult to maintain.

One of the main benefits of this exploratory effort was that the team learned how easy it could be to translate certain types of rules into handlers and vice versa. *The important thing, they realized, was to represent the reasoning accurately.* If the reasoning could be captured in one form, whether rules or procedures, going from one to the other was not nearly as difficult as they had anticipated.

In the end, the team members decided to press forward with developing the rules for quality control, rather than pursuing a wholly object-oriented approach. If it turned out later that re-implementing the rules as procedures was more convenient, they would do so. For now, they would stick to expanding the rules because they were more accessible to the project experts.

READINGS

Agha, G., and C. Hewitt. 1987. Concurrent programming using actors. In *Object-oriented concurrent programming,* eds. A. Yonezawa and M. Tokoro. Cambridge, MA: MIT Press.

Bobrow, D. G. et al. 1986. Common loops merging lisp and object-oriented programming. *Proceedings of OOPSLA-86,* Portland, OR.

Cox, B. 1986. *Object-oriented programming: An evolutionary approach.* Reading, MA: Addison-Wesley.

Fishman, D. et al. 1987. Iris: An object-oriented database management system. *ACM Transactions on Database Systems* 5, no. 1.

Goldberg, A., 1984. *SMALLTALK-80: The interactive programming environment.* Reading, MA: Addison-Wesley.

Goldberg, A., and D. Robson. 1983. *SMALLTALK-80, The language and its implementation.* Reading, MA: Addison-Wesley.

Lieberman, H. 1986. Using prototypical objects to implement shared behavior in object-oriented systems. *Proceedings of OOPSLA-86,* Portland, OR.

Meyrowitz, N. 1986. Intermedia: The architecture and construction of an object-oriented hypertext/hypermedia system and applications framework. *Proceedings of OOPSLA-86,* Portland, OR.

Rosch, E., C. B. Mervis, W. D. Gray, D. M. Johnson, and P. Boyes-Braem. 1976. Basic objects in natural categories. *Cognitive Psychology* 8.

Stefik, M., and D. G. Bobrow. 1986. Object-oriented programming: Themes and variations. *AI Magazine* 6, no. 4.

Stroustrup, B. 1986. *The C++ programming language.* Reading, MA: Addison-Wesley.

Young, R. L. 1987. An object-oriented framework for interactive data graphics. *Proceedings of OOPSLA-87.*

9

INTEGRATING A SECOND EXPERT'S KNOWLEDGE USING BACKWARD CHAINING

In the initial prototype described in the earlier chapters, forward-chaining rules made use of abnormal sensor readings to identify faulty components. In this case, the data drove the inferencing process. Now we have a slightly different situation, where we wish to use an expert's ability to work back from a hypothesis about a situation to the situation's cause. This problem is not data-driven but rather hypothesis-driven.

We'll address two new problems, the representation of a second expert's knowledge using backward chaining rules, and the integration of this new knowledge into the existing knowledge base. The key word here is integration. Both our forward- and backward-chaining rules use the same format and thus can address the same facts in the knowledge base. Consequently, we can use the same frames and slots that the forward-chaining rules used. In fact, most shells permit the same rule to work as either a backward- or forward-chaining rule, and all shells provide some mechanism for invoking further chaining from within the rules themselves.

TYPES OF EXPERTISE

Expertise exists in many forms. In the first part of this book, we worked with highly structured, theoretical knowledge—engineering knowledge about the operation of the canning plant. Now we need to work with a second type of expertise—experiential knowledge, often referred to simply as "know-how."

> George, one of the quality-control (QC) engineers at the canning plant, was now ready to contribute his many years of experience in interpreting qualitative observations of abnormalities in operations at the plant. These qualitative observations included the unusual sights, sounds, and smells that a good QC engineer must be able to recognize and then intuitively diagnose. George would begin with a hypothesis—his suspicions about the potential existence of a fault—and work back to a cause. The team immediately recognized an ideal situation for applying backward-chaining rules.
>
> One task of the implementation process would be the creation of frames representing in detail all the attributes of an operator observation, in this case, George's qualitative observations. A network of new, backward-chaining rules that captured the logic used by an expert (George) linking observations to specific problem causes (faulty machines) would also need to be implemented. As part of this process, methods of embedding requests to the user for further information (requests to line operators to make further observations) within these rules would be examined.

We'll introduce the following new paradigms to address expansion of the knowledge base:

- a backward-chaining subsystem (for performing QC analysis)
  - Rules that describe the mechanical causes of poor quality
  - Rules that identify faulty component behavior
  - Slots with which we can represent QC-specific observations

- a facility for querying the user for missing information during backward chaining

To reduce the interactions between new additions to an expanding knowledge base and the existing rules, it is good practice to build the backward-chaining subsystem as a stand-alone module. Similarly, the query facility we'll develop in this chapter is initially stand-alone. We will link these two modules with a simple developer's interface later in the chapter, then show how to combine them into an integrated end-user interface in Chapter 10.

In the plant, we began observing how George could link direct observations such as the discovery of an oily residue on the finished cans with machine failures such as a clogged washer nozzle. As we acquired this information, it was translated into backward-chaining rules, allowing the expert system to start with one of George's hypotheses for a coating problem (for example, poor washing of the cans) and then work back to primary causes (for example, clogged washer nozzles). Our plan of action was to expand the existing knowledge base by:

- representing the initial-observation component of George's QC knowledge with rules underlain by objects (frames and instances) to capture:

  · effects of one canning-line machine on another

  · definition of each possible cause of a QC problem

  · key physical observations that aid in confirming each QC problem

- devising procedures to query the operator about the observations we need him/her to make for us (programming procedures)

New rules would capture the train of thought used by George when he investigated a QC problem. New instances would represent George's qualitative observations. New procedures would enable the system to query the operator for key physical observations as they were needed by the rules during the QC analysis, emulating the points in the analysis where we observed George collecting that same information.

REPRESENTATION OF KNOWLEDGE CHUNKS

In many development situations, we need to represent physical observations about the state of the domain in the knowledge base. In the earliest chapters, this was accomplished with facts asserted into the knowledge base, for example a sensor informing us that "the pump is overheated." Later, we introduced frames and slots, allowing us to represent more complex attributes of these facts.

We can also use these same representational techniques to describe aspects of the expert's reasoning process. Experts often base their logic around **knowledge chunks,** points of collected information from which they build intermediate conclusions.

For example, the plant QC observations all center around cans that are moving down the production line. QC analysts observe the cans for particular sets of abnormalities and, using these observations, search for further information to confirm or deny developing hypotheses.

We can represent these types of observations in a number of ways. For example, we might define a set of rules, one for each possible observation.

The problem with using only rules is lack of descriptive power; we'd really like to define a number of attributes associated with each observation. We might add new slots to existing frames that describe the domain, for example, new slots describing the state of the cans (e.g. WASHER). Finally, we could define a completely new type of frame, one for each type of observation.

The third alternative, having a new type of frame, is usually best because of its simplicity and maintainability. Figure 9-1 shows an instance, CANS, of the new MANUFACTURED-ITEM frame. The CANS object serves to collect all QC observations together in one location rather than having them scattered throughout the knowledge base. This example is the most simple of approaches; at any given moment, only one set of observations about the cans exists for use by the rules. A more general approach would be to create a CANS child frame and create an instance for each new observation, providing a history of all observations made (and of course, some method of resetting the knowledge-base state by deleting all instances of CANS).

We will use facets to further define attributes of an observation. The RESIDUE slot of CANS (Figure 9-2) illustrates the use of a user facet, DEFAULT-OBSERVATION. In most applications, we will define some type of default value, primarily to enable a user to quickly re-initialize the knowledge base to a default "normal" state. In the case of the CANS instance, the values in the DEFAULT-OBSERVATION facet initialize all observations to be NONE; that is, the cans start an analysis with no manufacturing defects. As the operators observe abnormalities, the observations will be stored in these slots and used by the rules.

At times, it is desirable to specify additional layers of information concerning observations, for example, information on where an observation was made. To accomplish this, we might add a LOCATION facet to each

---

```
Instance: CANS
Parents: MANUFACTURED-ITEM
--Slots--
RESIDUE: NONE
ODOR: NONE
INNER-SURFACE: SMOOTH
OUTER-SURFACE: SMOOTH
COATING: OK
```

FIGURE 9-1. The CANS instance

Slot: **RESIDUE**
Instance: **CANS**
Values: NONE
Documentation: Crud on the cans, left for a variety of
   reasons, that (among other things) makes the contents
   taste bad...difficult to detect residue after coating
   has been applied, however.
Constraints: OILY SOAPY NONE
--User Facets--
DEFAULT-OBSERVATION: NONE

FIGURE 9-2. The RESIDUE slot

slot. This facet could contain a pointer to the specific component at which the observation was made. We could endlessly expand these detailed attributes, using combinations of slots and facets. For example, additional information about an observation, such as who made it and when, could be recorded. In the canning plant, this added level of complexity is unnecessary.

> NOTE: Only provide the level of detail in the knowledge base that is required to support the expert's logic.

Constraints on QC Observations

Another advantage of using frames and slots to describe observations is the ability to add constraints on the values the observations can take. Constraints enable the developer to limit the user's response to a set of pre-determined values. This is critical if we are going to have rules that can imply conclusions based on expected values. Slot constraints used in conjunction with object graphics benefit the developer by providing a base from which to implement prompts to the user that doesn't involve programming. This approach is much more straightforward than writing special prompting rules because it is both easier to modify and easier to check—all the prompts are grouped in one location.

Many different kinds of constraints are possible. If the inputs are numbers, the type (e.g., real, integer) and the range (e.g., 0 to 100) might be specified. If more qualitative values are being used, as in the plant, the actual acceptable values might be specified. All of the slots in the CANS instance

---

```
Slot: RESIDUE
Instance: CANS
Values: NONE
Documentation: Crud on the cans, left for a variety of
    reasons, that (among other things) makes the contents
    taste bad...Cannot really detect residue after coat-
    ing has been applied, however.
Constraints: OILY SOAPY NONE
--User Facets--
DEFAULT-OBSERVATION: NONE
```

FIGURE 9-3. Constraints on the RESIDUE slot

are defined with a constraint restricting their values to one of a fixed set of descriptive words (Figure 9-3). We can use this constraint to:

- ensure that operators will only enter observations that match the rule clauses

- aid in building the interface (e.g., menus, dials) through which the expert system can obtain information from the operator

Storing Plant-State Observations

Now we will add new slots to the canning-line component frames to represent the observations made by line operators. The values of these slots can be determined only by a human who physically goes to the machine in question and makes the observation. As we shall see in the next section, these new slots are needed by the QC rules and relate directly to various QC-specific problem states.

The values of those slots representing plant-state observations are heavily constrained, in much the same way as the new slots defined for the CANS instance. The possible values have been limited to those descriptors typically used by operators and QC engineers when they describe the behavior of particular plant components. For example, as shown in Figure 9-5, the NOZZLE slot of WASHER has been constrained to be either CLOGGED or OPEN. Similarly, the SOUND slot of PUMP (Figure 9-6) can be recorded only as CHUGGING, GRATING, or SMOOTH.

We have stored the QC observations in the CANS instance. However, in previous chapters, we defined slots whose values were based upon sensor

---

Frame : **PUMP**
Parents : **MACHINE**
Instances : **OIL-PUMP WASH-PUMP RINSE-PUMP**
--Slots (not all shown)--
RPM :
Constraints : LOW OK HIGH
User Facets : DEFAULT-OBSERVATION OK
PRESSURE :
Constraints : LOW NORMAL HIGH
User Facets : DEFAULT-OBSERVATION NORMAL
OPERATING-TEMPERATURE :
Constraints : LOW NORMAL HIGH
User Facets : DEFAULT-OBSERVATION NORMAL

FIGURE 9-4. The PUMP frame.

data. For example, as shown in Figure 9-4, all PUMP instances have slots for RPM, PRESSURE, and OPERATING-TEMPERATURE. In a similar manner, the plant-state observations will be stored in the various instances that define the component machinery of the plant.

Using Correct Terminology

From a knowledge engineering perspective, it is important to realize that the qualitative descriptors discussed above have very precise meanings for users such as our plant personnel, even though their definitions may seem a little

---

Slot : **NOZZLE**
Frame : **SPRAYER**
DEFAULT-VALUES :
CONSTRAINTS : OPEN CLOGGED
--User Facets--
DEFAULT-OBSERVATION : OPEN

FIGURE 9-5. The NOZZLE slot

Slot: **SOUND**
Frame: **PUMP**
DEFAULT-VALUES:
CONSTRAINTS: CHUGGING GRATING SMOOTH
--User Facets--
DEFAULT-OBSERVATION: SMOOTH

Figure 9-6. The SOUND slot

vague to us. For a line operator or QC engineer, when a pump's sound is described as "chugging" it means something very specific and quite distinct from, say, a "grating" sound. Were we to substitute a more scientific phrase such as "rhythmic changes in pitch" for "chugging," we would only confuse and alienate our potential users.

It is often critical to use precisely the right terminology when describing qualitative phenomena. Often, correct terminology can be determined only by carefully reviewing every detail of the knowledge base with the experts.

NOTE: In the canning plant representation, the default RPM of a PUMP instance (see Figure 9-4 above) is described as "OK," while the default PRESSURE of a PUMP instance is "NORMAL." When initially implementing these two slots, the team tried to standardize the terminology by specifying that NORMAL would be used for all situations where a component was operating correctly. However, when George saw the initial version of the PUMP frame using NORMAL for RPM, he became quite alarmed. The difference was significant, because a high rpm at the pump, while not normal, is still ok, whereas a value of high or low for pressure indicates a real problem. We had learned our lesson: Write down what the expert says exactly.

Backward-Chaining Rules

The typical process of building an expert system occurs in a cyclic pattern:

- create an initial set of frames, slots, and rules
- modify and add frames and slots
- modify and add rules
- run test cases

- modify and add frames and slots

- modify and add rules

- repeat the process

We may cycle through this process three, four, or more times in the course of building a prototype expert system. In the first couple of cycles, the basic structure is built. This initial structure is critical, because a well-designed frame hierarchy will make the knowledge base relatively easy to expand in the later development stages. At this point, however, we begin to extend the frame and rule hierarchy.

NOTE: Why do we use *backward-chaining* rules at this point? Forward-chaining rules are used when facts are being updated in the knowledge base and we wish to assess the resultant changes. Backward chaining is used when we wish to test a hypothesis or look for a causal chain from an observed state to its underlying cause. In the case of the plant QC observations, we begin with an observed problem, then backward chain to find a confirming succession of linked facts leading back to a confirmable problem. Our expert hypothesizes that a problem of a certain type exists, and the rules test to see if the facts support this hypothesis.

The rules presented in this section are one of many sets of backward-chaining rules linking QC observations to mechanical problems. These rules provide a representative sample of the general process of designing and implementing rules that link observations of problem events to their causes.

We'll alternately add rules and the slots discussed in the previous section that provide knowledge-base facts for those rules. Three basic types of slots will be added:

- slots representing **observations of events** occurring in the domain (e.g., line operators reporting phenomena such as foaming tanks or leaking lines)

- slots describing **physical qualities** of the product being analyzed in the domain (the cans being manufactured—the CANS instance)

- slots holding **intermediate rule conclusions** (preliminary results of the QC rules)

Converting Expert Statements into Backward-Chaining Rules

Diagnosing a specific QC problem on the canning line can be viewed as answering the questions shown in Figure 9-7. As each question is answered,

FIGURE 9-7. A simplified diagnostic algorithm

Situation	Example
Identify Problem	What is wrong with the way the cans were manufactured?
Identify Component	Which canning-line component malfunctioned?

Identify Causes:
   Local?
   Upstream?
	What caused the malfunction?
	Is this component faulty?
	Was the fault caused by a previous production step?

Find Cause Upstream	Where and how? (Restart cycle of questions.)

it is analogous to delving deeper and deeper into the knowledge base of rules during backward chaining. Our next task is to develop a set of backward-chaining rules that implement a segment of the QC analysis. These rules work back from QC problems to the faulty components causing those problems. We will begin with several observations made by George during the knowledge engineering sessions (the reasoning sequence is illustrated in Figure 9-8):

1. An oily residue on the cans will cause the cans' coating to bubble after it is applied.

2. Improper washing of the cans will leave an oily residue.

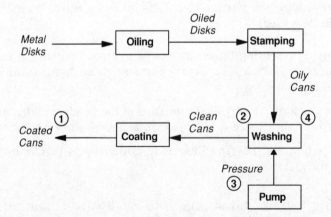

FIGURE 9-8. A portion of the canning line, showing where washing problems occur.

3. The washers must operate at a very high pressure (created by the pump) to remove all oil from the cans.

4. Clogged nozzles are a frequent cause of low washer pressure.

Each of the observations 1–4 results in a single rule being added to the knowledge base. We will now work backward through the resulting sequence of rules, trying to find the cause of a bubbly coating on the cans:

1. For cans that are being manufactured with bubbly coatings, we find that the rule BUBBLY-COATING (Figure 9-9) provides a connection between an oily residue and a bubbly coating on the cans.

2. We suspect an oily residue. We find that a RESIDUE slot value of OILY matches the consequent of the rule POOR-WASH-PER-FORMANCE (Figure 9-10).

3. We need to match the antecedent of POOR-WASH-PERFORM-ANCE. A search reveals that the consequent of the rule LOW-WASHER-PRESSURE (Figure 9-11) yields a machine object (washer) with PERFORMANCE slot value of POOR.

4. We now search for a match to the antecedent of the rule LOW-WASHER-PRESSURE. We find that the CLOGGED-WASHER-NOZZLE! (Figure 9-12) rule is such a match, since it results in a PRESSURE slot value of LOW. Finally, this rule seeks final confirmation of the fault by asking the operator (askOperatorWhenUnknown) to check the washer-in-question's nozzle.

```
Rule: BUBBLY-COATING
Rule Set: QUALITY-CONTROL
Documentation: Improper washing often leaves an oily
  residue; the Can-Coating sprayed on over this residue
  will bubble.
IF
  THE RESIDUE OF CANS IS OILY
THEN
  THE COATING OF CANS IS BUBBLY
```

FIGURE 9-9. The rule BUBBLY-COATING

Rule: **POOR–WASH–PERFORMANCE**
Rule Set: **QUALITY–CONTROL**
Documentation: When the cans are rough, oil stays in microscopic grooves and cannot be washed off.
IF
   ?WASHER IS A WASHER
   AND
   THE PERFORMANCE OF ?WASHER IS POOR
THEN
   THE RESIDUE OF CANS IS OILY

FIGURE 9-10. The rule POOR-WASH-PERFORMANCE

From this sequence of back-chaining steps, the inference engine has confirmed that the observed oily residue was caused by crud clogging the washer nozzle. (We could extend this logic to the crud itself, using observations to determine the precise type of crud and thus its origin, perhaps suggesting preventive maintenance.)

Note the call to the procedure askOperatorWhenUnknown in the antecedent of the rule CLOGGED-WASHER-NOZZLE! . This procedure queries the operator for information. We'll look further at this procedure in a later section of this chapter.

Rule: **LOW–WASHER–PRESSURE**
Rule Set: **QUALITY–CONTROL**
Documentation: Anytime you've got a washer that sprays at low pressure, it's not cleaning the cans properly.
IF
   ?WASHER IS A WASHER
   AND
   THE PRESSURE OF ?WASHER IS LOW
THEN
   THE PERFORMANCE OF ?WASHER IS POOR

FIGURE 9-11. The rule LOW-WASHER-PRESSURE

Rule: **CLOGGED-WASHER-NOZZLE!**
Rule Set: **QUALITY-CONTROL**
Documentation: The nozzles can easily get clogged with "crud," greatly decreasing the spray pressure on the cans. If the knowledge base does not already have an entry for the state of a WASHER NOZZLE, request that the operator enter a value, either CLOGGED or OK.
IF
  ?WASHER IS A WASHER
  AND
  askOperatorWhenUnknown ?WASHER "NOZZLE"
  AND
  THE FAULT OF ?WASHER IS CLOGGED-NOZZLE
THEN
  THE PRESSURE OF ?WASHER IS LOW

FIGURE 9-12. The rule CLOGGED-WASHER-NOZZLE!

> NOTE: One of the advantages of using backward chaining for this type of application is the ability of the backward chainer to request additional information. The forward chainer is driven by the facts that are available but typically will not evaluate rules when a fact is unknown.

Adding Linked Rules and Objects

Now let's look in detail at how an expert's observations are translated into new rules and associated frame slots. We'll again use George's observations:

1. An oily residue on the cans will cause the cans' coating to bubble after it is applied.

2. Improper washing of the cans will not remove all of the oil, leaving an oily residue.

3. The washers must operate at a very high pressure to clean the cans properly.

4. Clogged nozzles are a frequent cause of low washer pressure.

We begin with the statement:

1. An oily residue on the cans will cause the cans' coating to bubble after it is applied.

We start by representing the state of the cans being manufactured. Our rules do not contain references to detailed information at the level of individual cans—we are only concerned with the overall quality of can batches.

NOTE: *Only use the level of detail that is required.* In the canning plant we have represented all of the manufactured cans as a single CANS instance because the operators do their QC analysis only on randomly selected batches of cans. If they had to keep track of each batch, the situation would be more complex. For example, we might replace the CANS instance with a BATCH frame (it would still contain the same slot definitions as CANS); each batch of cans coming down the line would then be represented by a separate instance of the BATCH frame. Alternatively, we could keep the CANS instance intact but make its slot values batch dependent; the slots would become multivalued, and each value in those slots would be a batch-observation pair.

Because of the way our rules have been written, reflecting the way QC is actually performed on the plant floor, the cans may be considered a single object for purposes of inferencing. The wording of statement (1) above implies the need for two separate attributes of those cans, one to capture the type of residue on the cans (if any), and the other to describe the state of the cans' coating. Thus we need to represent at least two object-attribute pairs, which for consistency with the rest of our application we have chosen to represent by a MANUFACTURED-ITEM frame with a single instance, CANS (Figure 9-13 shows the BUBBLY-COATING rule).

First:

Define frame MANUFACTURED-ITEM

Define instance CANS

Add slots COATING and RESIDUE to CANS

Then add rule BUBBLY-COATING.

Next we have the statement:

2. Improper washing of the cans will not remove all of the oil, leaving an oily residue.

Rule: **BUBBLY–COATING**
IF
  THE RESIDUE OF CANS IS OILY
THEN
  THE COATING OF CANS IS BUBBLY

FIGURE 9-13. Rule for Action No. 1

Now we need to capture the phrase "improper washing." We already have a WASHER frame, with instances representing the different washers in the plant. It would be convenient if we could capture the concept of "improper washing" as a slot value on those instances. We will have to represent similar concepts, such as "improper coating" and "improper oiling," for other plant components as well.

One simple way to handle this representation need is to create a PER-FORMANCE slot, constrained to have one of two values, OK or POOR. Such a slot is easy for a user to interpret and can be used for any of the machines in the plant. Although our immediate need involves only the performance of washers, we place the PERFORMANCE slot on the MACHINE frame where it will be inherited not only by the WASHER frame (and therefore all of the WASHER instances), but also all other MACHINE frames and instances, anticipating the need for a similar slot on other types of MACHINE (Figure 9-14 illustrates the addition of this slot's corresponding rule).

Rule: **POOR–WASH–PERFORMANCE**
IF
  ?WASHER IS A WASHER
  AND
  THE PERFORMANCE OF ?WASHER IS POOR
THEN
  THE RESIDUE OF CANS IS OILY

FIGURE 9-14. Rule for Action No. 2

First:

Add slot PERFORMANCE to the MACHINE frame

Then add rule POOR-WASH-PERFORMANCE.

Now we turn to:

3. The washers must operate at a very high pressure to clean the cans properly.

> NOTE: The resulting rule, LOW-WASHER-PRESSURE (Figure 9-15) has been stated in the negative, as if the statement had instead read "The washers perform poorly if they operate at low pressure." Our re-phrasing is no accident, as we must always be careful to ensure that rule consequents match the antecedents and the antecedents match the corresponding consequents of connected rules. In this case, the consequent of the LOW-WASHER-PRESSURE rule must match the antecedent of the POOR-WASH-PERFORMANCE rule.

We must be able to store the (apparent) pressure of the washers' spray; we do this by first adding a PRESSURE slot to the WASHER frame, then adding rule LOW-WASHER-PRESSURE.

Next we have the statement:

4. Clogged nozzles are a frequent cause of low washer pressure.

We now must represent "clogged nozzles" in our knowledge base. There are several possibilities, among them being:

- Maintain a list of all washers with clogged nozzles.

- For all washers, add a yes/no slot that has a value of "yes" for those washers that have clogged nozzles.

- Add an attribute (slot) to all washers that describes the current state of their nozzles.

The first alternative is rather clumsy organizationally (where would we put such a list in our knowledge base of rules and objects?). The second alternative is acceptable, but it would be a little difficult to change if we later wanted to have a range of values that described degrees of being clogged (for example, a percentage with 0.0 being clear and 1.0 being totally clogged). The third alternative seems not to have the disadvantages of the

---

Rule: **LOW–WASHER–PRESSURE**
IF
  ?WASHER IS A WASHER
  AND
  THE PRESSURE OF ?WASHER IS LOW
THEN
  THE PERFORMANCE OF ?WASHER IS POOR

FIGURE 9-15. Rule for Action No. 3

other two, but it's not clear what to name the attribute ("nozzles-state," "nozzles-opening," and "nozzles" are all potential candidates). Ultimately, the choice is somewhat arbitrary.

We chose the last alternative over the second one for aesthetic reasons (we liked the way the resulting rules read), and defined a new slot called NOZZLES. We added the new slot to the SPRAYER frame, whereupon it was inherited by the WASHER frame and all WASHER instances. We then restricted the slot's possible values to CLOGGED and OPEN. This representation then allowed us to write the CLOGGED- WASHER-NOZZLE! rule, as illustrated in Figure 9-16.

First:

    Add slot NOZZLE to SPRAYER

Then add rule CLOGGED-WASHER-NOZZLE!

Rule: **CLOGGED–WASHER–NOZZLE!**
IF
  ?WASHER IS A WASHER
  AND
  THE NOZZLE OF ?WASHER IS CLOGGED
THEN
  THE PRESSURE OF ?WASHER IS LOW

FIGURE 9-16. Rule for Action No. 4

> NOTE: as a simple reminder to ourselves we have added an exclamation mark at the end of the rule's name to indicate that there is no further backward chaining from this rule. Establishing a set of naming conventions for rules will make later maintenance of the knowledge base much easier.

INTEGRATING RULES AND PROCEDURES

We now have an extended representation of the domain. So far in this chapter, we've added new slots to the objects that define the domain, as well as defined abstract objects that describe summary aspects of that domain (e.g., CANS). These additions have increased our ability to describe problems that may occur and to suggest new solutions to solving those problems. What we now need to do is improve the means by which the end user of the expert system updates and interacts with those new capabilities.

In this section, we'll use the canning-plant example for examining:

- points at which information must be supplied interactively by the user (our plant operator)

- methods for requesting that the operator supply this information during the backward-chaining process

Backward Chainer Requests for Information

An advantage of backward-chaining rules is that they can capture external data or observations *on an as-needed basis* during the inferencing process. Generally speaking, when the inference engine encounters a given slot whose value is unknown, that slot's value will need to be filled immediately with information not currently in the knowledge base. This is ideally suited to the physical observations described in this chapter, if we can devise a suitable way for the system to interact with the operator during backward chaining.

We've seen that at some point our quality-control (QC) rules depend on the kinds of physical observations that only a human being can make. These observations relate to mechanical symptoms of specific fault conditions, such as the irregular spray pattern of a clogged washer nozzle. Because they must be made individually by operators, these observations tend to be haphazard unless a particular type of problem is suspected.

We've accommodated these physical observations by extending our representation of the canning line with additional definitions for frames, instances, and slots. The new backward-chaining QC rules access those definitions during the inferencing process. Now we'll look at a procedure that can interact with the canning-line operator to query about specific mechanical symptoms. Such a procedure is the first step in constructing an end-user interface. In the next chapter, we'll discuss a variety of ways to extend this simple interaction.

The askOperatorWhenUnknown Procedure

The QC rules of this chapter begin with a known problem and work their way to other plant observations that help isolate the cause of the problem. These additional observations must be verified by a human observer. For example, earlier in this chapter we saw a chain of reasoning that stopped at the rule CLOGGED-WASHER-NOZZLE! (shown in Figure 9-12 in the previous section). In the CLOGGED-WASHER-NOZZLE! rule, the procedure askOperatorWhenUnknown is used to request input from the operator about the status of the nozzle of a washer when its condition (the slot-value) is unknown.

The askOperatorWhenUnknown function will be executed whenever it is encountered by the inference engine, such as when the antecedent of CLOGGED-WASHER-NOZZLE! is probed during backward chaining. If the function returns TRUE, the inference engine will continue processing as if there were an assertion in the knowledge base matching the function's name and its arguments. Otherwise, the inference engine will treat that particular clause—and thus that particular line of reasoning—as false, and attempt to find an alternative chain of reasoning (in this case, it will try to find an alternative set of values for the rule's variables or, failing that, try another rule).

The logic of askOperatorWhenUnknown is: If the value of an instance's slot is known, return TRUE and do nothing. If the slot's value is unknown, ask the user for the value. If the user provides a value, insert that value into the slot and return TRUE. If the user does not know the value, leave the slot unmodified and return FALSE. Figure 9-17 provides a flow chart that summarizes this logic.

If a user prompt is required, askOperatorWhenUnknown (Figure 9-18) calls an auxiliary function, queryOperatorForUnknownSlot.

The function queryOperatorForUnknownSlot (Figure 9-19) returns TRUE if the user inputs a value and FALSE if the user doesn't know the slot's value. First, queryOperatorForUnknownSlot sets the slot's value to whatever is contained in the slot's DEFAULT-OBSERVATION facet.

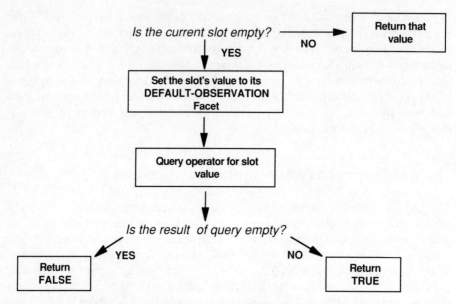

FIGURE 9-17. The logic flow of askOperatorWhenUnknown

```
--If current value of the slot is known, return that value.
--If unknown value, ask. Since this function performs slot
--access, it must replicate the behavior of the inference
--engine, in that it may be called with values of INSTANCE
--and SLOT which are incompatible(i.e.,SLOT isn't a slot of
--INSTANCE). So...we have to test to make sure SLOT is a
--slot of INSTANCE before doing anything.(In reality, the
--rules which call this fcn have been set up to insure that
--SLOT is a slot of INSTANCE, but it's best to be safe)
on askOperatorWhenUnknown instance, slot
   if isInstance(instance) and isSlot(instance,slot) then
      if getValue(instance,slot) is not empty then
         return "true"
      else
         return queryOperatorForUnknownSlot(instance,slot)
      end if
   end if
end askOperatorWhenUnknown
```

FIGURE 9-18. The askOperatorWhenUnknown function

```
function queryOperatorForUnknownSlot instance,slot
  put getFacetValue(instance,slot,"DEFAULT-OBSERVATION")
    into default
  put queryForSlotValue(instance,slot) into response
  --if value is unknown use DEFAULT-OBSERVATION and
  --Return FALSE
  if response is empty then
    putValue instance,slot,default
    return false
  else  --put user's response in slot and return TRUE
    putValue instance,slot,response
    return true
  end if
end queryOperatorForUnknownSlot
```

FIGURE 9-19. The queryOperatorForUnknownSlot function

In addition to providing a value for "resetting" the plant, the DEFAULT-OBSERVATION facet provides a default response for the user when prompting for unknown slot values.

The queryOperatorForUnknownSlot function uses yet another function, queryForSlotValue (Figure 9-20), to prompt the user for a slot's value. The function queryForSlotValue pops up a simple menu (using an existing function popUp—all systems have some facility for providing simple pop-up menus), listing the possible choices taken from the slots constraints, with an additional choice that allows the user to respond with "I don't know." If the user chooses the "I don't know" option, queryForSlotValue returns empty (which we translate to false).

In this example, when the user responds that the value is unknown we have chosen to place the default—normal operation—in the slot but return false to the rule, causing that rule to fail. However, we sometimes have situations where a specific action is required when neither the knowledge base nor the user can supply a value.

The easiest solution is to add a side effect to askOperatorWhenUnknown that produces a required action. For example, we might wish to put all queries that the operator could not answer into a special instance/slot in the knowledge base for later use. Another option would be to create a second rule set that runs if this first rule set fails. In the second rule set, we would have rules that provide alternative routes to finding the needed information. To find out whether the washer's pressure was low, for example, the new rules might examine secondary parameters, such as the rate at

```
function queryForSlotValue inst, slot, default
  --find constraints on slot value and make into a list
  --for menu
  put getFacetValue(inst,slot,"constraints") into constrnt
  put the number of words in constrnt into numOfchoices
  repeat with i = 1 to numOfchoices
    put word i of constrnt into line i of choices
    --make choice list
  end repeat
  put "DONT KNOW" into line (numOfChoices + 1) of choices
  put "Enter State of" & slot & "of" & instance into title
  --nice title
  return PopUp (choices,title)
end queryForSlotValue
```

FIGURE 9-20. The queryForSlotValue function

which fluid was being used—a lower than expected usage would imply low wash pressure.

Requesting Information from the User

Consider what happens when the following commands are executed:

    retractSlotValue "wash-pump","sound"

    askOperatorWhenUnknown "wash-pump","sound"

```
Slot: SOUND
Frame: PUMP
DEFAULT-VALUES:
CONSTRAINTS: CHUGGING GRATING SMOOTH
--User Facets--
DEFAULT-OBSERVATION: SMOOTH
```

FIGURE 9-21. The SOUND slot

```
┌─────────────────────────────────────────────────┐
│                                                   │
│         What is the SOUND of WASH-PUMP?           │
│                    CHUGGING                        │
│                    GRATING                         │
│                    SMOOTH                          │
│                   DONT KNOW                        │
│   OK                                    CANCEL     │
│                                                   │
└─────────────────────────────────────────────────┘
```

FIGURE 9-22. Menu of choices for SOUND slot

The retractSlotValue function will remove any current value for the SOUND slot of the WASH-PUMP instance. This will force askOperatorWhenUnknown to ask the user for the actual value. Using the values in the constraints facet (Figure 9-21), a menu (Figure 9-22) would appear. At this point the operator would go over to the wash-pump and listen for an unusual sound matching one of the choices. Then, after the user had chosen a value for SOUND, that value would be inserted into the knowledge base.

SUMMARY

In this chapter, we implemented a series of quality-control rules that could be made to interact with the user. This interaction was made possible through the addition of programming procedures embedded in the rules. These rules used backward chaining to test users' hypotheses about observations they have made, providing a complementary inferencing strategy to the earlier forward-chaining rules that are driven by changing facts in the knowledge base.

We saw that functions are used within a rule for two reasons:

• to perform a true/false test

• to interact with the user

The inference engine evaluated the function just like any other clause, except that instead of trying to find an instantiation of the clause in the knowledge base, the function was called directly. If the function returned FALSE, the inference engine behaved exactly as if it were unable to instantiate a normal clause.

10

PROBLEM RECOGNITION

So far in the development of the expert system, we have implemented rules that, given clear starting facts, either provide the user with advice or confirm a user's hypothesis. However, an important aspect of an expert's working process is the performance of procedures, tests, and measures, either to determine starting conditions or to answer intermediate questions.

In the previous chapter, the backward-chaining rules implement a strategy for *finding the causes of suspected problems*. The experience of an expert solving a problem was turned into backward-chaining rules that took an observed problem and helped a user discover the cause. The process, however, assumed that the end user could provide a valid starting condition for the diagnosis. The rules did not provide much interactive help to the inexperienced user in *finding or confirming the existence of those starting conditions*.

In this chapter, we'll use a backward-chaining strategy that begins with a suspected problem and, through suggestions to the users on heuristics to apply to the suspected problem, enhances their **problem recognition** abilities. Problem recognition expertise is often highly procedural, requiring a variety of tests to be conducted and specific conditions to be identified. We'll examine how programming procedures can be implemented to integrate these tests with the rules.

Continuing with the canning plant example, we'll extend the operator observation rules on quality control from the previous chapter. We'll refer to the operator observations as **fault conditions**. These fault conditions will be implemented using a new hierarchy of frames and instances, with one instance per fault condition. Additional rules will be written that link the fault-condition instances to the QC rules described in the previous chapter. Finally, we will write a set of procedures that query the user concerning the existence of specific faults and integrate these procedures with the rules.

ASSESSMENT

After implementing the quality-control rules described in the previous chapter, we reviewed them with George. We began the review with George sitting at the terminal selecting the observation "The can coating is bubbly." The interface translated the observation into the hypothesis

THE COATING OF CANS IS BUBBLY?

and initiated backward-chaining (using the rules developed in Chapter 9). After a moment, the system responded with the menu shown in Figure 10-1.

The inference engine had backward chained to the CLOGGED-WASHER-NOZZLE! rule (Figure 10-2) and was requesting operator confirmation using the clause

askOperatorWhenUnknown "WASHER-1" "NOZZLE "

which popped up the menu shown in Figure 10-1. Everything had worked perfectly.

However, George was clearly puzzled. "So what do I do if I am the operator? Should I know what to look for? What if I've never seen a clogged nozzle? What if I'm not even sure where washer-1 is, much less where the nozzle is located?" Nancy nodded, perhaps thinking of some of the operators whom she supervised. We immediately realized that the system was fine—as far as it went. However, we had become so used to working with someone with George's skills that we had neglected to incorporate ancillary materials to aid less experienced users.

What is the STATE of NOZZLE of WASHER-1?

OPEN
CLOGGED
DONT KNOW

FIGURE 10-1. Menu displayed by CLOGGED-WASHER-NOZZLE! rule

Rule: **CLOGGED–WASHER–NOZZLE!**
Rule Set: **QUALITY–CONTROL**
Documentation: The nozzles can easily get clogged with
  "crud," greatly decreasing the spray pressure on the
  cans. If the knowledge base does not already have an
  entry for the state of a WASHER NOZZLE, request that the
  operator enter a value, either CLOGGED or OK.
IF
  ?WASHER IS A WASHER
  AND
  AskOperatorWhenUnknown ?WASHER "NOZZLE"
  AND
  THE NOZZLE OF ?WASHER IS CLOGGED
THEN
  THE PRESSURE OF ?WASHER IS LOW

Figure 10-2. The rule CLOGGED-WASHER-NOZZLE!

After our review episode with George and Nancy, we got back to work. It was clear from George's comments that the system had to be able to help the operator by giving guidance on how to *identify* mechanical problems. (In the next chapter, we'll worry about telling the operator how to *fix* those problems.)

Because of its simplicity and frequent occurrence, we concentrated first on the problem of clogged nozzles. First, George told us about how to spot this problem visually. We dutifully followed him as he crawled around the washer machinery to the position necessary for seeing the spray pattern, even though it required coming dangerously close to the scalding washer spray. George claimed that he could *hear* an uneven spray pattern at a distance, even above the din of machinery, but we were unable to get him to be more specific than that. Next, George explained the procedure for shutting down a washer. This procedure was posted, but perhaps not as obviously as it could have been. Although none of it was very complicated, it was easy to see how an inexperienced operator could make a mistake, especially in the heat of the moment.

NOTE: The expression "a picture is worth a thousand words" is quite apt for both diagnosis and repair. In the last chapter of this book we'll examine the use of multimedia techniques for providing users with sound and pictures.

Finally, George led us directly to a detailed description of the clogging problem, buried inside two operations manuals. The language in the manuals was almost incomprehensible, although the photographs and diagrams were quite useful. The pages containing the most useful photographs and diagrams were well worn with use.

Implementation Approach

Expert system rules clearly need a way of querying an inexperienced user for information in a manner that provides adequate guidance. The required extensions to the knowledge base must be designed so that there is a logical integration with the rules already present. The new design must also take into account the iterative nature of problem identification. Iteration is needed because suspected problem investigation must sometimes be deferred. As questions are asked of the user about suspected problems, the user may have to answer "I don't know now." Later, the user will be able to obtain the requested information, *but only after backward chaining has finished.* Part of the design must account for this requirement for deferred information input.

Iterative processes such as fault confirmation are often a problem because of the time lag between the beginning and ending of the reasoning process. The critical factor to be evaluated is the granularity of the time change. If facts in the domain will undergo significant change during these delays, then a mechanism to account for these changes must be implemented (a detailed discussion of temporal effects is presented in the next section). Luckily, in most situations, the delays in the reasoning process are much shorter than the time periods in which domain facts are changing, obviating the need for special handling.

The following approach provides a stable, integrated platform for expansion:

- Build a frame hierarchy to represent the new, procedural knowledge.

- Modify the rules so that when they backward chain, they query the user about specific conditions, rather than requesting obscure facts.

- During backward chaining, have the inference engine save a history of questions that the user could not immediately answer.

- When providing advice, also provide the user with access to procedures explaining how to implement the advice.

Figure 10-3 shows the application of these new features to the canning plant expert system. The shutdown logic using fault trees was implemented in the first prototype. As we expanded the prototype (Chapter 9) we

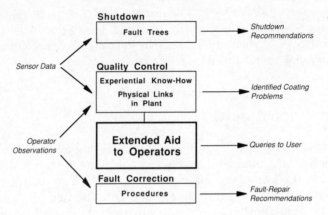

FIGURE 10-3. The quality-control architecture

implemented rules that aided in identifying quality-control problems using operator observations. Now we will expand the knowledge base by adding extended aid to the operators in the form of detailed queries for information and a facility for postponing required answers until the information can be gathered.

TEMPORAL EFFECTS ON REASONING

When reasoning about events that occur in the real world, we must always take into account the effect of passing time. In particular, temporal effects must be dealt with in two types of situation: when transitory processes are being evaluated and when nonmonotonic tests must be administered.

Transitory Processes

Understandably, temporal systems are considered to be difficult to analyze. A new level of complexity arises if the phenomenon being studied (in our case, the deterioration of the canning process) has transitory processes. In the canning plant, for example, suppose that the addition of bad wash mix to the wash tank has caused a momentary foaming of the wash mix. This can cause QC problems hours later, but because the foaming occurred previous to the analysis—and is only one of thousands of events in the plant that occurred in these intervening hours—it could be very difficult to pinpoint the wash mix as the cause of the observed problems.

Systems analyzing problems at nuclear power plants have this same problem. Often, the cause of a problem occurs many hours before the symptoms manifest themselves. To discover the cause of a problem, the system must have the ability to record when events occur and then reason about the order of their occurrences over time.

In the current implementation for the canning plant, none of the transitory processes was a problem. This is because all of the fault conditions are relatively static, in the sense that the operator can make observations at any time and obtain the same basic reading.

When reasoning with transitory events must be addressed, the first step is to add a mechanism for recording the time an observation was made: adding a time facet to all slots recording temporally affected data or keeping a temporally ordered list in the slot, with periodic readings paired with the time at which the observation was made, are possible approaches. Procedures or rules that can group observations by when they occur are then needed. Finally, additional rules and frames that establish causal links between observations and time lapses need to be added. The net effect is to produce a system that includes blocks of passing time as facts in the reasoning process.

Nonmonotonic Reasoning

In the world of theory and theorem proving, a fact remains true throughout the proof, or the proof is invalid. In the real world, however, situations are constantly in flux, and experts often change their mind in midstream. Welcome to the world of nonmonotonic logic, where a valve can be blocked at the beginning of a rule and, after a clause invokes a test procedure, unblocked when we reach the next premise clause. The ability to write rules in an environment where a fact changes from true to false or vice versa, is critical when working with almost any real-world situation, particularly situations involving **differential diagnosis**, a reasoning process that makes an assumption and then attempts to disprove it.

Let's look at an example of differential diagnosis at the canning plant. An operator believes that a valve between the wash-tank and the wash-pump is not fully open, because she has observed a low pressure in the system. The rule in Figure 10-4 makes use of nonmonotonic reasoning. The rule begins with the assumption that the wash-pump pressure is low, runs a test procedure that causes the valve to cycle, and then retests the pressure to see if it is now normal. In Figure 10-4, the rule tests pressure at the start and end of a procedure; if the pressure starts low and returns to normal, it provides evidence that the problem with the pressure was indeed the value. In nonmonotonic reasoning, a fact that was true at the start of the rule can become false during the inferencing.

Nonmonotonic reasoning is useful any time rules are addressing phenomenona that change during the course of a reasoning process. Modeling of transitory processes is useful whenever events that occurred in the past have a bearing on reasoning about events in the present.

Rule: **VALVE–CYCLE–TEST**
IF
  THE PRESSURE OF ?PUMP IS LOW
  AND
  THE OUTLET–VALVE OF ?PUMP IS ?VALVE
  AND
  runValveCycleTestProcedure ?VALVE
  AND
  THE PRESSURE OF ?PUMP IS NORMAL
THEN
  THE FAULT OF ?VALVE IS INTERMITTENT–CLOGGING

FIGURE 10-4. Nonmonotonic rule testing for faulty valve

CONCEPTS REPRESENTED AS OBJECTS

Up to now, the objects in our knowledge base represent only physical entities, for example, plant components such as washers, pumps, and the cans
that are being manufactured. It is often useful, however, to also represent
conceptual "objects." The representation of fault conditions is a good example of representing concepts with objects.

    All fault conditions share a number of attributes: They occur at some
specific physical location, they have an associated repair procedure, and so
forth. These fault conditions may be represented as frames and instances. As
we'll see, this representation provides a common structure for our knowledge about those faults, and collects all fault-specific knowledge in a single
locus in the knowledge base.

Defining a Conceptual Object Frame

Let's begin by reviewing George's major objections to the QC rules of the
previous chapter:

- No advice was given on how to confirm a fault condition.

- No help was given concerning where to look in the thousands of
  pages of operations manuals for additional, detailed help.

    We can meet George's objections by constructing a FAULT-
CONDITION frame (Figure 10-5) with separate instances for each distinct

```
Frame: FAULT-CONDITION
Parents: DIAGNOSTIC-FRAME
--Slots (not all shown)--
CONFIRMING-ACTION : "Do whatever necessary to find the
   fault"
Constraints: TEXT
Documentation: Tells the operator what to do to find the
   fault
MANUAL-REFERENCE :
Constraints: TEXT
Documentation: A place in the operator's manual to find a
   detailed description of how to do something
```

FIGURE 10-5. Initial FAULT-CONDITION frame

fault. Later in this chapter, we will integrate the new objects with the existing QC rules. Our new frame will require the following slots:

- CONFIRMING-ACTION: a way of confirming the fault's existence

- MANUAL-REFERENCE: a pointer to where to look for additional information, diagrams, and so forth

For now, CONFIRMING-ACTION will simply be text that we can print on the screen when asking the operator to confirm or deny the presence of a particular fault. MANUAL-REFERENCE will be another sentence describing where to go in the voluminous reference manuals available to the operator.

One simple fault occurs when a washer nozzle becomes clogged. To represent this fault, we define an instance of the FAULT-CONDITION frame, CLOGGED-NOZZLE, shown in Figure 10-6.

```
Instance: CLOGGED-NOZZLE
Parents: FAULT-CONDITION
---Slots---
CONFIRMING-ACTION : "Visual inspection: look for uneven
   spray pattern"
MANUAL-REFERENCE : "Chapter 15, pp. 197--222"
```

FIGURE 10-6. The CLOGGED-NOZZLE instance

```
Instance: LEAKING-PIPES
Parents:  FAULT-CONDITION
---Slots---
CONFIRMING-ACTION : "Look for pools of liquid on the floor,
  especially near pumps"
MANUAL-REFERENCE : "No reference in manual"
```

FIGURE 10-7. The LEAKING-PIPES instance

As we did for CLOGGED-NOZZLE, we can represent leaking washer pipes with the instance LEAKING-PIPES, shown in Figure 10-7.

However, these fault descriptions do not allow us any way of specifying that a fault has actually been found. What should we do, for example, if we find that washer-2 has a clogged-nozzle fault?

Locating a Fault Condition

This lack of expressive power in our FAULT-CONDITION frame immediately suggests the addition of another slot, FAULTY-COMPONENT, shown in Figure 10-8. Having such a slot will allow us to specify that a fault has

```
Instance: CLOGGED-NOZZLE
Parent:  FAULT-CONDITION
--Slots (not all shown)---
CONFIRMING-ACTION : "Visual inspection: look for uneven
  spray pattern"
CORRECTIVE-PROCEDURE : "Turn off flow to nozzle","Use a
  wire to clear the clogged nozzle holes","If the holes
  are not cleanable with a wire, remove nozzle head","Soak
  nozzle head in solvent for 30 minutes","Thoroughly clean
  nozzle head","Re-install nozzle head", "Restore flow to
  sprayer"
MANUAL-REFERENCE : "Chapter 15, pp. 197--222"
FAULTY-COMPONENT: WASHER-2
SUSPECTED-COMPONENT:
```

FIGURE 10-8. The CLOGGED-NOZZLE instance with new slots

Slot: **SUSPECTED—COMPONENT**
Frame: **FAULT—CONDITION**
Default—Values :
Documentation: "The place where askOperatorToFind thinks
    it might be"
Constraints: INSTANCE—OF **COMPONENT**

FIGURE 10-9. The SUSPECTED-COMPONENT slot

been found. If washer-2 has a clogged nozzle, for example, we can set the value of CLOGGED-NOZZLE's FAULTY-COMPONENT slot to WASHER-2. Because the FAULTY-COMPONENT slot will always contain a plant component represented in our object hierarchy, we will constrain it to be an instance of COMPONENT.

Similarly, what should we do if we *suspect* a particular fault exists at some component, but are not yet sure? One alternative would be to associate a **certainty factor** with each component present in the FAULTY-COMPONENT slot. Unfortunately, there continues to be a great deal of controversy on how to handle certainty factors. In general, alternative solutions are preferable when possible (usually the case). We have instead added a SUSPECTED-COMPONENT slot (Figure 10-9) that will serve as a temporary holding container (during our QC analysis) to store a list of all components that the rules indicate *might* be suffering from some particular problem. Additional information will be provided on how to further evaluate these choices, leaving the final decision up to the user. The SUSPECTED-COMPONENT slot will typically contain more than one value, while the FAULTY-COMPONENT slot will contain only a single value at the conclusion of analysis. A final slot, CORRECTIVE-PROCEDURE, will be discussed in the next chapter.

LINKING FAULTS TO RULES

In the previous section, we defined the FAULT-CONDITION frame. Each instance of this frame contains detailed information on a specific fault condition, including identification of the problem and methods for its repair.

We now need a way to link the FAULT-CONDITION instances to our quality-control (QC) rules. In this section, we'll examine one way of building this link by:

- referencing the new instances in the QC rules
- collecting information about suspected faults in a master list

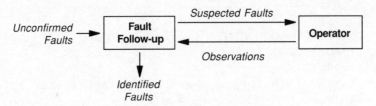

FIGURE 10-10. Interaction of fault conditions with QC rules

Fault Identification

Our fault-identification analysis will work as follows:

- During backward chaining we will query the user to try to confirm or deny specific fault conditions.

- Those faults that cannot be confirmed or denied (unconfirmed faults) will immediately go on a master list of "things to do."

- After backward chaining is complete, we'll follow up on the unconfirmed faults. As the operator finishes investigating particular faults, analysis will be resumed and those faults will be removed from the "things to do" list.

Figure 10-10 provides a summary of how the fault conditions will now interact with the QC rules, using observations to determine if unconfirmed faults should become identified faults.

To implement this procedure we will link the instances representing given fault conditions to the QC rules using backward- chaining rules. Let's look at exactly what we have to do to set up those links. We have already constructed a set of FAULT-CONDITION instances, each of which describes a particular mechanical problem on the canning line. Eventually, we will want our new rules to lead to conclusions such as

"washer-2 has a clogged nozzle."

"wash-mix-tank has leaking pipes."

Each of the problems mentioned above (clogged nozzle and leaking pipes) corresponds to a FAULT-CONDITION instance. Our first need, then, is to be able to cross-reference a plant component with the fault condition it is exhibiting. The statements above appear as rule-premise clauses in the form

THE FAULT OF WASHER-2 IS CLOGGED-NOZZLE

THE FAULT OF WASH-MIX-TANK IS LEAKING-PIPES

Rule: **FAULT-IDENTIFIED**
Rule Set: **FAULT-CORRECTION**
Documentation: We've confirmed a fault; update the KB.
IF
   ?FAULT IS A FAULT-CONDITION
   AND
   THE FAULTY-COMPONENT OF ?FAULT IS ?COMPONENT
THEN
   THE FAULT OF ?COMPONENT IS ?FAULT

FIGURE 10-11. FAULT-IDENTIFICATION rule

on which we can now backward chain. Thus, we first:

1. Add a FAULT slot to the COMPONENT frame. This slot will contain the name of the fault instance corresponding to a confirmed fault (e.g., the instance CLOGGED-NOZZLE). Because COMPONENT is high up in the frame hierarchy, the FAULT slot will be inherited by all instances in the knowledge base that represent plant components.

Now we need to ensure that the connection between the FAULT slot of a COMPONENT instance and the corresponding FAULTY-COMPONENT slot of a FAULT-CONDITION instance is made when a fault is confirmed. For example, if the FAULTY-COMPONENT slot of CLOGGED-NOZZLE has a value of WASHER-2, then the FAULT slot of WASHER-2 should contain CLOGGED-NOZZLE. To make this connection we:

2. Write a rule connecting the FAULT and FAULTY-COMPONENT slots—the FAULT-IDENTIFIED rule (Figure 10-11). The exact usage of this rule will be described in the next section.

Now we need a way to query the operator concerning the existence of faults. This leads to the third step of our implementation:

3. Write a rule that will alert the operator to the possibility of certain faults, FAULT-QUERY (Figure 10-12). The second and third clauses in this rule set the contents of information slots to local variables in the rule. The fourth clause is a test saying "Have we confirmed this fault or is it still unknown?" The final clause makes use of a new function, askOperatorToFind.

Rule: **FAULT–QUERY**
Rule Set: **FAULT–CORRECTION**
Documentation: We're trying to confirm a fault; we need to
  ask the operator to try and find it.
IF
  ?FAULT IS A FAULT–CONDITION
  AND
  THE CONFIRMING–ACTION OF ?FAULT IS ?ACTION
  AND
  THE MANUAL–REFERENCE OF ?FAULT IS ?REF
  AND
  UNKNOWN
     THE SUSPECTED–COMPONENT OF ?FAULT IS ?COMPONENT
  AND
  askOperatorToFind ?FAULT ?COMPONENT ?ACTION ?REF
THEN
  THE FAULT OF   ?COMPONENT IS ?FAULT

FIGURE 10-12. The FAULT-QUERY rule

The final clause invokes askOperatorToFind only after it has determined that no suspected components yet exist, that is, that no previous testing for a fault has been made. The purpose of askOperatorToFind is similar to the askOperatorWhenUnknown function of the previous section—both functions request information from the operator—except that askOperatorToFind also conveys instructions on how to gather the requested information. Using rule variables, this function asks the operator about the existence of a fault (?FAULT) at some plant component (?COMPONENT) and gives some advice on how to find the fault (?ACTION) and, if it is needed, a detailed discussion from the operations manual (?REF). The function evaluates the answer and returns TRUE or FALSE for the inference engine, eliminating the need for a final test of the component's FAULT slot value.

Consider what happens when the FAULT-QUERY rule is used to check out the possibility of a clogged-nozzle fault at washer-2. In this case, when the inference engine reaches the call to askOperatorToFind, the rule's variables will have been set to:

?COMPONENT   WASHER-2

?FAULT   CLOGGED-NOZZLE

Rule: **MIX–ON–FLOOR!**
Rule Set: **QUALITY–CONTROL**
Documentation: When the soap or rinse mix proportions are
  incorrect, foaming–over occurs, causing a reduction of
  washer performance.
IF
  ?WASHER IS A WASHER
  AND
  AskOperatorWhenUnknown ?WASHER "APPEARANCE"
  AND
  { THE APPEARANCE OF ?WASHER IS SOAP–MIX–ON–FLOOR
  OR
  THE APPEARANCE OF ?WASHER IS RINSE–MIX–ON–FLOOR }
THEN
  THE PRESSURE OF ?WASHER IS LOW

FIGURE 10-13. The MIX-ON-FLOOR! rule

?ACTION   value in CLOGGED-NOZZLE's CONFIRMING-ACTION slot

?REF   value in CLOGGED-NOZZLE's MANUAL-REFERENCE slot

askOperatorToFind will then ask the operator whether WASHER-2 has
a clogged nozzle. One advantage of the FAULT-QUERY rule is that it permits us to eliminate a number of rules, for example CLOGGED-WASHER-
NOZZLE! and MIX-ON-FLOOR! (Figures 10-2 and 10-13). All of the information contained in these rules, including the documentation, is available
in the various fault instances' slots and thus more readily accessible during
inferencing.

NOTE: When rules use OR in the antecedent, the clauses divided by the OR
are split into two rules by the inference engine. Some users prefer to write
two rules instead of using an OR (and some shells do not support OR). In
this case, each rule would check for ?WASHER as an instance of WASHER,
run askOperatorWhenUnknown, and then test one of the clauses here
separated with the OR.

Check out fault CLOGGED-NOZZLE at WASHER-1

CONFIRMED
NOT PRESENT
UNKNOWN

Directions: Look for uneven spray pattern
Manual: Chapter 7, pp. 313–371

FIGURE 10-14. The menu displayed by queryFinding for fault condition CLOGGED-NOZZLE

The askOperatorToFind Function

The FAULT-QUERY rule uses a new function, askOperatorToFind, that is similar in many ways to the askOperatorWhenUnknown function of the previous chapter. askOperatorToFind makes use of the new FAULT-CONDITION frame to prepare and ask questions. As backward chaining occurs, this function is called wherever a rule antecedent requires information on a parameter that is observable only by the operator:

- It first determines whether the fault is already on a list of "faults to find" (the global variable suspectedFaultList).

- If the fault is already on the list, it returns FALSE.

- If the fault is not on the list, the function sets the SUSPECTED-COMPONENT slot and queries the operator with the function checkFindings.

- If the operator finds the fault, it returns TRUE.

- If the operator can't determine immediately whether the fault exists, the function adds a description of the fault onto a list (suspectedFaultList), then returns FALSE, causing the rule to fail and no immediate confirmation of that fault to occur.

Figure 10-14 shows the menu that is displayed when askOperatorToFind is run for a typical case: trying to locate a clogged-nozzle at washer-1.

When the Answer is Unknown

We now need a way of asking the user whether any of the suspected faults that have been placed on the "deferred" list (suspectedFaultList) actu-

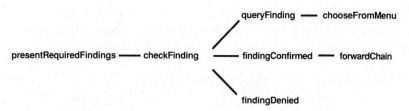

FIGURE 10-15. Calling sequence for the operator-advice functions

ally exist. After backward chaining has finished, the operator must investigate all suspected faults that could not be confirmed or denied while the inference engine was running.

When more evidence has been gathered and the operator is ready to restart the process of analysis for the suspected faults, the operator must run the function (presentRequiredFindings), a process similar to starting forward chaining with the forwardChain function. The algorithm used by presentRequiredFindings is:

- For each suspected fault, ask the operator to investigate that suspected fault.

- If the fault is confirmed, use forward chaining rules to offer advice on how to take corrective action.

- If the fault is denied, take that fault off the list of suspected faults.

- If the fault's existence is still unclear, take no action, leaving the fault on the suspected faults list.

This algorithm has been implemented using the function checkFinding to step through the list of suspected faults (suspectedFaultList). It asks the user to confirm or deny the presence of each potential fault.

Figure 10-15 illustrates a diagram of the calling sequence for present RequiredFindings and the functions it uses.

> NOTE: the forward chainer is invoked when a finding is confirmed; this is the mechanism used to provide advice. We could also have implemented presenting and checking findings with rules; in this case, the forward chainer would be invoked from a backward-chaining rule that confirmed the finding.

Each time the user is queried about a fault by checkFinding, the function queryFinding will be executed. queryFinding is the function that interacts with the operator by popping up menus and asking the appropriate question about a fault's confirmation or elimination. Based on the return value from queryFinding, the fault can be

- confirmed (execute findingConfirmed)

- eliminated as a possibility (execute findingDenied)

- unknown (do nothing, returning EMPTY)

If a fault is confirmed by the user (the CONFIRM option in the menu we just examined), the function findingConfirmed places the confirmed fault in the offending component's FAULT slot and puts the component's name into the fault instance's FAULTY-COMPONENT slot (as did our rule FAULT-IDENTIFIED). It then invokes the forward chainer using the fault-correction rules. These rules, which provide the operator assistance in correcting the confirmed fault, are described in detail in Chapter 11.

Alternatively, the user may have indicated that the fault wasn't found (by choosing NOT PRESENT). If this is the case, we want to ensure that the suspected fault is ignored for the remainder of the analysis. This is done by deleting the fault from the list.

Finally, the user may have chosen UNKNOWN from the menu. In this case, the fault remains on the suspectedFaultList list and can be tested at a later time.

Whenever there are suspected faults that cannot be definitively confirmed or denied, there must be a way to resume the fault check-out procedure. This may be done by re-running the function presentRequiredFindings, whenever the operator is ready, as many times as are needed to thoroughly investigate all of the suspected faults.

SUMMARY

In this chapter, we looked at how we could aid the end user by performing data-gathering tasks more consistently using rules that give hints and helps. Part of the problem with the Chapter 9 rules was their iterative nature—data requests for the rules often could not be fulfilled during the course of the backward chaining. A discussion of temporal effects examined problems with transitory processes and nonmonotonic reasoning. Frames that represented conceptual ideas, such as a problem description, were added to the knowledge base and then linked to the rules discussed in Chapter 9 using new rules and procedures.

11

TURNING KNOW-HOW INTO ASSISTANCE

I n the previous chapter we discussed ways we could assist the user in the performance of procedures, tests, and measures that determine starting conditions and answer intermediate questions.

In this chapter we'll use a combination of procedures and forward-chaining rules to enhance users' **problem solving** abilities. Problem solving, like problem recognition, is often highly procedural, requiring a variety of tests to be conducted and specific conditions to be identified. We'll examine how programming procedures can be implemented to integrate these tests with the rules. We'll start with the backward-chaining rules concerning quality control in the canning plant, described in the previous few chapters, and then add various types of procedural control and integration with forward-chaining rules.

REPAIRING FAULTS

In the previous chapter, we constructed a mechanism in which suspected faults are

- tested
- gathered into a list of "things to do"
- presented to the operator

Once a fault has been identified, it has to be repaired. In this section, we'll show how to make recommendations to the operator concerning the repair of identified faults. We'll look at the three steps of making those recommendations: representing the repair knowledge, displaying a repair procedure to the operator, and updating the knowledge base.

Storing Information about Fault Repair

Our first task is to represent knowledge about repairing fault conditions. We'll place this information in instances of the FAULT-CONDITION frame, because each instance already contains a description of some specific fault. We'll store the repair information in a new slot called CORRECTIVE-PROCEDURE.

For simplicity, we'll assume that fault repair consists of following a linear set of steps. The complete list of steps thus defines a clear-cut, sequential procedure that must be carried out by the operator. More complicated schemes are certainly possible, however—Chapter 15 discusses the addition of video and sound to the instructional tools.

The CORRECTIVE-PROCEDURE slot of FAULT-CONDITION contains information about how to fix a fault once it has been isolated. This slot (Figure 11-1) contains a list of sentences, with each sentence describing a step in the correction procedure. We would like to be able to:

- display the procedure

- have the operator perform the procedure step by step

- keep track of which steps in the procedure have been completed

---

Slot: **CORRECTIVE-PROCEDURE**
Instance: **CLOGGED-NOZZLE**
Values: "Turn off flow to nozzle", "Use a wire to clear the clogged nozzle holes", "If the holes are not cleanable with a wire, remove nozzle head", "Soak nozzle head in solvent for 30 minutes", "Thoroughly clean nozzle head", "Re-install nozzle head", "Restore flow to sprayer"
Documentation: A list of sentences, where each sentence describes a step to take in fixing the fault
Constraints: LIST

FIGURE 11-1. Slot CORRECTIVE-PROCEDURE of CLOGGED-NOZZLE

Take the CLOGGED-NOZZLE fault instance as an example. It contains a simple procedure for unclogging a washer nozzle. This procedure would be followed by the operator whenever we (the inference engine plus the operator) determine that a washer's nozzle was indeed clogged.

Correcting Faults

Once a fault has been identified by the user, there must be some way to invoke the proper procedure for fixing the fault. The overall architecture is shown in Figure 11-2. Repair procedures will be passed from fault conditions in the knowledge base to fault- correction logic that interacts with the operator. Based on information provided by the operator, the fault-correction logic will update the status of the fault conditions to reflect the operator's progress in repairing identified faults.

The fault-correction module has very specific requirements for how it must interact with the operator and update the status of fault conditions. In particular, it must be able to:

- bring up a menu that lists each step of the procedure

- let the operator check off specific steps as they are completed

- allow the menu to be redisplayed repeatedly, "remembering" which steps have been completed so far

- once all steps have been completed, recheck the identified fault to see whether it was corrected by the corrective procedure

- if the corrective procedure was not effective, mark that fault somehow as being "identified but not fixable."

Much of the complexity of the fault-correction module is caused by the operator's need to go back and forth between interacting with the system and actually repairing the fault. In other words, the repair of most faults will occur over an extended period of time, and the operator must be able to look at a repair procedure, mark one or more steps of the procedure as finished, go back to repairing the fault, reinvoke the fault-correction analysis, and so forth.

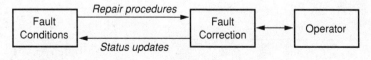

FIGURE 11-2. Correcting Faults

Our implementation of the fault-correction module uses a combination of rules and functions. First, rules detect the need for making a fault-repair recommendation to the operator and activate the recommendation process. Then, functions called by the rules control the display of a specific repair procedure and track the operator's progress in completing that procedure. Once the operator has finished the procedure, rules determine whether the procedure was successful and update the knowledge base accordingly.

We'll first look at the functions that display and track the completion of a repair procedure. Later, we'll describe the rules that interact with those functions to produce a complete fault- correction module.

Executing a Repair Procedure

Execution of the repair procedure for some specific fault condition is done in three steps, as summarized in Figure 11-3.

Rules begin the process by identifying a faulty component and then calling the function recommendProcedure, shown in Figure 11-4. This function formats the values in the CORRECTIVE-PROCEDURE slot of a given FAULT-CONDITION instance. A "completion" indicator is included during the formatting process for each step of the procedure, because we want to redisplay the procedure multiple times and must keep track of which steps have been finished. The function appends the formatted instructions to a global variable, requiredOperatorActions, that acts as a list of "things to do" for the operator. Finally, it calls the function updateFaultProcedure to evaluate how the operator is dealing with the procedure. Note that the global variable requiredOperatorActions, which contains the list of actions still pending, exists outside the knowledge base of objects and rules; it will not be saved with the knowledge base, but is recreated each session. This variable might also have been implemented as a slot on the CANNING-LINE frame if we had wished to save the information.

FIGURE 11-3. The steps of executing a repair procedure

Step	Description	Function Names
1	Setup procedure	recommendProcedure
2	Display and redisplay procedure	updateFaultProecdure queryFaultProcedure
3	Cleanup to-do list and knowledge base	isProcedureFinished procedureFinished

---

```
--Recommend PROCEDURE to operator for faultInstance at
--COMPONENT...Takes PROCEDURE (a list of sentences) from
--fault frame slot and reformats the list into
--(<sentence> <check>) where check is true or false (not
--yet completed by operator).  Finally, the result is
--added onto the requiredOperatorActions which contains
--all repair procedures to be performed.  The fault
--Instance and faulty component are placed at the front
--of the procedure list for later tracking.  Other
--functions present the user with the formatted list.

on recommendProcedure faultInstance, component
  global requiredOperatorActions
  put getValue(faultInstance,"corrective-procedure") into
    procedure
  put empty into resultList
  repeat with i = 1 to the number of items in procedure
    put item i of procedure into step
    --make a list of the form ("procedure",false)
    put list(resultList,step,"false") into resultList
    --"false"=not done
  end repeat
  put list(faultInstance,component,resultList) into
    actionItem
  --first check to see if this action is already on the
  --list
  if actionItem is not in requiredOperatorActions then
    --add a line with all info at top of global list
    put actionItem & return before requiredOperatorActions
  end if
  --see how operator is doing; pass the 1st action index
  updateFaultProcedure 1
end recommendProcedure
```

FIGURE 11-4. The recommendProcedure function

At first glance, the mechanism may seem unnecessarily complicated. However, although recommendProcedure is called only once for each fault, the remaining functions will be called multiple times for each fault until the repair procedure has been completed. A function (discussed later) brings up the menu shown in Figure 11-5 for subsequent repair work on a fault. This

```
┌─────────────────────────────────────────────────────────┐
│                                                           │
│          Choose Fault Procedure to Work On                │
│                  CLOGGED-NOZZLE                           │
│                  BAD-SOAP-MIX                             │
│                  BROKEN-THERMOSTAT                        │
│      OK                                    CANCEL         │
│                                                           │
└─────────────────────────────────────────────────────────┘
```

FIGURE 11-5. Fault selection menu for continuation of interrupted repair process

function then would call the updateFaultProcedure function, passing to
it the index number from the user's menu choice (e.g., BAD-SOAP-MIX
would be index number 2, based on the visual position in the menu and
the stored position in the variable requiredOperatorActions).

The updateFaultProcedure function, shown in Figure 11-6, controls the display and update of a user-selected fault condition.

It uses the function queryFaultProcedure to display a procedure
and perform all necessary bookkeeping for tracking which steps have already
been completed by the operator. This function, queryFaultProcedure,

```
--Run this to examine/update state of recommended action.
--Present multiple-choose menu; if finished, do
--bookkeeping. ACTION-ITEM should be a member of
--requiredOperatorActions. In general, FINISH-PROCEDURE
--must be customized to fit a particular application.

on updateFaultProcedure index
  --show user the steps for procedure indicated in master
  --list by index
  queryFaultProcedure index
  --check to see if operator finished all steps
  if isProcedureFinished(index) then
    --if all steps were finished, remove procedures from
    --master list
    procedureFinished index
  end if
end updateFaultProcedure
```

FIGURE 11-6. The updateFaultProcedure function

```
┌─────────────────────────────────────────────────────────────┐
│                                                               │
│           Fixing CLOGGED-NOZZLE at WASHER-1                   │
│  [√] Turn off flow to nozzle                                  │
│  [√] Use a wire to clear the clogged nozzle holes             │
│  [ ] If the holes cannot be cleaned with a wire, remove nozzle head │
│  [ ] Soak nozzle head in solvent for 30 minutes               │
│  [ ] Thoroughly clean nozzle head                             │
│  [ ] Reinstall nozzle head                                    │
│  [ ] Restore flow to sprayer                                  │
│           OK                          CANCEL                  │
│                                                               │
└─────────────────────────────────────────────────────────────┘
```

FIGURE 11-7. Procedure checklist for repairing a clogged nozzle

produces the menu shown in Figure 11-7—in this example, the operator has already checked off the first two steps of the procedure.

The function queryFaultProcedure (Figure 11-8) first finds the procedure in requiredOperatorActions. The procedure's list for repairing a clogged nozzle is:

"CLOGGED-NOZZLE ","WASHER-1","Turn off flow to nozzle","true",
"Use a wire to clear the clogged nozzle holes", "true","If the holes cannot be cleaned with a wire","false","remove nozzle head","false",
"Soak nozzle head in solvent for 30 minutes","false","Thoroughly clean nozzle head","false","Reinstall nozzle head","false","Restore flow to sprayer","false"

The first two elements are the fault instance (CLOGGED-NOZZLE) and the faulty component instance (WASHER-1). The remaining elements are the procedure steps followed by "true" (operator has completed the step) or "false" (no yet run). The first repeat loop formats the menu with either an empty box or a checked box. As the operator completes the procedures, this menu indicates what remains to be done by replacing the updated steps on the master list (requiredOperatorActions).

Next, the procedure is tested by the function isProcedureFinished (Figure 11-9) to see whether all steps of the procedure have been completed. The test is done by searching the procedure list; if "false" is found anywhere within the steps, it indicates an incompleted step and the procedure is not removed.

If the user has completed all steps of the procedure, the function procedureFinished (Figure 11-10) is run to remove the fault from the operator's list of things to do and reset all instance slots to their default values. The forward chainer could now be invoked using the fault-correction rules to test whether the fault has indeed been fixed.

```
on queryFaultProcedure index
  --actionitems: faultinstance, faulty component, pro-
  --cedures uses chooseMultiple menu for marking completed
  --steps of a fault's corrective Procedure...index allows
  --us to go into requiredOperatorActions and update it
  global requiredOperatorActions
  put line index of requiredOperatorActions into actions

  put item 1 of actions into faultInstance
  put item 2 of actions into component
  --keep only the procedures
  delete item 1 to 2 of actions
  put the number of items in actions into numActs
  --menu setup(items are pairs, sentence true/false)
  repeat with i = 1 to (.5 * numActs)
    put i * 2 into j
    if "true" is in item j of actions then
      --put √ in box if action completed
      put "[√]" & item (j − 1) of actions into line i of itms
    else put "[]" & item (j − 1) of actions into line i of
      itms
  end repeat

  put chooseMultiple(items,"Fixing" && faultInstance & "at" &
    component) into completedSteps
  --rebuild actions list, noting steps completed by the user
  put empty into updates
  repeat with i = 1 to (.5 * numActs)
    put item (i * 2) − 1 of actions into procedure
    put item (i * 2) of actions into testState
    if procedure is in completedSteps then
      put list(updates,procedure,"true") into updates
    else put list(updates,procedure,testState) into updates
    --PROCEDURE items look like (<sentence> <done?>)
  end repeat
  delete item 1 of updates
  put list(faultInstance,component,updates) into updates
  --finally, not completed procedures in master list
  put updates into line index of requiredOperatorActions
end queryfaultProcedure
```

FIGURE 11-8. The queryFaultProcedure function

```
function isProcedureFinished index
  --if "false" is in procedure list, some steps of the
  --procedure have not been completed
  global requiredOperatorActions
  if "false" is in line index of requiredOperatorActions then
    return "false"
  else return "true"
end isProcedureFinished
```

FIGURE 11-9. The isProcedureFinished function

```
on procedureFinished index
  --this runs when we've definately finished FAULT's
  --recommendedProcedure. actionItem should be a member
  --of requiredOperatorActions
  global requiredOperatorActions
  put line index of requiredOperatorActions into procedure
  put item 1 of procedure into faultInstance
  put item 1 of procedure into faultyComponent
  delete line index of requiredOperatorActions
  putValue faultInstance,"procedure-Finished?","YES"
  putValue faultyComponent,"fault",empty
  putValue faultInstance,"faulty-component",empty
end procedureFinished
```

FIGURE 11-10. The ProcedureFinished function

INTEGRATION OF FORWARD AND BACKWARD CHAINING

Often, it is desirable to use a mixed inferencing strategy that combines forward and backward chaining (sometimes called **opportunistic reasoning**). For example, during backward chaining, the user may be requested by a rule clause to enter a value. This fact potentially has implications for other facts now becoming true. In some cases, when there are forward-chaining rules that this fact can match on, maintaining the integrity of the knowledge base requires running the forward chainer when a fact is added.

The Fault-Correction Rules

The fault-correction rules, which are forward-chaining, are integrated with the backward-chaining QC rules to permit inferencing on new facts that the operator may enter. The basic idea behind these new rules is to manage the ebb and flow of advice and observations between the operator and the system once a fault has been identified. Once a fault is identified, that fact is inserted into the knowledge base and the fault-correction rules forward chain from that fact to the correction procedures.

The fault-correction rules begin with an identified fault. (In our implementation, an "identified fault" is a FAULT-CONDITION instance that has a plant component installed as the value of its FAULTY-COMPONENT slot.) The rules use four slots in FAULT-CONDITION instances to track the progress of a specific fault, as summarized in Figure 11-11.

Taken together, these four slots define a fixed path down which each identified fault must go. The layout of this path is illustrated in Figure 11-12; there is a fault-correction rule for each question on the path.

The rules implementing the flow chart in Figure 11-12 are shown in Figures 11-13 through 11-16.

The fault-correction rules would never chain together without some outside help. If the rule PROCEDURE-FINISHED-BUT-NOT-CHECKED is to fire, an external procedure must set the PROCEDURE-FINISHED slot from NO to YES. This is done automatically by the functions that control advice-giving; as soon as the operator indicates that the last step of a given procedure is finished, the PROCEDURE-FINISHED slot of the appropriate FAULT-CONDITION instance is set to YES, then forward chaining is started for the fault-correction rules.

FIGURE 11-11. The four slots of FAULT-CONDITION instances used by the fault-correction rules

Slot Name	Description	Initial Value
RECOMMENDATION-MADE	Has the operator been given the recommended procedure for fixing it?	NO
PROCEDURE-FINISHED	Is the recommended procedure finished?	NO
RECHECKED	Has the operator rechecked the fault to see whether the procedure was successful?	NO
FIXABLE	Did the procedure actually fix the problem?	YES

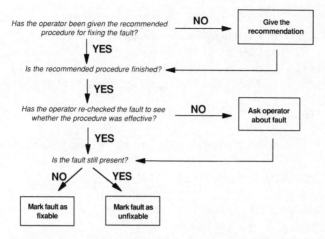

FIGURE 11-12. Flow-chart logic for fault-correction rules

In a similar manner, the fault-correction rules must be activated whenever a fault is identified and a plant component name is inserted into the FAULTY-COMPONENT slot of a FAULT-CONDITION instance. Once a faulty component has been identified, the RECOMMEND-PROCEDURE rule will be ready to fire. The forward chainer is invoked as a side effect of the function that is run when the operator confirms a fault.

```
Rule: RECOMMENDED-PROCEDURE
Rule Set: FAULT-CORRECTION
Documentation: If a fault has been identified, give advice
   on how to fix it.
IF
   ?FAULT IS A FAULT-CONDITION
   AND
   THE FAULTY-COMPONENT OF ?FAULT IS ?COMPONENT
   AND
   THE RECOMMENDATION-MADE OF ?FAULT IS NO
THEN
   recommendProcedure ?FAULT ?COMPONENT
   AND
   THE RECOMMENDATION-MADE OF ?FAULT IS YES
```

FIGURE 11-13. The RECOMMENDED-PROCEDURE rule

Rule: **PROCEDURE—FINISHED—NOT—CHECKED**
Rule Set: **FAULT—CORRECTION**
Documentation: Once a procedure is completed, the operator
   should see if the fault has been fixed (by the procedure).
IF
   ?FAULT IS A FAULT—CONDITION
   AND
   THE FAULTY—COMPONENT OF ?FAULT IS ?COMPONENT
   AND
   THE PROCEDURE—FINISHED OF ?FAULT IS YES
   AND
   THE RECHECKED OF ?FAULT IS NO
THEN
   askOperatorToFind ?FAULT ?COMPONENT
   AND
   THE RECHECKED OF ?FAULT IS YES

FIGURE 11-14. The PROCEDURE-FINISHED-NOT-CHECKED rule

Rule: **FAULT—FIXABLE**
Rule Set: **FAULT—CORRECTION**
Documentation: After rechecking fault, if it's not there
   anymore, reset the fault and mark as fixable.
IF
   ?FAULT IS A FAULT—CONDITION
   AND
   THE FAULTY—COMPONENT OF ?FAULT IS ?COMPONENT
   AND
   THE PROCEDURE—FINISHED OF ?FAULT IS YES
   AND
   THE RECHECKED OF ?FAULT IS YES
   AND
   UNKNOWN
      THE FAULTY—COMPONENT OF ?FAULT IS ?COMPONENT
THEN
   THE FIXABLE OF ?FAULT IS YES
   AND
   resetFault ?FAULT

FIGURE 11-15. The FAULT-FIXABLE rule

```
Rule: FAULT-NOT-FIXABLE
Rule Set: FAULT-CORRECTION
Documentation: If we've done everything we can and the
   fault's still there, mark it as not fixable.
IF
   ?FAULT IS A FAULT-CONDITION
   AND
   THE FAULTY-COMPONENT OF ?FAULT IS ?COMPONENT
   AND
   THE PROCEDURE-FINISHED OF ?FAULT IS YES
   AND
   THE RECHECKED OF ?FAULT IS YES
   AND
   THE FAULTY-COMPONENT OF ?FAULT IS ?COMPONENT
THEN
   THE FIXABLE OF ?FAULT IS NO
```

FIGURE 11-16. The FAULT-NOT-FIXABLE rule

CONTROLLING LOGIC FLOWS WITH RULE SETS

Observant readers will have noticed that each of our rules is associated with a particular **rule set**. A rule set defines as a functional group a related set of rules. So far, we've defined the following rule sets:

- SHUTDOWN
- QUALITY-CONTROL
- FAULT-CORRECTION

As far as the inference engine is concerned, each rule set is a distinct entity. When the inference engine runs, it is a simple matter to have it match and fire only those rules from a particular rule set (different shells treat this differently, but in general inferencing can be limited to a single rule set by passing an extra argument to the forward- and backward-chaining functions indicating the rule set to be used).

Why would we ever need to limit the inference engine in this way? If a rule in one rule set is ready to match and fire, why would we want to instruct the inference engine to ignore that rule, albeit temporarily? Although there are a number of possible uses for rule sets, three stand out:

- debugging—limiting active rules at any given time

- efficiency—fire only those rules pertinent to the moment

- control—control the order in which groups of rules fire

Ease of debugging is certainly an important reason for using rule sets—small sets of rules are easy to control and observe. By working only with small groups of rules at a time, it's easier to follow the effects of adding, deleting, and modifying rules.

Efficiency can be crucial in rule-intensive applications that cause the inference engine to look over a large search space. By enabling only those rules we are interested in, and disabling all others, inferencing is limited to a subset of existing rules. Such a strategy effectively reduces the search space during any single execution of the inference engine.

Control over the order of inferencing is often important, because applications frequently require one part of an analysis to occur before another part. For example, if one set of rules worked strictly from sensor data, and another set required physical observations from the user, we would probably want to run the sensor-based rules first.

In our canning plant application, we have employed rule sets in a number of ways:

- By running the PLANT-SHUTDOWN rules before the QUALITY-CONTROL rules, we replicate the priorities of the plant operators: The operators' first duty is to make sure the plant machinery is not damaged because of faulty operation.

- Once a mechanical fault has been identified, we run only the FAULT-CORRECTION rules. This replicates how an operator actually works: Until a fault is fixed, the operator will concentrate on its repair and ignore possible shutdown and quality-control problems.

- Our three rule sets are completely independent; thus, we are able to limit inferencing to only one rule set whenever we run the inference engine. This improves application performance significantly.

At this point, you may find it useful to go back over the rule-based discussions in previous chapters to see the actual details of how rule sets have been used so far.

SYSTEM INITIALIZATION

Once a fault has been corrected, we need to place our knowledge base in a "normal" state. We initialize the system at start-up, then re-initialize prior to each attempt at fault identification. Initialization consists of setting all of the slot values to their default values. In this section, we'll look at three types of system initialization:

- fault conditions
- quality-control information
- canning-line components

All three must be performed whenever we query the backward-chaining QC rules.

Initialization is tedious, because not all slots are initialized in the same way. Some component slots, for example, are initialized with the value in their DEFAULT-OBSERVATION facet, first introduced in Chapter 5. Other slots, such as the FAULT slot of plant components, should be initialized by retracting (setting to unknown) their current value(s). Still others, such as the MANUAL-REFERENCE slot of fault conditions, should not be changed at all.

The Need For Initialization

It is easiest to understand the need for initialization by considering concrete examples. Let's look at the QC rule OILY- RESIDUE (shown below in Figure 11-17). Note that if the RESIDUE slot of the CANS instance already has a default value (which is NONE, in this case), the antecedent of the rule will fail. On the other hand, if the RESIDUE slot is empty, that is, unknown, the function askOperatorWhenUnknown will execute and a menu will pop up during backward chaining to prompt the user for this slot's value.

Now consider the rule FAULT-QUERY, shown in Figure 11-18. This rule references no slots of canning-line component instances, other than FAULT (in the consequent clause). When beginning a QC analysis, we will want all FAULT slots to be empty, assuming there are no existing faults anywhere in the plant. Similarly, we will want all FAULTY-COMPONENT slots in FAULT-CONDITION instances to be emptied prior to starting a QC analysis.

Initialization Procedures

There are two types of initialization that must be performed prior to a QC analysis: resetting certain plant observations and initializing the state of all fault conditions in the knowledge base. Initializing fault conditions requires resetting several yes/no slots that are modified by the rules and removing pointers to suspected and confirmed faults. See Figure 11-19, which shows the initializeAllFaults function, for details.

Rule: **OILY-RESIDUE**
Rule Set: **QUALITY-CONTROL**
Documentation: The coating can't be applied properly if
   oil remains on the cans... check the odor prior to
   coating.
Direction: BACKWARD
IF
   askOperatorWhenUnknown "CANS", "ODOR"
   AND
   THE ODOR OF CANS IS OILY
   AND
   THE RESIDUE OF CANS IS OILY
THEN
   THE PERFORMANCE OF CAN-COATER IS POOR

FIGURE 11-17. The OILY-RESIDUE rule

Rule: **FAULT-QUERY**
Rule Set: **FAULT-CORRECTION**
Documentation: We're trying to confirm a fault; we need to
   ask the operator to try and find it.
IF
   ?FAULT IS A FAULT-CONDITION
   AND
   THE CONFIRMING-ACTION OF ?FAULT IS ?ACTION
   AND
   THE MANUAL-REFERENCE OF ?FAULT IS ?REF
   AND
   UNKNOWN
      THE SUSPECTED-COMPONENT OF ?FAULT IS ?COMPONENT
   AND
   askOperatorToFind ?FAULT ?COMPONENT ?ACTION ?REF
THEN
   THE FAULT OF ?COMPONENT IS ?FAULT

FIGURE 11-18. FAULT-QUERY rule

```
on initializeAllFaults
  put empty into requiredOperatorFindings
  put empty into requiredOperatorActions
  put frameAllInstances("faultCondition") into faults
  repeat for i = 1 to the number of items in faults
    put item i of faults into fault
    put getValue(fault,"faultyComponent") into component
    if component is not empty then

      --set slots to unknown by making value empty
      putValue fault,"faultyComponent",empty
      putValue component,"fault",empty
    end if
    putValue fault,"suspected-component",empty
    putValue fault,"procedure-finished","NO"
    putValue fault,"recommendation-made","NO"
    putValue fault,"fixable","YES"
  end repeat
end initializeAllFaults
```

FIGURE 11-19. The initializeAllFaults function

To initialize the plant, we go through a subset of all slots on COMPONENT instances and install the values of those slots' DEFAULT-OBSERVATION facets. Initializing COMPONENT instances is more difficult than it might seem at first, because there are slots defined at many places in the frame hierarchy. Another possibility would be to loop over all slots in all instances of COMPONENT, installing the DEFAULT-OBSERVATION facet's value if the facet is present. We prefer the first implementation because it is more explicit, even though it invites error due to someone forgetting to add a new slot or frame type to the initialization list.

NOTE: Exactly what happens when a slot's values are all retracted is highly implementation dependent—not all shells have the same behavior. Some shells are content to leave the slot empty. Other shells will install a default value inherited from parent frames, if such a default exists. Finally, some shells distinguish between putting "nothing" in a slot and retracting the value— retracting the value has the special meaning "unknown."

```
on initializeQCObservations
  retractSlotValues "cans","residue"
  retractSlotValues "cans","coating"
  retractSlotValues "cans","odor"
  retractSlotValues "cans","innerSurface"
  retractSlotValues "cans","outerSurface"
end initializeQCObservations
```

FIGURE 11-20. The `initializeQCObservations` function

To initialize quality-control observations, we simply go through a selected list of slots on the CANS instance and retract any slot values that are present (see Figure 11-20). This assumes that the slot values are completely unknown.

RULE PRIORITIES

Earlier in this chapter we described the use of rule sets for controlling the order in which rules fire. In many rule-based expert system shells, one alternative to using rule sets to control the order of rule firing is to use **rule priorities**. Rule priorities typically are specified by assigning individual rules a numeric value; then, if two rules are simultaneously available for firing by the inference engine, the rule with the higher priority will fire first. Rule priorities are attractive because they offer a simple mechanism for simulating procedural control over the order of rule firing: By assigning different priorities to different groups of rules, one group of rules can be made to fire before the other group.

However, in general we advise against the use of rule priorities unless they are unavoidable. A perceived need for rule priorities is often an indicator that:

- Logic flows have not been clearly defined.

- Rules that would eliminate the need for priorities are missing.

- The problem is highly procedural and inappropriate for rules.

In most cases, it is preferable to group rules according to their function—much as we have done with our rule sets—and activate those *groups* of rules in a specific order by using external procedures. The use of external procedures to control groups of rules is clearer and more straightforward and, in the long run, will make the system easier to debug and maintain.

> NOTE: Expert system shells with weak pattern matching (e.g., those shells that back chain on a variable value rather than on fixed symbolic pattern) often require the use of priorities to ensure that the rules chain is a fixed order.

SUMMARY

This chapter describes various techniques that help turn an expert system prototype into a useful piece of software. First, a complete module is presented for giving procedural advice to the user and tracking the user's progress in following that advice. The integration of backward- and forward-chaining rules is shown through the intersection of hypothesis testing and the rendering of assistance in solving discovered problems. The use of rule sets is discussed as a way of organizing a knowledge base and controlling the ebb and flow of advice to the user. Finally, an initialization scheme for the canning plant application is described in detail.

READINGS

Chandrasekaran, B. 1983. "Towards a taxonomy of problem-solving types," *AI Magazine* 4, no. 1.

Genesereth, M. 1984. "The use of design descriptions in automated diagnosis," *Artificial Intelligence* 24: 411–436.

Shneiderman, B. 1987. *Designing the user interface: Strategies for effective human-computer interaction.* Reading, MA: Addison-Wesley.

Weiss, S. , and C. Kulikowski. 1984. *A practical guide to designing expert systems.* Totowa, NJ: Allanhead.

12

VALIDATION
AND DELIVERY

The validation and delivery of an expert system is similar in many ways to that of a traditional software system, with all of the attendant problems: A clear, easy-to-use interface must be designed; system veracity must be confirmed; users must be trained; hardware and software must be maintained; and communication with the external environment must be established. The similarities shouldn't be too surprising because, at one level, an expert system is simply another computer program to be used by individuals in their day-to-day work routine.

In this chapter, we'll examine the steps that lead to the implementation and use of an expert system in the end-user environment. Much of what we will talk about here applies equally well to any software system that is built using an incremental approach based on testable prototypes. As AI software development tools such as object-based graphics and symbolic debuggers spread to more conventional programming environments, the incremental approach has become more and more widespread, because the development approach is heavily influenced by the software tools that are used. When the tools support (and even encourage) interactive development, the overall development cycle will closely parallel that for an expert system project, even if the subject matter of the system is decidedly conventional.

INSTALLATION ISSUES

The transformation of the final prototype into a delivered expert system occurs over a period of many months, going through a number of major approvals during that period. The table in Figure 12-1 illustrates the steps, the concerned parties, and the approximate time periods for completion (these time periods are for a medium-sized system comparable to the example used for the canning plant—larger systems will take correspondingly longer periods in all categories).

This table represents a relatively aggressive schedule in actually fielding a working system. Depending on the nature of the domain, the shakedown period may be quicker, but is more likely to be longer—it just depends on how much confidence users and management have in the expert system's advice combined with the level of criticality of the work on which the advice is being given. Users will hardly be willing to adjust parameters in a nuclear power plant on the system's say-so after six months, but they would probably be fairly willing, after the same period of installation time, to take advice on recommending insurance claims for further investigation.

Distribution of the expert system to multiple sites is likely to take at least as long as the table indicates. Even with traditional software systems, distribution throughout a large company can typically take as much as four to five years. Given the more experimental nature of expert systems, a longer

FIGURE 12-1. Completion steps for final acceptance of an expert system

Description	Involved Parties	Time
Final debugging	Development team	2 weeks
Validation/Tuning	Developers, experts, end users, management	2–4 weeks
Training	Developers, end users, maintainers	2 weeks
Installation and field test On-site debugging/tuning	Developers, experts, end users	2 weeks 2 weeks
Shakedown	End users, developers	6–12 months
First round expansion: delivery to 3–5 sites*	Maintainers	6 months
General delivery to all sites*	Maintainers	18–24 months

* These two categories are for expert systems that will be distributed to a large number of sites

period of time is likely to be required because more testing will be required, the suspicions of local managers and users will need to be overcome, and system tuning to each individual site may require special considerations.

Testing

To a large extent, then, the testing of an expert system should be an ongoing process during the entire development cycle. As we have seen in previous chapters, the development of an expert system is an interactive process in which the knowledge engineers work as closely as possible with the experts to produce a working system. Prototypes of specific modules are developed and then shown to the experts as they are completed. Control structures that integrate those modules are also tested and demonstrated to experts during their development. It is likely that several different user interfaces will have been built during prototype development, and will have also undergone tests of varying degrees of rigor with both experts and potential users.

   If development has been done correctly, testing of the completed prototype will largely involve making sure that the system is usable outside the laboratory. Unfortunately, however, thorough testing is rarely done during development. In many respects, software testing can be compared with writing documentation:

   • No one really wants to do it, especially the developers.

   • It can be tedious and boring.

   • It's usually done at the end of the development cycle.

No matter how much you might think the prototype has been tested during development, the testing will probably have been haphazard, at best. Also, the real world always has unexpected problems ranging from the simple (e.g., set points in a manual used in implementation don't match those used on the factory floor) to the serious (e.g., logical flaws in rule chaining under certain unusual conditions) to the sublime (e.g., the location chosen for the equipment at the end-user site has no power outlets). Realistically, the "completed" prototype will need an extensive going-over before it is truly fielded.

Validation

Validation occurs in three phases: validation of test cases before final debugging; validation of "all" (it really will take months to find *all* the unusual circumstances) cases at time of installation; and long-term fine tuning over the first year. Only after this last year or so of testing will the expert system be truly validated and useful as an integral part of the end users' routine.

Three groups take part in this validation effort: the experts in the domain, the end users, and management.

Expert Validation

To the extent possible, the test cases should reflect specific problems that have very specific answers. The system's output should be compared with the "correct" answers as supplied by the experts and the results tabulated for later comparison. Concise descriptions of the conditions under which the system's advice breaks down and is no longer valid should be recorded; if necessary, separate logic may have to be added to the system that reflects these conditions, advising the end user when the system may not be giving correct advice.

Bringing in outside experts to test the system may also be useful. Their impressions of the system may provide new insights; at the least, the approval of the system by outside experts will enhance the system's respectability and the confidence people have in its use. Where there are substantial differences in expert opinion, it may be advisable to have "second opinions" inserted into the knowledge base (yet another alternative to confidence factors: Give the user several choices, but annotate them).

End-User Validation

The initial end-user validation requires testing the system's overall usability with a representative sample of those people who will eventually be using the system. The overall aim of this validation should be twofold:

- to correct deficiencies in the user interface
- to determine training requirements for the system

These two points are complementary. Improving the user interface should make it easier to train new users. The proper type of training, on the other hand, can decrease the need for an elaborate—and error prone—user interface.

The end-user validation should be performed after the expert validation. *Allow plenty of time*; this will be the last chance for extensive experimentation with the system before it goes on-line.

Where possible, the end-user validation should be performed with cases taken from the expert validation process. Concentrate on making sure that the user interprets the expert advice correctly. Determine whether the system's advice would result in the proper actions being taken by the user in response to that advice. Where doubts exist, the user's interpretation of the system's output should be cycled back to the experts and modifications made to the way the user interface displays the advice.

After the system installation, on-going validation consists of regularly scheduled comparisons between actions users took, recommendations the system made, outcomes of the users' actions, and explanations of any discrepancies among these three.

Management Approval

Obtaining management approval is not really "validation" in the technical sense. Nevertheless, it is as important to the project's schedule and budget as technical validation is to the expert system's usefulness. There should be two stages of management approval:

1. agreeing on the validation procedure and schedule

2. giving the go-ahead for field installation and testing

Approval of the validation procedure, including objective criteria for success and failure, should be obtained before the start of either expert or end-user validation. *The importance of obtaining management's participation and approval in advance cannot be overemphasized.* While discussing the validation procedure, a realistic timetable and budget should be set up for the installation and testing period, as well as for the initial validation.

Management was keenly interested in devising acceptance criteria for the prototype after validation. By working directly with management, everyone involved gained a deep appreciation of how difficult it was to come up with an objective way of judging the prototype's advice. In some cases, the prototype might be of value to the operator even when it came up with the wrong answer. This was especially likely when the system was helping the operator locate mechanical faults in the plant; clearly, just helping the operators be methodical about tracking down problems was going to be a big benefit of the system. The same was true of observing quality-control problems; just using the system would make the operators more aware of quality problems in general, even if the system itself was only partially successful in isolating the specific sources of those problems.

The net result of working with management personnel was that they came to view the system as a tool for increasing quality in the plant, not as something that needed to be given a pass/fail grade. Working with management beforehand caused attention to be focused on where the system performed well instead of where it performed poorly. When the time came to proceed with the field installation, obtaining management's approval was a mere formality.

Training

For the field test, training of end users doesn't necessarily have to be a long and drawn-out affair. With at least one member of the development team in day-to-day contact with the users during initial testing, on-hand help can compensate for a lack of extensive training by clearing up problems as they occur. In addition, a core group of end users—those involved with the end-user validation—may already be familiar with the system. Nevertheless, end-user training shouldn't be ignored, as a lack of proper training can cause problems such as:

- users not using the system because they don't understand how to use it

- users misinterpreting the advice given by the system

- users not appreciating the system's benefits to *them* and thus underutilizing the system

Training of end users is only part of the problem, however. A more difficult and time-consuming category of training concerns long-term maintenance of the system. Inevitably, changes in the end-user environment will require modifications to the system over time. Probably few, if any, of the developers will be associated on a permanent basis with the system, and eventually it will be necessary to start bringing in the people who will be responsible for long-term maintenance of the system. Maintenance costs will be greatly reduced in the long term if these individuals participate in the system's validation. This participation should also include preliminary training in the development software used by the project. Investing in software training to support an unproven piece of software is somewhat of a risk, of course; if, on the other hand, the system goes on-line permanently, the potential benefits will outweigh the training costs by a large margin.

User Interface

When installing the final user interface, feedback during the validation period from all three groups of testers—experts, users, and management—will provide a final "tuning" on the usability and reliability of the interface. In general, the following design guidelines can be used to provide evaluators and designers alike with implementation direction:

- realistic interface
  · looks like something the users are used to
  · not familiar, but an improvement over existing environments without sacrificing clarity of using something familiar

- cognitive models
  - show users underlying cause and effect linkages
  - graphical illustrations of inferencing process tied to domain models
- clear demarcation between inputs and outputs
  - requests for information from rules
  - user updates of domain status
  - user queries concerning *why* questions are asked or advice given
- appropriate graphics
  - color should be mapped to meaning (e.g., red = abnormal, green = normal)
  - realistic schematics

To illustrate these principles, we'll examine how an interface for the plant was implemented.

After some experimentation with different formats, the development team decided to lay out the interface as follows:

- Below the menu bar, the screen is split in half horizontally, the top half containing a plant schematic and the bottom half dedicated to textual information and advice.

- The top half of the screen (the plant schematic) is highlighted in various ways to indicate the status of particular plant components.

- The bottom half of the screen contains detailed recommendations and data on the values of component-specific parameters.

A rough design sketch is shown in Figure 12-2, along with some of the behavior of the interface when various items are selected by the user.

The top line of the screen contains a menu bar (shown as white lettering on black background) with the main choices available to the user: initialize the expert system, examine the current recommendations, and quit (that is, return to the operating system). Initialization corresponds to resetting all parameter values to their defaults and removing the latest set of conclusions from the expert system, as described in Chapter 11. When recommendations are requested, the choices in the lower-right window are given to the user; the current recommendations are time-stamped for the user's benefit, because the recommendations change over time and the user might be unsure whether the expert system's analysis needs to be re-executed.

The plant schematic is highlighted in various ways to indicate the general status of plant components. When a component is selected (using the mouse), two options are available: display detailed parameter data (which appears in the lower-left window) or "zoom in" on the immediate area of that component. When

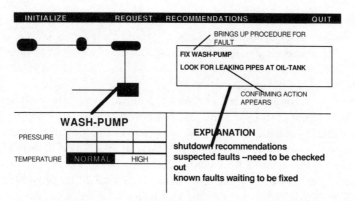

FIGURE 12-2. The design sketch for the final end-user interface of the canning-line application

zooming occurs, many plant components become visible that are not present when the entire canning line is being displayed (see the discussion of composites in Chapter 13).

NOTE: The plant schematic is constructed by modifying the Model Editor software, described in Chapter 13. Briefly put, this software allows the display of a set of relations (in this case, as defined by values of the DOWNSTREAM slot) between objects in the knowledge base (plant components). Along with the graphical display, the Model Editor allows full control over what is to happen when the user selects one of the objects in the display. For more details, see Chapter 13.

When detailed parameter data is displayed in the lower-left window, it is presented as a simple table. The display is time-stamped to show the user when the display was constructed, because the display corresponds to a snapshot of one small section of the knowledge base. Each row of the display corresponds to a single parameter, and the possible values of that parameter are shown. The current value of each parameter, taken directly from slot values in the knowledge base, is indicated by highlighting the appropriate value in the row.

The recommendation displayed in the lower-right window is the most complex. Here the user is presented with three separate options:

- display shutdown recommendations (from the shutdown rules of Chapter 4)

- show selected faults (the "things to do" list from Chapters 10 and 11)

- show any known faults that need to be corrected (instances of FAULT-CONDITION, as described in Chapter 10)

> Selecting any one of these three then results in a cascading set of pop-up menus presenting the appropriate list of known faults; selecting one of these would bring up the procedure for correcting that particular fault, as described in Chapter 10.

Notice that this interface is relatively simple. First, the graphics are not complicated—they could even be implemented with character graphics on a standard PC. More important, however, is the use of **data filtering:** The information presented is only a small fraction of all the information contained in the application's knowledge base. In fact, most of the knowledge base is never accessible by the end user. The aim is to present only that information that is directly relevant to the user performing his or her job. All other information that could be displayed is, for purposes of the end-user interface, ignored, even though it may be critical to how the expert system performs its analysis.

IMPLEMENTATION ISSUES

Decisions about implementation occur at all stages of a project's development. Ideally, of course, they occur sooner rather than later, but many factors can cause early decisions to change: the expert system becomes larger than expected, it addresses new problems not originally envisioned, or it is more successful and thus in demand at more sites, to mention but a few. The two major decisions affecting delivery are the hardware that it will be delivered on and the corresponding software environment.

Hardware Platform

The delivery hardware is frequently different from the development hardware. The prototype may have been developed on an engineering workstation running Unix, for example, yet the delivered version must be delivered on PC-compatible computers running DOS. In many cases, the delivery hardware will consist of computers that are already being used for other purposes, and the expert system will have to coexist with existing applications.

Certain vendors have long recognized the importance of providing a wide variety of compatible hardware and software options. Texas Instruments, for example, has an integrated set of expert system development tools using hardware ranging from PCs to highly sophisticated Lisp workstations. Using a similar strategy, Sun Microsystems sells a line of compatible workstations ranging in capability from just above PC to just under supercomputer.

For expert systems, the most important hardware delivery issues include:

- integration with other computers
- execution speed
- quality of the graphical display

NOTE: We have left politics out of this discussion, but, unfortunately, corporate policies standardizing on a particular family of computers often make this part of the decision process moot.

For delivery, integration with other computers is needed for a variety of reasons. Access to an external data base may be required, or regular reports may need to be filed by the expert system with a centralized data base. In certain cases, another processor may be needed for compute-intensive tasks that can safely be performed in the background.

Execution speed is frequently a problem, especially if the expert system is to be delivered on personal computers. Sometimes, a smaller machine that seems perfect for delivery may simply not be up to the task of handling the amount of calculation that is required. With the advent of 386-based personal computers capable of addressing large amounts of memory, execution speed is much less a problem than it was a few years ago. On the other hand, the speed and memory requirements of expert systems will likely grow at least as fast as the capabilities of general-purpose hardware, so this particular delivery issue is unlikely to go away for the foreseeable future.

The quality of the delivery system's graphical display is also a frequent problem, since most development environments have high-quality graphics facilities. Often, a prototype is developed with a sophisticated user interface, with little thought given to the hardware on which the final system will be delivered. This may cause a sizable mismatch in graphics capabilities when the time comes to field a deliverable version of the system. Like execution speed, however, the quality of graphical display is less of a problem than it once was—the availability of inexpensive, high-resolution displays for general-purpose hardware has lessened the urgency of this particular delivery issue.

Software Porting

Many expert systems will eventually have to be ported to another software environment for final delivery. Such a port may involve a complete redesign of the software implementation, even if the basic structure of the knowledge base remains the same. The reasons for the port usually revolve around improving performance and/or portability, but may simply reflect the cost of licensing the development software on all of the delivery machines.

With a ported system, the thorniest questions have to do with where maintenance should be performed. The delivery version often has to be re-coded "from scratch" in a procedural language. If major changes must later be made to the delivery version, there will be no built-in software development tools to support making those changes. In particular, the rapid-prototyping capabilities of the development software will no longer be available. Many people therefore opt for maintaining two versions of an expert system. When using two versions, all changes to the system are first performed and tested on the original version using the original software development tools, then carefully ported over to the delivery version.

At its most basic level, an expert system consists of three modules:

- the knowledge base
- the inference engine
- the user interface

The difficulty of porting varies widely from module to module. (For our purposes, any user-supplied programs that exercise procedural control over rule firing or perform other types of custom problem-solving may be considered part of the "inference engine.")

In most cases, porting the knowledge base—which mostly consists of rules and object definitions—is not a difficult task. There are many ways to implement a frame-like representation in almost any language. And, as we saw in Chapter 8, even translating rules into their procedural equivalents can be very straightforward.

Similarly, porting the inference engine is usually not too difficult. In most expert systems, people find that their final inferencing strategy is relatively simple. It may take quite a lot of experimentation with different techniques to decide on the details of how the inferencing should work, but the final product is usually pretty simple.

By far the most difficult part of the port will consist of re-implementing the user interface. It is here that the differences between software environments become the most obvious. Common graphics standards among different manufacturers are still the exception rather than the rule. Unfortunately, even so-called "standards" such as XWindows provide developers with only a bare minimum of functionality.

SUMMARY

This chapter explored the issues surrounding the validation and delivery of an expert system, looking in detail at the steps involved in moving the finished prototype through testing to distribution: testing and validation by the experts, the end users, and management; training; and the design of an end-user interface, using the canning plant application as an example.

PART

IV

MODELING THE
ENVIRONMENT

13

SUPPORT OF MODEL-BASED REASONING: MODEL EDITORS

R eal-world environments are often complex, and models of these systems are correspondingly complex. Complexity arises primarily because of the many interconnections between the components that constitute the system. If each time a change is made to the knowledge base the developer must manage these interconnections manually, when the knowledge base is expanded or modified, errors are bound to occur. One solution to this problem is automation of the low-level maintenance of knowledge base consistency.

Shortly after the start of the Phase II prototype effort, Nancy tried to add several new frames and instances to the model. At the same time, she decided that the pump names should be changed to more closely reflect their designations on the plant floor. Using the basic instance-renaming feature of the expert system shell, she proceeded to make her additions and modifications. Much to her surprise, when she tested out the rules, a number of previously working diagnostic routines now inexplicably did not produce any results.

As we all examined the modified system, it dawned on us that a number of vital connections between machines had been lost by the name changes. The downstream slot values of components feeding the renamed pumps no longer contained the correct pump names. Nancy then corrected these downstream slots and connected up the new instances. The total time taken for these simple name changes—change, testing, problem discovery, and repair—had been several days.

Part of the problem was remembering all of the things that had to be done when adding a new component instance to the canning line representation. Deleting existing component instances was even more error prone than adding them. The worst part of the problem, however, was our inability to visualize the status of the new representation during the implementation process. We had no way of telling how far we had progressed, other than making a hand drawing of the line as the knowledge base was extended.

Realizing the scope of the changes that were to come, we recognized a need for new tools enabling us to better visualize the existing relationships between components in the knowledge base. We especially desired a mechanism that would take our desired changes and make all of the correct things happen: additions, slot value changes, deletions, etc.

One solution to managing a complex knowledge base is to build a customized editing facility that can translate a simple user command (for example, the deletion of a frame) into the complete set of changes that must be made in the model—that is, removal or alteration of all references to that frame and its children in other knowledge-base objects. We refer to such a facility as a **model editor.**

Renaming the objects using a graphical editor would have allowed Nancy to make only a single change, the name of a graphical object. The editor would then have made all the connections and updates occur automatically.

Let's begin with the definition of an editor. An **editor** is a facility that translates high-level requests into the lower-level actions of maintaining consistency within a data environment—in our case, the frames, instances, slots, and slot values represented in the knowledge base. This maintenance includes adding and deleting objects. The details of how objects are maintained may vary considerably from model to model, depending on the precise definition of "object" for a specific application, but the basic design principle of all editors is the same: Provide the user with a representation with which they are comfortable, irrespective of the underlying mechanism for representing the data.

A **graphical editor** is an editor that presents the user with a graphic picture of the knowledge base. A graphic representation can be as simple as the names of objects connected by lines representing slot values linking the objects. Often, the term **structure editor** is used to describe graphical model editors, because the editor uses special knowledge about the graphical structure of the data being manipulated. For example, in the plant model, arrows might be drawn between components to represent connections and flow directions, based on the value of each component's DOWNSTREAM slot.

We'll start by examining the basic design principles required for implementing a model editor in the context of building a simple graphical editor for the canning-line application, then show how this example can be modified for use in a wide variety of other situations.

Model editors seldom exist at the beginning of a project, as the need for them arises only when the knowledge base begins to reach a level of complexity that is difficult to visualize using tabular display. The first step is recognizing the need for an editor. This need is proportional to the overall complexity of the knowledge base. Typically, complexity occurs with as few as 30 or 40 objects, increasing as the number of attributes the objects contain and the number and type of links between the objects increase. As the number of connections and cross-references increases, knowing exactly what is in the knowledge base becomes increasingly difficult. At the same time, making modifications to the knowledge base becomes increasingly tedious and error prone. These difficulties are especially prevalent when those making the modifications—typically, the experts or maintainers—are not the individuals who did the original implementation.

The building of a model editor need not be a long and drawn-out affair. Most model editors are primitive at the start, evolving over time as the need arises for increased representational power. They seldom prove more trouble than they are worth, as they will save many debugging hours caused by small errors, for example a mistyping made during a manual update of the knowledge base.

MODEL EDITOR DESIGN

No matter what the specific requirements for the editor, the first design decision will be whether the editor will incorporate graphics. The two reasons for not using graphics would be either a lack of a graphic capability in the implementation environment or the characteristics of the knowledge itself.

Graphic images work best when there are explicit relationships between the knowledge-base components. If the knowledge base is flat—in essence just a list of object names—then graphics contribute very little to the editing process. A good example of a flat data structure is a personnel database that contains employee names, addresses, and salaries. However, in most expert systems, flat data is seldom present, so we'll only be discussing graphical editors.

The editor design will consist of two parts: the editor which creates objects and fills in attribute values, and the elements composing the graphical interface.

Design Criteria

Editors are built to serve many purposes. The first step in designing an editor is to examine the full set of capabilities that an editor can have and then choose what is required for the particular problem. The following capabilities are all useful, but not always necessary, to an editor:

- graphical interface
- ability to view and modify the knowledge base
- representation of different types of objects
- representation of multiple relationships between objects
- edit options extensible by nontechnical users
- mechanism ensuring internal consistency of the knowledge base

A model editor must be simple to learn and use. A rough design goal is that it should be possible to teach a complete novice the basics within 15 minutes. Even though this goal may not be attainable, it should be adhered to as long as possible; such a limitation will help keep the editor usable and prevent its becoming an overly complex tool for the developer.

Careful design of the graphical interface can aid both learning and use. The interface should strive to match the terminology and visual layout with which the users are already familiar. Another goal of the interface is to provide strong conceptual models of how the domain functions. For example, a control room for a processing plant contains electric switches for controlling pumps, valves, and tank levels. A graphical interface can show these same components as dynamically changing entities: As a tank fills, its level changes on the screen; as a valve opens, the connecting pipe is filled with a pattern or color.

The editor should enable the user to add, delete, and modify objects. Visual cues should indicate to the user where to press or click in order to select a component for editing. In any case, access to action menus should be quick and unambiguous. Menu bars along the top of the screen are commonly used for this. In other systems, many of these commands are located on the objects themselves—when the object is selected, a menu of actions to perform on that object is displayed.

To actually perform an action on an object, two styles of editing are commonly used, modal and nonmodal. In a **nonmodal** system, you select an object to edit, then select an edit action from the command menu. To delete an object, either the object would be highlighted, enabling the user to choose "delete" from a visible command menu (e.g., a menu bar), or a menu would appear containing a delete option. Repeated deletes require a repetition of these two actions, selection and deletion. In a **modal** system, you first select the mode in which you wish to operate; again, let's choose delete from our action menu (note that using a mode precludes having the action menu associated with the object—the disadvantage is that you cannot easily customize delete for individual objects or object classes). Now, every object selected will be deleted. Modal systems are quite powerful when repetitive actions are desired; however, many people find them confusing, and there is always the danger of something unexpected happening if you forget which mode you are using.

The editor should *display relationships* between objects in the knowledge base. Moreover, it must be relatively easy to define and modify such a relationship. Color or other differentiating characteristics allow the simultaneous display of multiple relation types.

The model editor should be *extensible*. New types of graphic representations will have to be added from time to time, and such additions have to be simple and quick. Different types of icons, colors, and fonts are examples of additions that might be required. Similarly, it is usually desirable to expand and/or modify the library of objects accessed by the editor. All such expansions should be straightforward and uncomplicated. New object types usually have to be added over time. If the editor isn't defined properly, such additions can be very time consuming, as well as subject to programmer error. The editor should let the user define new component types and make those available for inclusion in a layout.

The editor's maintenance of *internal consistency* must be transparent to the user. Simple graphic changes on the screen should cause the correct changes, connections, and so on to be established without the user having to participate.

Finally, when an action is taken by the user, there should be no doubt in the user's mind as to what has just happened inside the knowledge base. The principles of *WYDIWYS* (what you do is what you see) and *WYSIWYG* (what you see is what you get) say that the graphic interface should show you the changes as you make them and that these changes should represent internal knowledge-base changes. Thus, if a new graphic appears on the screen, the user should know, as intuitively as possible, what that new graphic means in terms of the layout being modeled, even if the user has no technical understanding of what is contained there. If the user changes the knowledge base directly—for example, changing a slot value—the corresponding graphics in the model editor should change accordingly. Similarly, when the user manipulates the model editor's graphics, the corresponding changes to the knowledge base should be made automatically.

Figure 13-1 illustrates an interface for a model editor that aids users in building connections between components. Connecting two components fills in their UPSTREAM and DOWNSTREAM slots and shows the connection graphically with an arrow. Deleting a component from the diagram

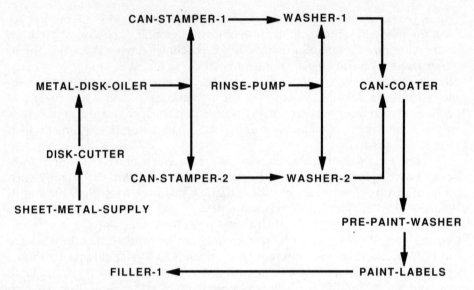

FIGURE 13-1. Simple graphic editor using plant layout with arrows for can flows (character-graphic representation, AXLE)

removes it from the knowledge base and removes the name from any related components' UPSTREAM and DOWNSTREAM slots. Adding a picture of a component on the screen creates it in the knowledge base.

> NOTE: A graphical model editor must maintain consistency between the objects in the knowledge base—their names and attribute values—and their graphical representation on the screen.

Adapting an Existing Editing Facility

Given the required functions of the model editor and the work required to implement one, the team's first reaction was to explore the use of an existing software tool for doing the editing. The company already owned several CAD and data-base packages, and it was felt that perhaps knowledge-base editing could be accomplished using the built-in editing facility of one of those packages. As shown in Figure 13-2, the plan was to translate part of the canning plant knowledge base into a data file recognized by one of those packages, manipulate the data, then translate the information back into the format of the knowledge base.

A little experimentation showed that such a dual-package approach was unwieldy for the model of the plant. Translation of the instance/slot representation

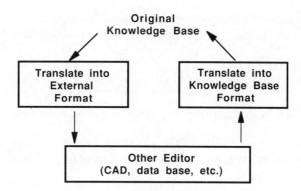

FIGURE 13-2. Using a second software package to edit the knowledge base

was relatively easy; each instance/slot value became a variable (such as a spread-sheet cell) in the external format. However, representing relationships such as downstream was virtually impossible. Furthermore, it meant that two different versions of the knowledge base had to be maintained dynamically: If changes were made to one, the corresponding change had to be made to the other. In the end, difficulty with maintenance and translation made the external editing option impractical. The editor would be built using graphics that could interact directly with the knowledge base.

The temptation to try to use existing external editors is often strong and not always misplaced. Spreadsheets offer the perfect example of simple editing environments that can be readily interfaced to the knowledge base through a translation facility. When the data are tabular in nature (this is applicable to both the static model and output from the expert system), then using a spreadsheet may well be the best interface solution, particularly when the end users are accustomed to this interface in their normal work. As we'll see in the next chapter, a spreadsheet makes an ideal input and output format for a knowledge-base simulation.

However, knowledge-base representations usually contain information about the relationships between components, and when these multidimensional characteristics must be displayed and edited, a graphical representation within the knowledge-base environment is almost always the best solution. Certainly, in terms of the work involved in building and maintaining a translation facility, building an editing facility within the development shell is the most time- and cost-effective approach.

In many cases, the expert system rules will be working primarily with an external data base. Obviously, manipulation of that part of the data will be done in the data-base environment. However, the knowledge base may still contain frame relationships—data from the database will be loaded into the knowledge base in the form of instances. The generic frames and their relationships can still be manipulated successfully using the editor.

DEFINING GRAPHICAL OBJECTS

Building a model editor requires the definition of several types of graphical objects:

- *icons*—pictorial/character representations of objects in the knowledge base

- *commands*—menus of user-selectable options (e.g., menu-bar, pop-up, and fixed menus)

- *display canvas and viewport*—regions on the screen that contain graphic objects

- *connectors*—representations of relationships between the objects (e.g., lines and arrows)

Chapters 6 and 8 provide an overview of the features of an object-oriented graphic system. In this section, we'll further explore those features to see how they can be applied to building a graphical editor.

Icons

Early graphic hardware consisted of an ability to draw characters and lines. A basic graphic capability was obtained by defining an extended character set containing special graphic shapes. However, almost all hardware now offers a software environment where individual areas of the screen can be set to white or a color (black on a monochrome monitor). This feature permits the drawing of pictorial representations of most objects—an **icon**. In the canning plant, we might draw pictures of simple objects such as tanks or complex objects such as stamping machines and sprayers.

The use of graphic icons enables developers to replace text with more universal representations. The uses of an icon in place of text range from schematic diagrams requiring standard symbols to interfaces that will be used by multilingual audiences.

Icons can be either **static** or **dynamic**. A static icon is a picture that remains the same no matter what the state of the object it represents. A dynamic icon, on the other hand, changes as the object state changes. Examples of dynamic icons include a gauge with a moving dial or a tank that contains inner regions that darken as it fills. Although a basic model editor will use only static images, editors that are adapted to serve as multipurpose interfaces often contain a combination of both static and dynamic icons. In this chapter, we will be working with editors containing only static icons.

Commands

Commands are requests by the user for some action to take place. They appear on the screen primarily as text, though an icon can take their place if the meaning will be clear to the users. Using a picture in place of text is particularly useful in systems that will be used in situations where more than one language is spoken.

Commands appear in an **action menu**. Often, it will be useful to have the action menu appear as a menu bar along the top of the screen. Using this placement, commands can be accessed easily. If desired, the addition of new components to the layout can be made one of the choices in the menu bar, with a pulldown menu giving the choices of component type. Other possibilities include vertical menu bars or pop-up menus.

Canvas and Viewport

Let's do a quick review of the material on object graphics from Chapter 6. A **canvas** is a conceptual object defined as an infinitely expandable, rectangular drawing region. This canvas object, defined as a frame, also has an associated **viewport** on the screen that contains built-in graphics operations that operate on that region. Usually, the viewport will have a border drawn around it and will have some mechanism for scrolling the contents when they are too large to display fully. The canvas frame contains attributes, defined as slots, such as the viewport size, location, title, and so forth.

Let's look at the canvas on which the model editor is built. Figure 13-3 shows the EDITOR-CANVAS frame, which will serve as the template for the model editor. Initially, we have defined the canvas with a set of top-level commands pertaining to the editor, such as connecting and disconnecting objects. These commands pop up in a menu when the canvas is selected with the mouse (MENU-RIGHT slot), for example, "Exit Canvas." In later examples, these commands will instead be defined as a menu bar placed above the canvas. Their placement at the beginning of the design on the canvas background allows for more rapid prototyping of required functionality for the editor commands.

Object Image

Each object represented on the canvas has an associated image object—an instance of the EDITOR-OBJECT-IMAGE frame (Figure 13-4). This frame

```
Frame: EDITOR-CANVAS
Parents: CANVAS
Instances: EDITOR-LAYOUT-CANVAS
--Handlers--
close deleteAllImages Delete drawImages Move Open
  Redisplay Reshape SetTitle
--Slots--
BORDER:SINGLE
BORDER-COLOR:LIGHT-BLUE
DOCUMENTATION :"L(Enter)Add"
HEIGHT:200
IMAGES:EDITOR-MENU-IMAGE-521 MENU-ED-1
LEFT:0
MENU-LEFT:
MENU-RIGHT:
  "Exit Canvas", SendMsg *CurrentCanvas* Close,
  "Redisplay Canvas", SendMsg *CurrentCanvas* Redisplay,
  "Display Canvas", DisplayFrame *CurrentCanvas*,
  "Reshape", SendMsg *CurrentCanvas* Reshape,
  "Delete Canvas", SendMsg *CurrentCanvas* Delete,
  "Change Title", SendMsg *CurrentCanvas* SetTitle
MOUSE-LEFT-FN : ModelEditorLeftfn
MOUSE-RIGHT-FN : CanvasRightFn
TITLE :"Class Menu"
TOP : 1
WIDTH : 300
```

FIGURE 13-3. The EDITOR-CANVAS frame

is similar to the CANVAS frame in that it defines a region on the screen. In this case, however, that region is relative to the canvas viewport region and the image refers back to the canvas. The EDITOR-OBJECT-IMAGE frame will serve as our graphical template when we place plant component icons on the canvas layout. Each instance of EDITOR-OBJECT-IMAGE will graphically correspond to an instance of COMPONENT's child frames. Note that we are not monitoring specific slots in the editor but rather are concerned with the object itself and the relationships defined by its slots (e.g., DOWNSTREAM). Thus, the image is only associated with the instance and not an instance/slot pair.

When we wish to add new instances to our model, we must first select

```
Frame: EDITOR-OBJECT-IMAGE
Parents: BASIC-IMAGE
Instances: EDITOR-OBJECT-IMAGE-1   EDITOR-OBJECT-IMAGE-2
--Handlers--
ConnectObjects DeleteObject DisconnectObjects
  DisplayConnections DisplayObject Move
--Slots--
BORDER : NONE
CANVAS :
DISPLAYED-OBJECT :
HEIGHT : 40
LEFT : 1
MENU-LEFT :
MOUSE-LEFT-FN : PrintInstanceInfo
MENU-RIGHT :
  "Move image", SendMsg *CurrentImage* Move,
  "Display Object Instance", SendMsg *CurrentImage*
     DisplayObject,
  "Display Object Downstreams",
    SendMsg *CurrentImage* DisplayConnections,
  "Delete object", SendMsg *CurrentImage* DeleteObject,
  "Connect to Downstream", SendMsg *CurrentImage*
     ConnectObjects,
  "Disconnect from Downstream",
    SendMsg *CurrentImage* DisconnectObjects
MOUSE-RIGHT-FN : DefaultRightButtonfn
TEXT-COLOR : WHITE
TITLE :
TOP : 1
VALUE :
WIDTH : 40
```

FIGURE 13-4. The EDITOR-OBJECT-IMAGE frame

the frame whose instance we are to create. The menu containing the frames from which we can add new component instances to the layout requires a slightly different graphical representation. Several alternatives are possible, including a pop-up menu and a fixed menu (a selection of choices remaining visible on the screen at all times) containing a user-specified set of choices. For consistency with our frame-based editor design, we have chosen to

---

```
Frame : EDITOR-MENU-IMAGE
Parents : BASIC-IMAGE
Instances : EDITOR-MENU-IMAGE-521
--Slots--
BORDER : NONE
CANVAS :
DISPLAYED-OBJECT :
LEFT : 1
MENU-RIGHT :
MENU-LEFT :
MOUSE-LEFT-FN : PrintFrameInfo
MOUSE-RIGHT-FN : CreateNewComponent
TITLE :
HEIGHT : 30
TOP : 1
VALUE :
WIDTH : 40
```

FIGURE 13-5. The EDITOR-MENU-IMAGE frame

build the choice menu using graphic images, with one instance of the EDI-TOR-MENU-IMAGE frame for each choice (Figure 13-5). The EDITOR-MENU-IMAGE is similar to the EDITOR-OBJECT-IMAGE except that it is associated with a frame instead of a frame instance.

This frame will serve as our template when we make component choices available to the user. Each instance of EDITOR-MENU-IMAGE will have a corresponding frame in the COMPONENT inheritance hierarchy, as illustrated in Figure 13-6.

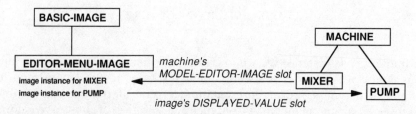

FIGURE 13-6. One-to-one correspondence between image instances and component frames

Screen Layout

The model editor is defined by one or more canvases (viewports on the screen). The following are options for the screen layout:

1. Only graphic objects representing instances are shown on a single graphic canvas. Limit: there is no facility for adding new objects, only, for editing of existing objects.

2a. Option 1 plus an action menu containing commands. These may be in either text or icon format.

2b. Option 1 plus a simple action facility for creating new objects; an additional canvas with graphic objects that represent frames. Selecting these graphic objects creates a new instance and adds it to the layout canvas of option 1.

3. Option 1 and one or more of option 2. A very common layout for a model editor is to have a layout canvas; one or two action canvases containing icons that, when chosen, are duplicated on the layout (typically a set of component frames and a set of relation frames); and a menu bar containing text commands (often the case when the editor is used as an end-user interface, as is the case with the simulation model discussed in the next chapter).

A good starting setup for a model editor is a layout of the objects and access to user actions (Figure 13-7). The layout contains a graphical representation of both the components and the logical connections between them. The choice-menu images (actions), instances of the EDITOR-MENU-IMAGE frame, are lined up on the left-hand canvas. The component images, instances of EDITOR-OBJECT-IMAGE, are arranged in a network-like layout on the right-hand canvas.

We'll refer to the left-hand viewport in Figure 13-7 as the **action menu**. We'll refer to the right-hand viewport as the **design layout**. Often,

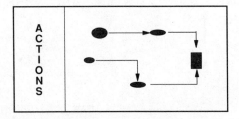

FIGURE 13-7. The Model Editor canvas layout

the action menu will actually be several viewports, for example, one for relations and one for component choices.

Composites

The factor that most limits the use of a model editor is the physical size of the screen. No matter how compact the icons, no matter how small the font, most situations will require more objects on the screen than can be displayed simultaneously. We can, of course, put in a scrolling mechanism that allows us to change the view by moving vertical and horizontal markers on the canvas edges. Although this allows us to add new objects and move about the layout to observe different areas, the entire layout cannot be viewed at a glance.

One solution is the use of different levels of abstraction:

- **visual** abstraction—display multiple objects as a single entity

- **structural** abstraction—represent multiple objects as a single frame

- **behavioral** abstraction—represent multiple objects as a single frame with associated behavioral changes

The simplest of these levels is a visual abstraction. In much the same way that we can create an exploded view of a car, showing breakdowns of the engine, wheels, and so on, we can collect groups of objects together and assign a single icon or label to that group. Figure 13-8 illustrates a simplified view of the plant with the components for stamping and washing (WASHER-1, WASHER-2, CAN-STAMPER-1, CAN-STAMPER-2) grouped into a single visual entity, STAMP-AND-WASH. Grouping objects reduces screen complexity and allows users to view the total layout.

This is a visual abstraction only, because none of the underlying representation changes. The same instances, both image and displayed objects, remain in the knowledge base. To build the composite view, we have two

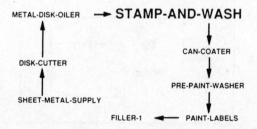

FIGURE 13-8. Composite object STAMP-AND-WASH

options: add a new slot and special composite-draw handler to our existing image frame or create a new image instance for the composite (in this case a STAMP-AND-WASH image) to temporarily replace the multiple image instances it represents.

In the next level of abstraction, structural abstraction, we begin to make changes to the displayed objects in the knowledge base. In addition to adding a new image instance, we also add a new "pseudo object" to be displayed—STAMP-AND-WASH, a child of the MACHINE frame. This new entity will have downstream and upstream slots the same as any other components, and their values will be those shown by the connecting arrows—in Figure 13-8 above, METAL-DISK-OILER and CAN-COATER. This second level of abstraction permits us to include the composite object in the expert reasoning process. Rules can now refer to this specific object in place of (or in addition to) the components it is abstracting.

The third level of abstraction is behavioral abstraction. At this level, the actual behavioral characteristics of the object are changed. This is by far the most complex level to implement, because you can create anomalies in behavior by connecting composites that are at different levels of abstraction. For example, in the canning plant you might end up with a pipe at no abstraction level feeding into a composite of tanks and machines at this third level of abstraction; for this intersection, no logically correct behavior is possible. (One way to implement this level of abstraction is to associate new handlers for the messages this entity inherits from the MACHINE frame.)

In general, visual abstraction is a useful and often necessary tool. Deeper levels of abstraction are powerful techniques but have limited usefulness because of the complexity of implementing and enforcing logical structures that include simultaneous multiple abstraction levels.

Linking Graphic Objects to the Displayed Object

Now that we have examined why we wish to associate graphic objects with component objects in the knowledge base, let's examine a possible mechanism by which the linking might be done. In Chapter 6, where we introduced object graphics, the graphic image and the displayed object were linked such that changing the slot value of the displayed object caused the image to update. Now, however, we wish the image to reflect characteristics of the object itself, not just display a particular slot value. To modify this behavior, we'll need to examine how the displayed object (component) and its image object (image) are linked one to the other.

All images have two slots, DISPLAYED-OBJECT and VALUE. The DISPLAYED-OBJECT slot contains either a paired value (the monitored instance and slot) or just an object name (either an instance or a frame). For the model editor, this slot contains either an instance or frame name. Because we are not monitoring a slot value, the VALUE slot will not be used.

(This is not entirely true—we have two options for how the image appears. Either it can be an icon with a graphic representation of the object, or we can place the name of the displayed object in the value slot and thus "trick" the graphic system into displaying our displayed object's name on the canvas. It mostly depends on how the graphic system has been implemented and how much we wish to modify it.)

Often, we wish to reference the image from the displayed object. For example, in a large, complicated layout, we may not wish to save the dozens or even hundreds of image instances. To facilitate this link, we can add an additional slot, MODEL-EDITOR-IMAGE, to the COMPONENT frame (and thus all children of that frame). The MODEL-EDITOR-IMAGE slot will contain the name of the graphic image—an instance of EDITOR-OBJECT-IMAGE or EDITOR-MENU-IMAGE—representing that component in the model editor.

Let's continue with the example of not saving all the graphic images each session. The only important information that these images contain is their location on the canvas. In order to save this information, we can now add a facet to the MODEL-EDITOR-IMAGE slot named **region**. When we save the knowledge base, these position facets will contain the position of the displayed objects' associated graphic.

When the knowledge base is reloaded, we can re-create the graphic layout by creating graphic instances and setting their position to the value stored in the region facet.

NOTE: As you may have guessed, a simple graphic system could be built using no graphic image instances but instead adding a number of facets to an image slot on the displayed object. The important thing to remember is that the design levels represented by object, slot, and facet are flexible; when more detail is required, a slot may become a frame and its facets, slots, thus permitting a new level of facet detail to be added. In the same way, we can turn frames back into slots, as we have done in this example, when that will reduce the size of the knowledge base without interfering with functionality.

REPRESENTING RELATIONSHIPS

The model editor is designed to represent a collection of physical objects and the links between those objects. Links between objects can represent a wide variety of relationships. In the case of a communication system, for example, the links might represent wires running between pieces of communications equipment. In a scheduling problem, the components now become tasks to be completed and the links represent start-and-end dependencies between those events (for example, the situation where one task can only begin after its predecessor has ended).

In the canning plant, the links between components represent three different types of physical flow:

- the flow of *cans* moving between successive stages in the production process (conveyor belts)

- the flow of *liquid* between a tank and a sprayer (pipes)

- the flow of *pressure* between a pump and a sprayer (hoses)

We'll use the DOWNSTREAM slot to define these links between components, then display those links on the model editor's schematic.

Relationships can take two forms, **unidirectional** and **bidirectional**. An unidirectional relationship only goes in one direction, for example, inheritance. A bidirectional relationship is one in which each element affects the other. We can define many different types of relationships within these two categories, including:

- Bidirectional

  symmetric ("Next to" is a symmetric relationship because the same relationship holds in both directions between two objects; e.g., if a is next to b, then b is next to a.)

  inverse ("Upstream/downstream" is an inverse relationship because one object of the pair has the opposite relationship to the other object; e.g., if a is upstream of b then b is downstream of a. Another common inverse relationship is part/whole.)

- Unidirectional:

  inheritance (A child frame inherits attributes and values from a parent, but the parent does not inherit any information from the child.)

A good implementation test for a unidirectional relation is seeing if cross-references are required on the relation participants. In a frame inheritance scheme, for example, only the parent needs to know about the children because the child can never actively pass information back to its parents.

When drawing directional links, the easiest method is simply to draw arrows. For example, an arrow drawn from component A to component B would represent the fact that B is one of the values in A's downstream slot. A more elaborate technique is to animate the connection, perhaps by drawing a line and moving icons along the line in the appropriate direction. Interface issues such as these depend on the intended audience; developers require much less in the way of alluring interfaces than end users do.

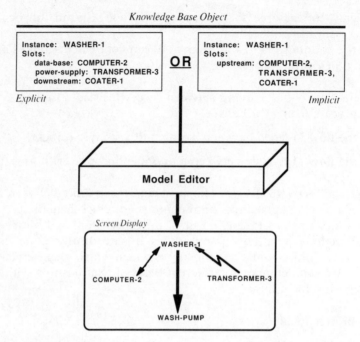

FIGURE 13-9. Slot representation of **implicit** and **explicit** relationships

Explicit versus Implicit Representation

Relationships between objects in the knowledge base can have two basic methods of representation: **explicit** or **implicit** (Figure 13-9).

If the relationship differences are explicit, the information defining each type of link is stored separately. One simple way to indicate this in the knowledge base would be to use different slots for defining those relationships. In our example, we have only the slot UPSTREAM but we could have easily defined others. For example, a POWER-SUPPLY slot could indicate from where a given component receives its supply of electricity, while a DATABASE slot might indicate from where the component receives operations data.

If the relationship differences are implicit, the type of relationship will depend on the types of components being connected. The connection between a tank and a sprayer will always be a fluid connection, for example, while the connection between a stamper and an oiler will always be a transportation link (here, a conveyor belt carrying cans). When representing these links implicitly, a single slot such as DOWNSTREAM can be used, but the entries in that slot will be interpreted differently depending on the details of which two components are being connected.

Granularity

All computer models are representations of some aspect of the real world. As such, they must achieve a balance between accuracy and the needed level of detail, because of the impossibility of exactly representing every aspect of the real system. The expert system developer must strive to have everything in the model that the expert logic (rules) will need to reason on, but no more. The level of detail that the model requires is the **granularity.** Granularity is a factor in all aspects of knowledge-base design.

In the case of relations, we want to define our representation of the knowledge only at a level required by the rule logic. For example, if our rule logic needs to know only about the existence of a relationship, and not what type it is, then placing information about type in the knowledge base is a wasted effort. This might be the case in a situation where all links are unique; that is, no two objects are linked by more than one type of relation. Thus, if the object pair has any type of link, the rules can implicitly use this information as the general fact "the objects are connected."

> At the plant, the team personnel tried a number of different approaches before they came up with a working solution. When they began looking at the different types of relations, it appeared that the operators actually used information about the different types of relations; at any rate, they felt uneasy about calling all of the links between components simply "downstream." The initial strategy turned out to be a hybrid of the explicit and implicit approaches.
>
> The single DOWNSTREAM slot, as initially specified, was allowed to remain. However, a type facet was added to the slot to provide explicit information about the link. This facet could take on one of three values: source-of-pressure, move-cans-from, supplies-wash-mix-to. This initially seemed to work, and all of the downstream relations were so defined.
>
> However, as the team members tried to create upstream slots in the same manner, they discovered that more than one link type existed for a number of the components, making it impossible to specify a single type. They were now faced with disparate types of link pairs (Figure 13-10). For example, the upstream relation of RINSE-PUMP to WASHER-2 was type SOURCE-OF-PRESSURE, whereas the relation of CAN-STAMPER-2 to WASHER-2 was type MOVE-CANS-FROM.

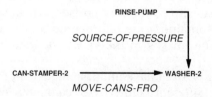

FIGURE 13-10. Flow diagram of component with disparate upstream link types

> Fortunately, before further changes were required, a decision was made that the information on link type would not be used in the rules and thus could be ignored in the slot definition. If, however, future expansion of the rules determined a need for link-type information, this issue would need to be resolved.

One possible solution to the upstream dilemma at the canning plant is the use of multipart relations. When the relationship between objects has three or more elements, we would like a concise way of stating this. For example, we would like to say "The source of pressure for washer-2 is the rinse-pump." Using slots and facets, as we have seen, can be quite awkward. Some shells and languages (for example, GoldWorks and Prolog) provide a mechanism for defining these relations. In such a situation, we might define the relation **SOURCE** as

SOURCE ?MATERIAL ?OBJECT1 ?OBJECT2

which we interpret as

the source of some ?MATERIAL for ?OBJECT1 is ?OBJECT2

As an example, **?MATERIAL** might represent cans or pressure and **?OBJECT1** and **?OBJECT2**, components of the canning line.

IMPLEMENTING THE MODEL EDITOR: EXAMPLE FUNCTIONS

Now that we've defined all the elements that constitute the editor, let's put them together by writing a set of functions that implement a simple model editor. Figure 13-11 shows the process of displaying a particular component layout using the model editor. The function modelEditor is used to start the process. We'll begin by looking at how the editor establishes the editing environment.

Initializing the Display

Each time a different model is to be edited, an initialization process must take place. The first time in a session that the editor is used, the initialization first opens each of the editor viewports. Next, the initialization function finds the frame containing the information for the layout the user has selected and draws the images in the viewport. Finally, the relations are drawn.

Because we may wish to have multiple models of the knowledge base (for example, to test different connectivity configurations) we'll begin by defining a new frame, LAYOUT, with an instance (Figure 13-12 shows a canning-line layout) for each configuration.

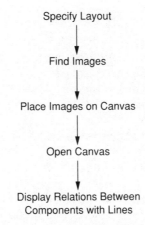

FIGURE 13-11. Process of placing components in graphical editor

The new frame has a single slot, COMPONENTS. All of the component instances that will be included in the graphic editor display are stored in this slot. Each of those components already has an associated graphical image, so when we initialize the editor with a particular layout, the function goes through the components, finds their images, and displays them on the canvas.

When a user wishes to use the editor, he or she runs the function modelEditor (Figure 13-13), providing the function with the name of the layout instance, for example, CANNING-PLANT. The function takes the list of components to be included in the layout from the layout's COMPONENT slot and iterates through these components to find their associated images

---

Instance: **CANNING–LINE**
Parents: **LAYOUT**
--Slots--
COMPONENTS: **SHEET–METAL–SUPPLY DISK–CUTTER METAL– DISK–OILER CAN–STAMPER–1 CAN–STAMPER–2 WASHER–1 WASHER–2 RINSE–PUMP CAN–COATER FILLER–1 PRE–PAINT–WASHER PAINT–LABELS**
Constraints: INSTANCE–OF **COMPONENT**
Documentation: All of the components in a particular line. Allows us to have several lines loaded simultaneously

---

FIGURE 13-12. The CANNING-LINE instance of LAYOUT

```
on modelEditor layout
  --setup canvas then find and place images on it
  put "Connection Diagram for" & layout into title
  sendMsg "editor-layout-canvas","setTitle",title
  --layout is an instance representing the plant,
  --e.g.,CANNING-LINE
  put getValue(layout,"components") into layoutComps

  --get all the images associated with the components
  --in the layout
  repeat with i = 1 to the number of items in layoutComps
    put item i of layoutComps into component
    put getValue(component,"model-editor-image") into
        item i of images
  end repeat

  --put the images onto the editor layout canvas
  putValue "editor-layout-canvas","images",images

  --Next, open the canvases, causing the viewports
  --to be displayed
  sendMsg "editor-menu-canvas","open" --action "menus"
  sendMsg "editor-layout-canvas","open" --layout

  --Finally, draw the lines representing relations
  --between objects
  drawObjectCanvasLines "editor-layout-canvas"
end modelEditor
```

FIGURE 13-13. The modelEditor function

(using the component's MODEL-EDITOR-IMAGE slot). These images are collected and, by placing them in the canvas' IMAGE slot, are displayed on the canvas' viewport when the canvas is sent an OPEN message.

Connecting and Disconnecting Objects

Once the objects have been displayed in the viewport, we want to indicate relations between the objects by drawing lines or arrows. The function drawObjectCanvasLines (Figure 13-14) loops through all the components represented on the canvas and, when a DOWNSTREAM slot value

```
on drawObjectCanvasLines canvas
  put getValue(canvas,"images") into images
  repeat with i = 1 to the number of items in images

    --get the images component instance
    put item i of images into compImage
    put getValue(compImage,"displayed-object") into component
    --get the component's connections (downstream slot)
    put getValue(component,"downstream") into dwnStrms
    repeat with i = 1 to the number of items in dwnStrms

      --now get each downstream's image
      put item i of dwnstrms into downstream
      put getValue(downstream,"model-editor-image") into
        dwnStrmImage
      --get two images' positions from slot, draw line
      connectCanvasImages compImage,dwnStrmImage,canvas
    end repeat
  end repeat
end drawObjectCanvasLines
```

FIGURE 13-14. The drawObjectCanvasLines function

is discovered, draws a line between the two related components' images. Depending on the application's details, different types of relations could be represented, indicated graphically by using different colors or line patterns (we don't show that here; however, you would have an additional argument after "canvas" with the relation type or line type).

The function connectCanvasImages actually draws the line or arrow, using the values in the images' TOP, LEFT, WIDTH, and HEIGHT slots to determine the endpoints of the line drawn with whatever draw function comes with the shell software. The model editor should also have the capability of aiding the user in establishing new relationships between components. In this editor, the user begins making the connection by selecting the component that will be the upstream component (the next section discusses image selection in detail). To make the connection between two components, we must execute four sequential steps (Figure 13-15):

1. The user begins by selecting a component image in the viewport. In the example, the user has selected the image (EDITOR-OBJECT-IMAGE2) that represents a component, WASH-TANK, and a menu of choices is presented, one option of which is *Add Downstream*.

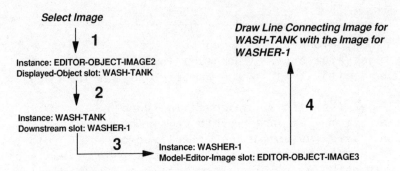

FIGURE 13-15. Steps required for graphically connecting the WASH-TANK to WASHER-1

2. The editor now locates the image's DISPLAYED-OBJECT instance, WASH-TANK, and presents a menu of valid choices for a downstream component (here is a good place to use slot constraints; for example, we might restrict the DOWNSTREAM slot of all tanks to accept only instances of WASHER). The user selects WASHER-1, which is placed in the DOWNSTREAM slot of WASH-TANK by the model editor.

3. The model editor now goes to WASHER-1, and finds *its* image. The editor may also place WASH-TANK in WASHER-1's UPSTREAM slot, if such a slot exists.

4. The model editor draws a line on the canvas between the image for the WASH-TANK and the image for WASHER-1.

When *Add Downstream* is selected, the source component's image is sent a connect message in the form:

sendMsg image,"connect",imageToConnectTo

which translates into

sendMsg "EDITOR-OBJECT-IMAGE2","Connect","EDITOR-OBJECT-IMAGE3"

The connect handler, illustrated in Figure 13-16, uses the steps outlined above to connect the two components and their respective images.

The connect message might also use a filter for gathering only those downstream components that can be connected. In **2** in Figure 13-16, we could have placed a filtering test that, as we iterated through the images to get their displayed objects, used the constraint facet on the source component's downstream slot. Only components that matched this constraint

```
on connect editorObjectImage,otherImage
  --connect two instances together by connecting their
  --images if otherImage is not given, then present
  --user with a menu

  --** 2 ** Picking valid component choices to connect to
  if otherImage is empty then
    put getValue("editor-layout-canvas","images") into images
    --put the number of items in images into counter
    repeat with i = 1 to the number of items in images
      --using images on canvas, collect all their components
      put getValue(item i of images,"displayed-object")
        into instance
      put instance into item i of components
    end repeat
    --use components as menu choices,pick downstream to
    --connect to
    put popup(components,"Pick downstream object") into
      component2
    if component2 is empty then exit connect

    --** 3 ** get the image of the component we'll be
    --connecting to
    put getValue(component2,"model-editor-image") into
      otherImage
  end if

  --update downstream slot of the first component with
  --second component
  put getValue(editorObjectImage,"displayed-object")
    into Component1
  putValue component1,"downstream",component2

  --** 4 ** connect the images with a line
  connectCanvasImages editorObjectImage,otherImage,"editor-
    layout-canvas"
end connect
```

FIGURE 13-16. The connect function

would then be presented in the choice menu. This use of a filter illustrates how a function can be used to constrain possible connections (an alternative to the slot constraints mentioned above). If the logic is complex enough, or the implementors wish to avoid programming, another alternative is to implement these filter constraints using rules.

When the user selects the *Remove Downstream* option, the message disconnect is sent. Disconnecting two components is the exact inverse of the connect message, erasing the line and removing the target component from the source's downstream slot.

Object Selection

A model editor should have a range of possible actions to take when an object is selected. In the previous section on connections, we assumed that clicking on an image produced a menu of editor options for the component associated with the selected image. Instead of associating the choices with the object itself, they could have been defined in a command menu such as a menu bar. The choice depends both on the conventions for a particular hardware/software implementation environment and the style preferences of the developer—both approaches have strong adherents.

Before we can redefine the actions that take place when an object is selected on the editor layout, we need to understand the dynamics of what occurs when an object is selected. When an object is selected by clicking the mouse over its sensitive region, a system-defined function is executed. We as developers thus need to associate the mouse-sensitive region on the screen (the image) with the behavior we wish for the editor.

If the editor is being implemented in a windowing system in Lisp or C, the window system itself will provide some type of access to the functions that are called when an image is selected. We'll assume here that you are using a shell that supports a graphics system where this function has been linked to a slot on a frame (most of the mid- to high-end shells have this feature). This type of connection can be made relatively easily by a programmer for situations where predefined graphics frames of this type do not exist.

The object graphic system should supply some type of slot that contains a default mouse function—MOUSE-FN slot (note: some implementations, such as GoldWorks, instead let the user define a handler on the frame for this same purpose). Whenever the image is selected, the function in its MOUSE-FN slot is invoked. For our editor, we have defined our own function, presentMenu, and placed it in the MOUSE-FN slot.

The presentMenu function (Figure 13-17) presents the user with a menu of choices taken from the contents of another slot, the image's MENU-RIGHT slot (Figure 13-18). When the user makes a choice, the associated

```
on presentMenu instance
  put getValue(instance,"menu-right") into menuItems
  put the number of items in menuItems in numItems
  --two items for each choice: prompt,action
  repeat with i = 1 to (.5 * numItems)
    --put all of the user-prompts together in a choice list
    --by selecting the odd items, e.g., 1, 3, etc.
    put item (2 * i - 1) of menuItems into item i of choices
  end repeat
  put popup(choices,"Select Action") into choice

  repeat with i = 1 to (.5 * numItems)
    --find user's choice in entire list
    if item (2 * i - 1) of menuItems = choice then
      --and execute the second element, the corresponding
      --action
      do item (2 * i) of menuItems
      --and stop iterating once choice has been found
      exit repeat
    end if
  end repeat
end presentMenu
```

FIGURE 13-17. The presentMenu function

action is evaluated. Again, many shells, such as IntelliCorp's KEE, define these slots. In others, such as GoldWorks, the user can add these slots himself, as we have done in this example.

The format for the MENU-RIGHT slot is

"user prompt" action,

where action can be a function or message.

If presentMenu is replaced with another function name (in the image's MOUSE-FN slot), that function—which may or may not use the MENU-RIGHT slot—will be used instead. Thus, there are two ways to change the selection behavior of an image:

- To provide a new set of choices, change the MENU- RIGHT slot.

- For arbitrary selection behavior, change the MOUSE-FN slot.

Slot: **MENU—RIGHT**
Frame: **EDITOR—OBJECT—IMAGE**
Documentation: Defines what appears when the default
   MOUSE—RIGHT—FN is run. Form is (prompt function—call).
   In the default buttonfn, canvas and image—instance are
   set to the canvas and image just moused.

DEFAULT—VALUES :
   "Move image", SendMsg *CurrentImage* Move,
   "Display Object Instance", SendMsg *CurrentImage*
      DisplayObject,
   "Display Object Downstreams", SendMsg *CurrentImage*
      DisplayConnections,
   "Delete object", SendMsg *CurrentImage* DeleteObject,
   "Connect to Downstream", SendMsg *CurrentImage*
      ConnectObjects,
   "Disconnect from Downstream", SendMsg *CurrentImage*
      DisconnectObjects

FIGURE 13-18. The MENU-RIGHT slot defines the menu that appears on user selection of an image

The image's selection behavior can thus be changed by modifying slots, rather than by modifying source code. This of course assumes that some alternative MOUSE-FN functions are lying about (another alternative would be to write rules that perform some type of action, and place the forwardChain or backwardChain command in the MOUSE-FN slot).

For instances of the EDITOR-MENU-IMAGE frame, we bypassed the MENU-RIGHT slot by putting the function name createComponent in the MOUSE-FN slot, replacing presentMenu. This new function, createComponent, creates an instance of the selected image's displayed object, then places the new instance onto the layout (createComponent ignores the MENU-RIGHT slot altogether; thus for clarity we've emptied the MENU-RIGHT slot in EDITOR-MENU-IMAGE). We'll take a detailed look at createComponent in the next section.

An alternative implementation of the graphics would use messages and handlers instead of function names and slot values. For example, we might change the selection behavior so that mousing on an image caused a select message to be sent to that image (instead of executing the function contained in the image's MOUSE-FN slot). In this case, the default select handler would have the same behavior as the current presentMenu function; to change the selection behavior, one would go in and modify the select handler.

Either alternative is satisfactory. Dynamically changing a handler, however, is difficult or impossible for nonprogrammers. We prefer the method of using a function name as a slot value, because it gives nonprogrammers an easy way to change an image's behavior dynamically: Simply change the MOUSE-FN slot and the image's behavior changes immediately. If a library of function names and behaviors is supplied by the developer, end users can pick the behavior they desire, insert the function in the MOUSE-FN slot, and immediately have the benefit of the new behavior.

Adding New Objects to the Layout

New objects are created and added to the layout by selecting an image, representing one of the object frames (not the instances in the layout) in the knowledge base, from a menu. When a selection is made, it is the equivalent of saying "I want to add one of these to the layout." Since choices represent frames in the knowledge base, selecting a choice causes the model editor to create an instance of that frame along with a corresponding image that is an instance of EDITOR-OBJECT-IMAGE, and draw that image on the layout canvas.

The following steps occur in the process of creating a new instance:

1. A name for the new object must be assigned, either automatically (as is done in the example) or as specified by the user.

2. The new instance must be created with the assigned name.

3. A new graphical image instance must be created to represent that new instance.

4. A cross reference must be established between the new instance and its image instance by filling in respective slot values on both instances.

Only after all four steps have been performed can we actually place the graphical object on the screen. This bookkeeping is the essence of why a model editor is useful: the user said "I want one of those on the layout," and all required links and graphics operations were performed automatically.

In this simple model editor, we keep these four operations as simple as possible. The createNewComponent function (Figure 13-19) performs these four steps. We start by getting the frame represented by the image the user clicked on, making a name for the new instance (the frame name followed by a random number, e.g., PUMP44), and then creating an instance

```
function createNewComponent image,canvas,layout
  --creates a new picture and a new instance of frame.
  --Component is placed

  if layout is empty then
    put "editor-object-canvas" into layout
  end if

  put getValue(image,"displayed-object") into frame
  --create name e.g. PUMP44
  put frame & random(30000) into newInstanceName
  createInstance(frame,newInstanceName)

  --create the new image instance, args are image frame,
  --canvas
  put createImage("editor-object-IMAGE",layout) into newImage

  --cross-ref component and image
  putValue newImage,"displayed-object",newInstanceName
  putValue newInstanceName,"model-editor-image",newImage

  --Finally, we add the new instance to the COMPONENTS
  --slot of layout
  addValue layout,"components",newInstanceName
end createNewComponent
```

FIGURE 13-19. The createNewComponent function

of the frame (using a standard shell command). Next, we create the corresponding image instance (a name is automatically generated in this version) on the layout canvas and fill in the cross-reference slots between component and image. Finally, we have to add the new component to the COMPONENTS slot of the layout instance.

Moving and Reshaping Images

Once a set of graphical images representing the layout has been placed on the screen, there must be some way to move and reshape those images.

Moving images is effected by having the user drag the image around with the mouse until it is properly positioned, with a final mouse click to fix the image's position. Resizing images is similar to moving them, except that only one corner of the image moves at a time, the user compressing or stretching a rubber-band rectangle on the screen to set the new dimensions. When a new size has been set, the results are stored in slots on the image.

A complication arises when moving or reshaping represents a change not only in the visual representation but also in the functional definition of the object. The model editor must constrain changes in the graphics to reflect real constraints in how the actual object can be changed. For example, in a computer-aided design (CAD) package, moving a graphical object on the screen may have to be translated into a change in the physical location, the capacity, or the status of the displayed object. Without constraints, the object could be made larger or smaller than is physically possible. In these cases, where exact measurements are important, we may also want to prompt the user for a position instead of dragging the mouse to place the object, because the exact location of the object is important.

ADDITIONAL USES OF GRAPHIC EDITORS

Graphic editors are usually built by the development team as an aid to expansion and testing. However, they can also provide powerful and unexpected benefits to end users. A good example of a model editor serving purposes other than the original intent was work done with NASA at the Johnson Space Center. While the expert system was originally built as a diagnostic system, the engineers soon discovered that the developers' model editor, combined with the expert system, permitted them to quickly test hardware design changes—the system was now considered an excellent design tool by certain end users.

Although this story illustrates an unexpected but successful secondary use of an existing expert system, attempts to adapt an existing implementation to a so-called similar application are fraught with difficulty. Particularly within a company, there is the temptation to take a successful application and try to re-implement it in a related facility. This is actually a very successful strategy in general, but adequate time and facilities must be provided. Too often, the assumption is made that the re-implementation will be simple and quick—often a false premise.

Porting the Expert System to Other Manufacturing Domains

One afternoon we were talking with George and Nancy about various ways to extend the prototype. Nancy asked about using the system for other types of canning lines. "There's a guy named Tom over in our department who saw your demo last month," she said. "He's really excited about the possibility of using the software in some of the plants down South. He thinks most of it should transfer over pretty easily." We groaned, knowing how fragile the software was and how

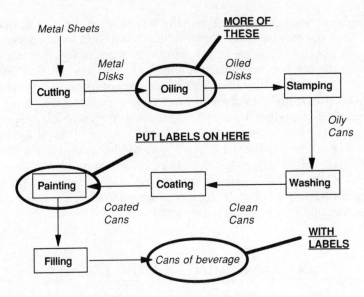

FIGURE 13-20. Tom's sketch of the other canning plant, showing required modifications

obscure it could be sometimes . "Tom thinks he can go in and change a few names, add some different equipment types (Figure 13-20), and it will be just like one of the other plants. He was really impressed during the demo when you showed how easy it was to expand the knowledge base."

We quickly put our heads together and produced a modified structure for the existing knowledge base (Figure 13-21). However, as we began to implement the changes, we realized that Tom's plant, built ten years before "our" plant, had a somewhat different set of problems. When we talked to one of the experts at

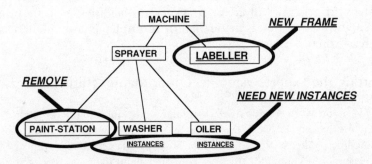

FIGURE 13-21. Nancy's new object hierarchy required to represent the new plant

that plant, he informed us that, although the layout appeared similar, most of the machines were different models and had different failings and test requirements. We soon realized that, although we could use the basic frame structure and interfaces of the original expert system, the encapsulated diagnostic expertise in the rules would in large part have to be redone, starting with some basic knowledge engineering with the new experts. Happily, we would still be able to make use of the tools that we had built, such as the model editor.

SUMMARY

This chapter examined the purpose of a graphical model editor, the elements of which it is composed, and the specific functions used in implementing one. The model editor tightly integrates object graphics with the concept of WYSIWYG (what you see is what you get) to provide users with a seamless view of the knowledge base from the perspective of a cohesive model—component objects linked graphically and functionally by relations.

14

MODEL-BASED REASONING: SIMULATION

I n previous chapters, we defined an object hierarchy describing the components of the canning production line. By specifying a set of attributes for those components that describe the flow of materials between the components, we built a model of the plant. In the previous chapter we formalized the model-building process by creating a graphical editor. However, we still have no capability for dynamically modeling (simulating) the flow of materials through the plant.

In this chapter, we'll explore the application of traditional discrete simulation to expert-systems problems. The simulation implementation will be based on object-oriented programming techniques, using frames and handlers as discussed in Chapter 8.

SIMULATION REVIEW

Many applications require the use of simulation. Briefly put, simulation is the process of using a computer to model a real-world process. Simulation provides an environment (the computer model) for testing theories about some particular system without actually running that system. The computer model provides the user with information about how the real-world system operates under the simulated conditions.

In this chapter, we will examine where and why simulation might be appropriate in expert systems. We'll also look at methods with which we can add simulation features to our expert system application. Because so much material has already been written on simulation, only a short overview will be included here.

In order to effectively build many expert system applications, not only the experts' knowledge but also the domain in which they operate must be constructed. Simulation provides a description of that domain. Because simulation modeling has in the past been such a laborious task, oversimplification of the problem domain has occurred in many finished models. This is not surprising, given the fact that a reasonable simulation can in itself require a major allocation of time and resources. What is lost is not always initially obvious, but long-term adverse effects can include the inability to adequately test the expert's abstracted reasoning; blocks of time spent building a set of test scenarios that is too small to produce a reliable finished system; and difficulty in convincingly communicating the benefits of the final system.

Traditional simulation can be enhanced by a knowledge base environment and in turn used as an advanced expert-system-building tool. Ongoing improvement of simulation techniques involves the integration of graphic animation, traditional simulation representation, and the knowledge representation techniques described in the previous chapters.

Historically, simulation has appeared to have an important role in design processes, yet simulation is still considered arcane enough that many projects that could benefit from this technique go without. A great many would-be users of simulation have relied on their own judgment and experience for the evaluation of their systems. Unfortunately, while this approach is adequate in the simplest systems, it is likely to result in incomplete analysis in more complex applications.

This is not to say that simulation has never been used in the design, implementation, and even use of large, complex systems. Frequent avoidance of simulation has been more a commentary on the fact that existing simulation languages are difficult to use and validate and even more difficult to explain in convincing terms to persons not versed in the use of them.

Systems may also have quite involved flow and control structures, easily described by English-style rules but difficult to model using traditional programming languages (e.g., GPSS) and almost impossible to model accurately. The approach to simulation described in this chapter examines how the integration of object programming, object graphics, and frame representations can aid in the development of a relatively easy-to-use simulation environment.

Need for a Test Environment

At the plant, the team's recognition of a need for a dynamic simulation of the canning line grew out of a series of small problems. The first hint of a problem came shortly after beginning the second-level prototype. Even as the team members were exploring the need for a model editor to deal with the growing complexity of model interdependences, they were also finding operational discrepancies in their layout of the plant.

As we began to add new rules to the system, George was searching for some way to accurately test the changes we were making. On several occasions, the addition of new rules had created unexpected side effects when existing rules chained to them, and we knew that some automated mechanism should be put in place to keep retesting the working parts of the system as changes occurred. Our first "simulation" for testing the rules was actually a hardwired set of assertions; to simulate a fault, we would choose that fault's name from a menu and this would in turn run a function that inserted a number of values throughout the knowledge base, simulating the component states that would appear in the plant if that fault had occurred.

Our simple simulated fault approach worked fine at first, when we were only testing 10 or 12 conditions. However, as the knowledge base continued to expand and an increasing number of rules—and thus potential faults to be diagnosed— were added, building and maintaining these fault simulations became increasingly difficult.

The final blow to our fault-simulation system came when we began to enter rules that tested for linked fault conditions. Now we wished to simulate faults that had dual causes, and we were facing a combinatorial explosion of fault possibilities. The only possible solution was to generate faults automatically. And this would be possible only if we had an accurate dynamic simulation of the canning line, where an introduced fault would automatically propagate itself. At this point, work on the model editor was expanded to add simple, and then increasingly sophisticated, simulation capabilities.

Simulation Design

The design of the simulation module is governed by the design of the total system, which will be split into two parts: the expert system discussed in previous chapters, and the actual model for tracking the movement of items between objects (the simulation). Although split into separate conceptual entities, both parts are in fact fully integrated, because they share a single representation—the frame system. As a result of this integration, the expert system can use the simulation to develop test scenarios, but the simulation can also be used for design extensions, making use of the expert system.

First, to provide test scenarios for our expert system, the simulation model can invoke our experts' rules to diagnosis problems as they occur

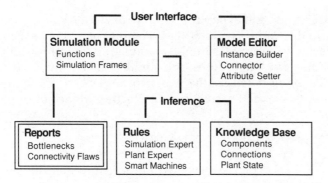

FIGURE 14-1. Flow of information in test environment

in the simulated plant operations. Second, by altering the model, we can observe the effect of these changes through the actions of the diagnostic system. In work done at NASA, testing the concept of a partially automated space station, a model of the life-support system was used initially for testing diagnostic rules, but secondarily to examine design decisions that would make the diagnostic process more comprehensive and efficient. Ideally, a cycle of diagnostic rule development, domain modification, and rule modification takes place, leading not only to a more comprehensive expert system but to a more effective domain environment as well.

Object Programming

An object-based expert system integrates object-programming concepts with deductive reasoning by implementing facts as objects (frames). Because simulation is concerned primarily with the way in which objects function and interact one with another, simulation integrates easily with the object-oriented nature of frame-based languages (IntelliCorp's SIMKIT, for example).

Using object-oriented programming techniques, a simulation system can be implemented that requires no programming expertise to use. The underlying principles are based on the fact that all objects in the system behave in a predictable manner, such that joining any two objects together will always result in a working simulation (though possibly an illogical system).

Figure 14-1 portrays the structure of our expert system environment with the inclusion of a simulation capability. In the previous chapter (Chapter 13) we discussed the operation of a model editor, a facility that enables the user to interact with schematic representations of their domain—in effect, a graphic interface for creating the knowledge base (creating component instances and their relations to other components). Figure 14-1 shows the inference engine and expert rules in relation to the editor and simulation module, with the simulation in effect becoming the interface through which users interact with the application. By simulating typical functioning of the plant, including random failures, the simulation can invoke the rules and interact with the user (either the expert or a plant operator) in a manner similar to how the expert system would function in the actual plant.

The Importance of a Correct Model

In order to test an expert system, we must ensure that our model of the domain is correct. In the canning plant, we have to be sure that the processes and faults in the knowledge base correspond to those of the actual canning plant.

For example, suppose that an operator observes that the washer pressure is low and physically traces the problem to crud in the washer nozzle; does the expert system correctly lead an operator to the same fault? Remember that a computer model of the real world will run just as happily with an inaccurate model as with a well-fashioned one—the only difference is that in the former case, the data from the simulation will be inapplicable to the problem at hand.

Once we're confident that the model is correct, we can try out various scenarios—for example, machines breaking or performing poorly—and see how our expert system diagnoses the problem. Obviously, we do not want to actually break the machines in the plant; thus, we turn to the simulation.

SIMULATION DESIGN

The simulation has been designed to allow the user first to build an accurate model of the plant and then to change certain aspects of the plant's operation to simulate faults. We have divided the simulation problem into two topic areas:

- modeling time by establishing a calendar of discrete events
- the mechanics of running the simulation, using object handlers

We start with the plant components, the frame objects that represent machines. To simulate changes in the plant over time, we have defined activities that occur at discrete points in time; these occurrences are **events**. The events must be scheduled to occur at a specific time, in much the same way that we might schedule a meeting in an appointment book—in fact, we'll place all events in a **calendar** slot. Our events must now be executed in the correct order, so we will maintain time using a simulation **clock**—another slot. As the clock advances (i.e., as the slot value is advanced

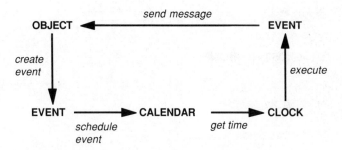

FIGURE 14-2. Sequence of message calls between simulation objects in one clock cycle

incrementally), events on the calendar will be executed at their scheduled time.

Figure 14-2 shows the sequence of actions that occur in the simulation. Each of the objects in boldface—object, event, calendar, and clock—are represented in our simulation system by frames. The actions, such as "create event," are represented by functions and handlers.

The rest of this chapter will describe how such an architecture might be implemented.

EVENT CREATION

The first step in building a simulation is representing the concept of an **event**. An event is the occurrence of an action at a specific time.

In the canning factory, each event involves a component. For simplicity, in this example we'll look only at a single type of event, a component sending an item to the next component downstream in the canning line. In this example, the item being sent is a batch of cans.

Every time a new action is to be taken, a new event (a new EVENT instance) must be created. All events that take place in the simulation are modeled as instances of the EVENT frame. This section will examine the EVENT frame and the program code required to create and initialize an EVENT instance.

We'll begin by defining an EVENT frame (Figure 14-3) with slots to represent the following information:

- start and end times—a number (slots: START-TIME and COMPLE-TION-TIME)

- a plant component, for example, WASHER-1—a COMPONENT instance (slot: OBJECT)

- the item being moved, for example, can-batch-2—text (slot: ITEM).

```
Frame:  EVENT
Parents:  DIAGNOSTIC-FRAME
--Slots--
START-TIME :
COMPLETION-TIME :
OBJECT :
ITEM :
```

FIGURE 14-3. The EVENT frame

The createEvent Handler

Events represent scheduled occurrences of activities. In the next section we'll discuss the creation of a schedule—here we'll only refer to the schedule as the location of our handler. Let's look now at the createEvent message, which is attached to the SCHEDULE frame. The createEvent handler (Figure 14-4) creates an instance for each new event required by the simulation. The function includes code for three alternative event representations:

1. Events can be created as **instances of the EVENT frame**. This is the alternative that we've chosen. Event creation is performed by the createInstanceEvent function (discussed later in this section). Advantages of this representation include better integration with the graphics system and rules and the existence of an "audit trail" (once created, the event instances are all available for inspection at any time).

2. Events could be modeled as **simple lists** (Figure 14-4b). This is the fastest and most efficient way of representing events; however, one disadvantage of this method is that no record of an event remains after the event code executes.

3. An event can be modeled as a **structure** (Figure 14-4c). A structure is similar to a frame (in fact, structures are often used as the underlying representation of a frame), but is defined within the programming language, not the expert system shell. A structure is more efficient than a frame, but, because it has more organization than a simple list, it executes more slowly. Examples of structures include: in Lisp, a defstruct or flavor; in HyperCard, a card with fields and buttons; in C, a record with fields.

```
on createEvent schedule,component,item
  --handler for SCHEDULE. Creates an event instance
  --containing information on object and scheduling times,
  --Returns the new event.
  put getValue(component,"duration") into dur
  --time in the simulation is stored in a "CLOCK" slot
  put getValue(schedule,"clock") into Time
  --** 1 ** here is where alternatives would go
  --create a new event instance and return its name
  return createInstanceEvent (component,dur,Time,item)
end createEvent
```

(a)

```
--LIST: simplest and fastest, but least flexible approach
--**2**
component & "," & dur & "," & Time & "," & item
```

(b)

```
--RECORD:flexible structure, clear,slower than list
--**3**
createDefstructEvent component,dur,time
```

(c)

FIGURE 14-4. (a) The createEvent handler (b,c) alternate record structures

In general, neither of the two latter alternatives allows easy integration with the knowledge base. Neither alternative allows simple access to either the rule system or graphics system images. We have chosen to represent our events as instances for illustrative purposes (among other reasons); in this application, our aim is clarity, not efficiency.

Many simulations are sufficiently large that several thousand (or more) events are created during a single run. In such a case, the speed of event creation becomes paramount, and a very efficient representation must be

```
function createInstanceEvent component,dur,startTime,
   itemName
  --Create an instance and fill in the slots.
  put component & "-Event" & random(30000) into eventName
  createInstance eventName, "event"
  --Install slots... use default duration of 0
  putValue eventName,"startTime",startTime
  putValue eventName,"completionTime",(startTime + dur)
  putValue eventName,"object",component
  putValue eventName,"item",itemName
  --return the new event
  return eventName
end createInstanceEvent
```

FIGURE 14-5. The createInstanceEvent function

devised. If efficiency is a significant issue, representing events as instances will almost certainly be unacceptably slow.

The createInstanceEvent Function

The createEvent handler calls the function createInstanceEvent (Figure 14-5). This function manages the actual instance creation; it then fills in the slots of the new event according to the arguments for originating object, event duration, start time, and the item being moved through the plant. Naming conventions for the new event are the object name and an arbitrary event number, for example WASHER-1-EVENT-23. Naming conventions provide the developer with a quick check for whether the simulation is functioning correctly.

MODELING TEMPORAL EVENTS (CALENDAR)

Now we need to order our events in time by scheduling them on a **calendar.** Our calendar is similar in concept to the ones hanging on most peoples' walls. Events occur at a certain point in time—on a wall calendar, a day or a time marked within that day. Thus our calendar should show the time at which an event occurs. Wall calendars also have some label that defines the action that is occurring; our simulation calendar will also associate the time with the thing happening—in the case of our plant, a machine completing an action. Finally, the calendar should show the object of the action. Thus, in the same way that we can write on our wall calendar "Ed, meet Elizabeth at 6:00 on October 28," we can place an event on the calendar with the information "RINSE-PUMP BATCH16 120" (120 minutes after the start of the simulation, the rinse pump will finish processing batch16).

To implement our mechanism for handling time we will have to

- create a SCHEDULE frame
- add slots for representing
  - information about time
  - the events that will occur at a future time
- define handlers to manage the events and the schedule

Schedule

We'll start by defining the occurrence of events in the plant as a **schedule of events**, implemented as the SCHEDULE frame. Because simulations enable users to try out many different scenarios, we will structure the simulation environment such that each simulation scenario is an instance of the SCHEDULE frame. Thus, each instance of SCHEDULE will contain

- slots for representing
  - a calendar of current events
  - the units of time being used (for example, minutes)
- handlers for
  - creating new events
  - scheduling existing events
  - executing existing events

Let's look at how we've implemented the SCHEDULE frame (Figure 14-6).

This frame includes the following slots:

- a list of the events that will occur in the "future" (CALENDAR)
- the current (simulated) time (CLOCK)
- a speed factor used in running the simulation faster than real time (TIME-COMPRESSION)
- the smallest unit of simulation time for example hours, minutes, seconds (TIME-UNITS)

```
Frame: SCHEDULE
Parents: DIAGNOSTIC-FRAME
Instances: CURRENT-SCHEDULE
--Handlers--
advanceClock createEvent execute scheduleAllEvents
  scheduleComponent
--Slots--
CALENDAR :
Constraints: LIST
Documentation: A list of the events which will occur at
  some point in time.
CLOCK :
Documentation: Keeps track of relative time in a
  simulation. Each loop of the simulation advances the
  clock.
STOP-TIME : 400
Constraints: NUMBER
Documentation: If this slot has a value, the simulation
  will stop when the  clock reaches this time.
TIME-COMPRESSION : 10
Documentation: A number by which the actual time is
  divided during simulation.
TIME-UNITS : MINUTES
Constraints: MINUTES HOURS DAYS
```

FIGURE 14-6. The SCHEDULE frame

Current Schedule

For illustration of the simulation features defined in this chapter, we'll use the instance CURRENT-SCHEDULE (Figure 14-7).

The global variable *CurrentSchedule* has been bound to the value "CURRENT-SCHEDULE." As we'll see in later sections, many simulation functions assume that the schedule instance being simulated is found in *CurrentSchedule*.

SCHEDULE maintains an ordered list of events. By looking at CALENDAR, the user can see the events that are scheduled to occur at some future time. In Figure 14-7, the simulation has been running for 50 minutes, and batches of cans are currently at the SHEET-METAL source, CAN-STAMPER-1, WASHER-1, WASHER-2, CAN-COATER, and PRE-PAINT-WASHER (the contents of the calendar slot).

Instance: **CURRENT–SCHEDULE**
Parents: **SCHEDULE**
––Handlers––
advanceClock createEvent execute scheduleAllEvents
  scheduleComponent
––Slots––
CALENDAR: **SHEET–METAL–SUPPLY1–EVENT–25 CAN–STAMPER–1–**
  EVENT–24 WASHER–1–EVENT–23 CAN–COATER–EVENT–22 PRE–
  PAINT–WASHER–EVENT–21 WASHER–2–EVENT–20
CLOCK : 50
STOP–TIME : 500
TIME–COMPRESSION : 10
TIME–UNITS : HOURS

FIGURE 14-7. The CURRENT-SCHEDULE instance

NOTE: When the CALENDAR is empty, there are no active events, and thus
the simulation cannot run.

As an example of using the calendar, let's create an event involving
the plant component WASHER-1 and add the event to the CALENDAR of
CURRENT-SCHEDULE (Figure 14-8).

The displayed completion time for the event (Figure 14-9) is (approximately) the number of minutes after plant start-up on the current day (40
minutes after 8:00, or 8:40). We keep a record of the start time against future
need, but will ignore it for now. The component of the assembly line at
which the event will take place is WASHER-1; the ITEM involved is the
batch of cans BATCH04; the event will be WASHER-1 sending BATCH04
on to the next machine at time 50.

Slot: **CALENDAR**
Frame: **CURRENT–SCHEDULE**
Values: **WASHER–1–EVENT–23**
Constraints: INSTANCE–OF **EVENT**
Documentation: The events currently scheduled to be
  executed

FIGURE 14-8. The CALENDAR slot of CURRENT-SCHEDULE

```
Instance:  WASHER-1-EVENT-23
Parents:  EVENT
--Slots--
START-TIME  :  40
COMPLETION-TIME  :  50
OBJECT  :  WASHER-1
ITEM  :  BATCH04
```

FIGURE 14-9. An event instance on the calendar

NOTE: Events on the calendar (Figure 14-9) are scheduled to be executed at the time indicated by the value in the COMPLETION-TIME slot.

This is a critical point—determining when events are executed by the simulation. In our simple simulation, we are only concerned with when activities complete. Remember: Nothing is really happening, it's a simulation, so start times are only important if some type of animation or inferencing about time is taking place—not the case in this example.

The Calculated Time

When the simulation runs (the next section describes the actual process of running the simulation), it will use the event instance's COMPLETION-TIME slot value in conjunction with the SIMULATION frame's CLOCK slot value to determine when the event should be executed.

NOTE: Initially, we've based the simulation clock on the computer's internal time-of-day clock. This approach is very useful for systems that are polling for real-time data. Later sections will discuss the use of a simulated clock to compress the time in which the simulation runs.

We have assumed the existence of a function that will return a unique integer giving the current time. The exact units and values will depend on exactly what kind of software you are using; in our case, we have used HyperCard's function the seconds, which returns the number of seconds

```
function compressedDuration schedule,duration
  --calculate new duration w/schedule's TIME-COMPRESSION
  --slot
  put getValue(schedule,"TIME-COMPRESSION") into compress
  return max(1, round(duration / compress))
end compressedDuration
```

Figure 14-10. The compressedDuration Function

elapsed since midnight on 1 January, 1904. Other software will provide similar numbers, sometimes in sixtieths of a second. Whatever the case, the important thing is that we are using a unique integer to represent the current time.

The TIME-COMPRESSION Slot

In addition to simulating events, in some cases we want to shorten the time taken between events, a process known as **time compression**, because it makes the simulation execute in less time than the period being simulated.

We can scale an event's duration to achieve time compression. The scaling factor is contained in the TIME-COMPRESSION slot of CURRENT-SCHEDULE. If the value of this slot is 1, the simulation will run at the same speed (real time) as the actual plant.

The compressedDuration Function

The function compressedDuration (Figure 14-10) contains the mechanism for compressing time in the simulation. The compressedDuration function would be called in the SCHEDULE frame's createEvent handler (shown previously in Figure 14-4) after getting the component's duration. This function divides DURATION by the TIME-COMPRESSION of SCHEDULE; it then rounds the compressed duration to an integer. The value returned by compressedDuration is then passed to the function createInstanceEvent, also described previously in this chapter.

Why Events Are Needed

In this section, we'll examine the simulated origination of batches of cans. In order to understand the origins of batches, we first need to see how the

---

Instance: **CURRENT–SIMULATION–PARAMETERS**
Parents: **SIMULATION–PARAMETERS**
--Slots--
SOURCE-INITIALIZATION : **SHEET–METAL–SUPPLY1** BATCH01,
  SHEET–METAL–SUPPLY2 BATCH02 BATCH03 BATCH04 BATCH05

FIGURE 14-11. The CURRENT-SIMULATION-PARAMETERS instance

simulation is initialized. Let's start with another new frame, SIMULATION-PARAMETERS.

The instance CURRENT-SIMULATION-PARAMETERS (Figure 14-11) contains a single slot, SOURCE-INITIALIZATION, that defines the starting conditions for the plant. This slot contains components and the items that are at each given component when the simulation starts—in this example, the batches of sheet metal available in pre-line storage at the time of plant start-up.

All components referenced by SOURCE-INITIALIZATION must be instances of the SOURCE frame. In the canning plant, there are two SOURCE instances: SHEET-SUPPLY-METAL1 (Figure 14-12, shown after initialization) and SHEET-SUPPLY-METAL2.

Instance: SHEET–METAL–SUPPLY1
Parents: SOURCE
-- Slots --
BREAKDOWN–FREQUENCY : 6000
CAPACITY : 30
CONTENTS: BATCH01
DOWNSTREAM : DISK–CUTTER
DURATION : 10
FAULT :
MAINTENANCE : UNNEEDED
MODEL–EDITOR–IMAGE : EDITOR–OBJECT–IMAGE–499
ON–CRITICAL–PATH : YES
PERFORMANCE : GOOD
SHUTDOWN : UNNEEDED
STATE : OK
UPSTREAM :

FIGURE 14-12. The SHEET-SUPPLY-METAL instance

As noted in the documentation of the SOURCE-INITIALIZATION slot, the function initializeSources will install the batches into the CONTENTS slot of the SOURCE instances referenced by SOURCE-INITIALIZATION.

These batches will serve as the "seeds" of the simulation. The batches are placed in the CONTENTS slot (a new slot defined on the COMPONENT frame) of SHEET-SUPPLY-METAL. By sending the appropriate start-up messages to SHEET-SUPPLY-METAL, we can start those batches rolling down the canning line.

The function initializeSources (Figure 14-13) uses the CONTENTS slot. This function steps through the values of the SOURCE-INITIALIZATION slot, installing the start-up items in each component's

```
--Initialize sources by scheduling them to send items.
--When a source sends an item, it also schedules itself to
--send another item. The SOURCE-INITIALIZATION slot contains
--subitems of the form <source component, items>
on initializeSources lineComponents
  global currentSchedule,currentLayout
  if lineComponents is empty then
    put getValue(currentLayout,"components") into components
  end if

  put getValue("current-simulation-parameters",
      "source-initialization") into initPairs
  repeat with i = 1 to the number of items in initPairs
    put item i of initPairs into Values
    put word 1 of Values into instance
    delete word 1 of Values
    --check if the initcomponent is on this line
    if instance is in components then
      --initialize the component's CONTENTS slot
      putValue instance, "contents",Values
      --component schedules itself
      sendMsg currentSchedule,"scheduleComponent",instance,
          last item of Values
    end if
  end repeat
end initializeSources
```

FIGURE 14-13. The initializeSources function

```
on sendItem component, itemName
  put getValue(component, "downstream") into downstream
  if downstream is not empty then
    sendItemControl component,downstream,itemName
  end if
end sendItem
```

FIGURE 14-14. The sendItem handler

CONTENTS slot. It then sends each component a sendItem message, cre-ating an event and adding it to the schedule. This process initializes the simulation, putting the first events on the calendar for factory start-up. The handler definition of sendItem for COMPONENT instances is displayed in Figure 14-14.

Because sendItem uses functions that will not be explained fully until the next section, our description will be somewhat cursory. The essence of sendItem is that it finds a downstream component (using the func-tion sendItemControl) that is ready to accept a new batch. Once such a component is found, the current schedule is sent a scheduleComponent message. The new batch is also put into the downstream component's CON-TENTS slot—this is the equivalent of starting that machine's processing of the item. Now, if another item comes along, that machine will be busy until the completion time, when another sendItem moves the item on down the line.

The handler scheduleComponent (discussed in the next section) cre-ates a new event and places it onto the calendar. This new event will, at some future time, send the scheduled ITEM from the component to one of the component's downstream components.

INITIALIZING THE SIMULATION

The initializeSimulation function (Figure 14-15) summarizes the ini-tialization process that must occur before the simulation can be run.

The following steps constitute the initialization process.

1. Initialize the global variables currentSchedule and current-Layout with the instance names appropriate for this scenario.

2. Remove all CONTENTS slot values (put "empty" in them) for com-ponent instances included in the layout to be simulated.

```
on initializeSimulation sched,layout
  global currentSchedule,currentLayout
  if sched is empty then
    put "current-schedule" into currentSchedule
  else put sched into currentSchedule
  if layout is empty then
    put "canning-line" into currentLayout
  else put layout into currentLayout
  --initialize content slots
  put getValue(currentLayout,"components") into line
  repeat with i = 1 to the number of items in line
    putValue item i of line,"contents",empty
  end repeat
  putValue currentSchedule,"calendar",empty
  putValue currentSchedule,"clock",0
  deleteAllEvents
  initializeScources lineComponents
end initializeSimulation
```

FIGURE 14-15. The initializeSimulation handler

3. Put values in the CONTENTS slot of all components in the simulation that act as external sources of material, for example, sheet metal for manufacturing the cans (start-up values are defined in the SOURCE-INITIALIZATION slot of CURRENT-SIMULATION-PARAMETERS).

4. Initialize the calendar by scheduling each source component with an item of material for transfer to one of its downstream components (send each source component instance a sendItem message in the initializeSources function).

Now that the simulation has all start-up requirements fulfilled, we'll explore ways of adding a dynamic element to the simulation—the ability to model changes to the environment over a simulated period of time.

RUNNING THE SIMULATION: REAL TIME

We can now represent the occurrence of an event at a particular time. We still need to incorporate a dynamic component into our model, however, to simulate time passing.

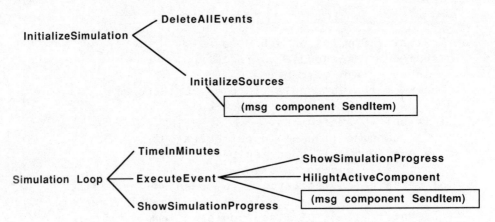

FIGURE 14-16. The function calls for initializing and running the simulation

Executing Events: The Simulation Loop

For most applications, it is desirable to run the simulation for a block of time. Our algorithm for running the simulation is as follows: Go into a continuous loop; during each iteration, perform these steps:

1. Calculate the current time and fetch the current schedule's calendar (we saw previously how individual events are assigned times and placed on a calendar).

2. Stop looping if the calendar contains no more events.

3. Find all events with a start time earlier than the current time.

4. Execute the events found in step 3 above and remove those executed events from the current schedule's calendar.

Event creation and scheduling occurs during event execution; now we'll take a look at this mechanism for tracking and executing a large number of events over an extended period.

Let's begin by examining a function-call diagram for the simulation functions. Figure 14-16 shows the functions for initializing and running the simulation.

The simulationLoop Function

The function simulationLoop (Figure 14-17) iterates continually, checking each event on the calendar and executing those that complete before or at the current time, until:

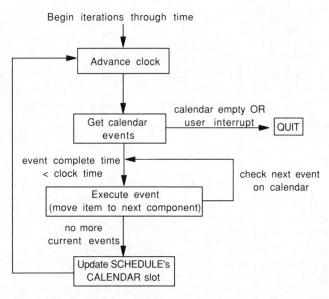

FIGURE 14-17. Flow of control in the simulationLoop function

- there are no more events waiting on the calendar or

- the user signals a stop

The numbered comments in the source code (Figure 14-18) for this function correspond to the numbered text items that follow. When the LOOP in simulationLoop begins executing:

1. Get the current calendar (from the CALENDAR slot of current-Schedule) and the current time (with the advanceClock handler). Initialize the list of events to execute, along with the new calendar.

2. If the current calendar is empty, RETURN from the LOOP (quit).

3. Go through the current calendar of events. Divide the events into those ready to be executed—executionList—and those that will execute in the future—newCalendar—by comparing completionTime to currentTime.

4. Install all future events—newCalendar—back onto the calendar. Execute those events ready to be executed—executionList. Print (display) the calendar, using the function showSimulation Progress.

```
on simulationLoop
  global userWantsToStop, currentSchedule
  --main loop of the simulation --look for event times
  --if the simulation is stopped for any reason, restart
  --this fcn... will restart the simulation where it was
  --stopped.
  repeat forever

    --** 1 **
    --initialize local variables for this iteration
    put getValue(currentSchedule, "calendar") into calendar
    put empty into executionList
    put empty into newCalendar
    sendMsg currentSchedule, "advanceClock"
    put getValue(currentSchedule, "clock") into Time

    --** 2 **
    --continue looping until no events are left on calendar
    if calendar is empty or userWantsToStop is true then
      exit repeat
    end if

    --** 3 **
    --find all events ready to execute on calendar
    repeat with i = 1 to the number of items in calendar
      put item i of calendar into event

                                                --(continue)
```

FIGURE 14-18. The simulationLoop function

The advanceClock Handler

The simulation clock (that is, the CLOCK slot of currentSchedule) is updated in simulationLoop when we send currentSchedule the advanceClock message (Figure 14-19). This message returns the new current time.

Note that advanceClock obtains the real-world time from the computer's internal time-of-day clock using *the seconds* and converts it to minutes.

```
    if getValue(event,"completion-time") <= Time then
      --ready to execute
      put event &"," after executionList
    --wait till later
    else put event &"," after newCalendar
  end repeat


  --** 4 **
  --execute collected events
  --(these in turn will add things to schedule)
  --create new sched
  putValue currentSchedule,"calendar",newCalendar
  put the number of items in executionList into
      numItems
  repeat with i = 1 to numItems
    executeEvent item i of executionList
  end repeat


  --Finally, PRINT a calendar report
  if executionList is not empty then
    showSimulationProgress "LOOP:the calendar is"&
        getValue(currentSchedule,"calendar")
    end if
  end repeat
end simulationLoop
```

FIGURE 14-18. (continued)

How Events are Executed

In the remainder of this section, we'll take a detailed look at how events are executed. Let's look at the calling sequence for executing events:

- In simulationLoop, for each executable event, call the executeEvent function.

- From executeEvent, send the event's OBJECT a sendItem message. This initiates the process of moving an item from an object to one of its downstream objects.

```
on advanceClock schedule
  putValue schedule,"clock",(the seconds/60)
end advanceClock
```

FIGURE 14-19. The advanceClock handler

- From the object's sendItem handler, call the sendItemControl function. This function controls the evaluation of available downstream components.

- From within sendItemControl, the following messages may be sent:

  · to components downstream of the sender:

  assessState
  —is the downstream component available (In the canning line, check if the CONTENTS slot contains an item.)

  acceptItem
  —if the component is available, then schedule the next activity for that component with the item and place the item in the new instance's CONTENTS slot.

  · to the sending component:

  CleanUp—remove the item from the sending component's CONTENTS slot.

  Wait—in situations where no downstream component is available, schedule the component to continue trying to send until a machine becomes available.

On the factory floor, all of the components have real-world analogs to these standard sets of messages (remember, though, that handlers with the same name may have different actions for different components). For example, a stamper feeds into a washer. Each of these components is defined as an instance of its class (e.g., WASHER-1 is an instance of WASHER). The sequence of events would be for the stamper to run its sendItem handler, which invokes the washer's assessState handler and, if that returns a value of true, then invokes the washer's acceptItem handler. Finally, the stamper's cleanUp handler would run.

Programming with objects allows us to define different code for the stamper's assessState handler and the washer's assessState handler. Stamper's handler will test to see whether an item is in its CONTENTS slot;

```
on executeEvent event
  --all events in our simple simulation are sendItem
  --messages
  showSimulationProgress "EXECUTING EVENT:"& event
  --highlight the component being executed
  highlightActiveComponent event
  put getValue(event,"item") into itemToSend
  sendMsg getValue(event,"object"),"sendItem",itemToSend
end executeEvent
```

FIGURE 14-20. The executeEvent function

washer's handler might test for both occupying items and the availability of washer fluid. The net result is that any component in the system can be invoked with an assessState handler and perform the action appropriate to its function.

The executeEvent Function

Events are executed with the function executeEvent (Figure 14-20), which sends the sendItem message (Figure 14-21) to the component associated with an event (the component is stored in the event's OBJECT slot). The sendItem message starts a chain of messages that ultimately will result in EVENT's ITEM being passed to the next component in the canning line, simulating the batch of cans being sent to the next processing station.

Figure 14-22 shows two handlers implementing the sendItem message. You may find it valuable to work through this section with frequent references to this diagram.

```
on sendItem component itemName
  put getValue(component, "downstream") into
    downstreamComponents
  if downstreamComponents is not empty then
    sendItemControl component,downstreamComponents,itemName
  end if
end sendItem
```

FIGURE 14-21. The sendItem handler

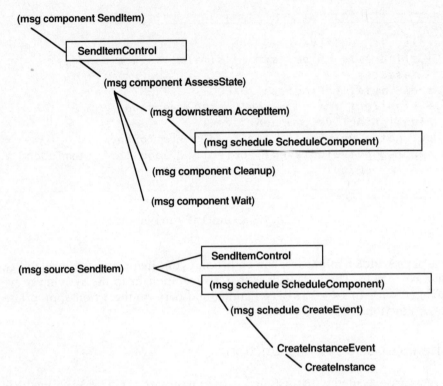

FIGURE 14-22. The send Item messages for COMPONENT and SOURCE

The function sendItemControl, used by the sendItem handler, implements the following algorithm, where ITEM is the item being sent to one of the components in the list downstreamComponents and COMPONENT is the component trying to send the item downstream:

1. If the function is called with ITEM set to empty (not set to any value), then set ITEM to the last thing in COMPONENT's CONTENTS slot (CONTENTS is thus a FIFO, a queue whose first item in is the first item out).

2. For each DOWNSTREAM component in downstreamComponents:

2a. Send DOWNSTREAM an assessState message, which returns the value OK if we can send the item downstream. Put the returned value in downstreamState.

2b. If downstreamState is OK:
    Send DOWNSTREAM an acceptItem message. This in turn sends a scheduleComponent message.
    Send COMPONENT a cleanup message.

Stop the loop through downstreamComponents, returning OK.

2c.   If downstreamState is WAIT:
Send COMPONENT a wait message.
Stop looping through downstreamComponents, returning "WAIT."

The sendItemControl source code is shown in Figure 14-23; the comments correspond to the preceding algorithm steps.

A simple version of an accessState handler is shown in Figure 14-24. The handler performs a test to see whether the component is busy by checking whether the CONTENTS slot is empty. If the slot value is empty, then the handler returns OK; otherwise it returns WAIT.

The acceptItem handler shown in Figure 14-25 is equally simple—accepting an item entails putting a new event on the schedule (scheduleComponent message) and placing the moved item in the downstream component's CONTENTS slot.

The scheduleComponent handler (Figure 14-26) creates a new event for a component containing the item itemName and adds the event to the schedule's calendar.

The cleanUp handler (Figure 14-27) removes the item from the upstream component's CONTENTS slot; in this simple case, we assume that a machine can hold only one item at a time, so putting "empty" into the CONTENTS slot is equivalent to removing the item.

The Calling Sequence for Executing Events

Finally, let's take one last overall look at the execution of events for one temporal cycle:

- In the SimulationLoop function, for each executable event (events whose time matches the CLOCK time), run the ExecuteEvent function.

- From within executeEvent, get the event's component (from the OBJECT slot) and send that component a sendItem message.

- From within that component's sendItem handler, run the send ItemControl function.

- From within sendItemControl, send the following message sets:
  - to components downstream of the sender,
    AssessState
    AcceptItem (which sends scheduleComponent)
  - to the sending component,
    cleanup or
    wait

```
on sendItemControl component,downstreamComponents,item

--** 1 **
  --Get the last thing in CONTENTS if not passed
  --an item (FIFO)
  if item is empty then
    put last item of getValue(component,"contents")
        into item
  end if

--** 2 **
  --simple case -- try each component until one accepts
  --then quit
  --an accept is either OK, WAIT, or NONOPERATIONAL
  repeat with i = 1 to the number of items in
      downstreamComponents
    put item i of downstreamComponents into downstream

    --** 2a **
    --How is DOWNSTREAM doing?
    sendMsg downstream,"assessState"
    put the result into receiveState

    --** 2b **
    if receiveState is "OK" then
      showSimulationProgress "SEND-ITEM:"&component&&
          item&downstream
      sendMsg downstream,"acceptItem",item
      sendMsg component,"cleanup",item
      --quit the loop
      exit repeat
    end if
  end repeat

  --** 2c **
  if receiveState is "WAIT" then
    sendMsg component "wait",item
    showSimulationProgress "ITEM waiting"&&item&&
        component&&downstream
  end if
end sendItemControl
```

FIGURE 14-23. The sendItemControl function

```
on assessState component
  if getValue(component,"contents") is not empty then
    return "WAIT"
  else return "OK"
end assessState
```

FIGURE 14-24. The assessState handler

```
on acceptItem comp,item
  global currentSchedule
  putValue component,"contents",item
  sendmsg currentSchedule,"scheduleComponent",comp,item
end acceptItem
```

FIGURE 14-25. The acceptItem handler

```
on scheduleComponent schedule,component,item
  put getValue(schedule,"calender") into calendar
  sendMsg schedule,"createEvent",component,item
  --returns new event
  put the result & "," & calendar into newCalendar
  --add event to calendar.
  putValue schedule,"calendar",newCalendar
end scheduleComponent
```

FIGURE 14-26. The scheduleComponent handler

```
on cleanUp component,item
  putValue component,"contents",empty
end cleanUp
```

FIGURE 14-27. The cleanUp handler

This cycle will continue to run as long as events remain on the calendar. Each cycle will continue to place events on the calendar until the source components no longer have any items in their CONTENTS slots and all other items have worked their way through to the end of the line.

The function SimulationLoop, as developed in the preceding section, used a simple mechanism for advancing simulation time: It read the computer hardware's time-of-day clock and then executed any events whose START-TIME slot value was less than (earlier) or equal to the time read from the clock. When an event was created, the start and end times stored on the event were relative to the computer's internal time clock.

In this section, we will work out a more efficient technique for advancing simulation time, useful when long time periods are to be simulated. This technique involves

- sorting the simulation CALENDAR from earliest to latest COMPLE-TION-TIME each time a new event is created

- setting the simulation CLOCK to the COMPLETION-TIME of the event at the front of the CALENDAR (the "earliest" remaining event)

- processing all events on the CALENDAR whose COMPLETION-TIME equals the value of CLOCK

As we'll see, the new technique is considerably more efficient in terms of the length of time the simulation takes to simulate a block of time. Consequently, it is more suitable for simulating a large number of events occurring over a long period of time. The clock advances immediately to the next event to be executed on the simulation calendar; if large intervals of blank time (when no event is starting or stopping) exist, they will be skipped. Our original technique, on the other hand, advanced the clock in concert with the computer's real-time clock. Thus, many simulation cycles had no event active.

Real-time simulations are tedious if the simulated times are long compared with the time required for computing the simulation. Use of the actual time *is* appropriate, however, if the simulation is being fed data in real time by external data sources, for example, when used in a training scenario where end users are interfacing with the simulation as if it were the real plant.

Changes for the New Simulation Time Method

To implement the new technique for advancing simulation time, we have modified a number of the functions and handlers of the preceding sections.

We've appended a "2" to the names of these modified functions and handlers. Thus the new version of simulationLoop is called simulationLoop2, the advanceClock handler becomes AdvanceClock2, and so forth.

To clearly indicate the modifications themselves, we have inserted the comment

—— ** Alternative #2 **

in the source code of these functions and handlers wherever these modifications exist.

To implement the new time-advancing technique, we have made substantive modifications in three places. All three modifications occur in handlers of the SCHEDULE frame:

- advancing the clock (advanceClock)

- scheduling new events (scheduleComponent)

- applying the test to decide whether events should be executed (execute?)

All other necessary changes to functions and handlers involve name changes only. For example, simulationLoop2 sends the advanceClock2 message, whereas the original simulationLoop sends advanceClock.

The simulationLoop2 Function

The new function simulationLoop2 uses the same algorithm as simulationLoop:

1. Calculate the current simulation time and fetch the current schedule's calendar.

2. Stop looping if the calendar is empty.

3. Find all events with a start time earlier than the current time.

4. Execute the events found in step 3 above and remove those executed events from the current schedule's calendar.

The only differences from the original simulations are, as mentioned above, changes in the called functions advanceCheck2 and execute-Event2.

Actually, there is one other change: The original loop required a < = comparison between the simulation clock time and the event start time. A less than or equal test was used because in a large simulation events might

```
on advanceClock schedule
  putValue schedule,"clock",the seconds/60
end advanceClock
```

FIGURE 14-28. The advanceClock handler

pile up more quickly than the system could process them. For example, if there were a dozen events each scheduled for 342 and 343 minutes past midnight, and the system could process six events per minute, it would be minute 344 (real time) before the minute-343 events could be handled. The new simulation loop would simply take as long as needed to process the minute-342 events and thus uses an = comparison. Only after all of those events were process would the loop advance the simulation time to minute 343.

Changes to the advanceClock Handler

In the original function simulationLoop, the advanceClock handler (Figure 14-28) was used to update the value of the CLOCK slot of the currently active schedule instance. This handler determined the new value of CLOCK by calling the function timeInMinutes. This function used the computer's real-time clock to calculate the simulation time.

The new top-level function simulationLoop2, sends the schedule an advanceClock2 message (Figure 14-29), which sets the new CLOCK slot value for currentSchedule. This function is the real change from our original simulation loop. Unlike advanceClock, which used fixed increments of real time to set the clock, advanceClock2 grabs the first event in the schedule instance's CALENDAR slot and advances the clock to that event's

```
on advanceClock2 schedule
  put item 1 of getValue(schedule,"calendar") into nextEvent
  if nextEvent is not empty then
    put getValue(nextEvent,"completion-time") into nextTime
    putValue schedule,"clock",nextTime
  end if
end advanceClock2
```

FIGURE 14-29. The advanceClock2 handler

completion time. Now, by definition, the next event is ready to execute as well as all other events with this start time.

We also have to modify slightly another SCHEDULE message, scheduleComponent, the message sent by the acceptItem and sendItem handlers. Formerly, new events were added to the end of the calender. Ordering events by time on the calendar was not important because the start times for all events were checked at each loop of the simulation. Now, however, advanceClock2 expects that the first event on the calendar will be the next to execute; now, when a component is scheduled, the calendar must be sorted so that the event at the front of the list contains the component next to complete activity and sends its material downstream.

INTERFACE

Finally, we must look at the simulation interface. Of course, we really don't need any particular interface to run the simulation. The components are represented by instances, the simulation code is represented by messages on these objects, and the calendar and clock have been defined as new instances. Thus, we can run the simulation by sending a message to initialize, then starting the simulation loop.

The previous chapter discussed in detail a model editor. The interface for this editor is one possibility for our simulation—the decision depends on what we wish to do with the simulation. If we are simply going to use a set configuration, with very occasional changes to the layout, then a more simple input/output interface is possible. However, if part of our modeling purpose is to try out different configurations, then we are going to have serious problems with anything short of a graphical editor. Figure 14-30 illustrates a highly graphic interface to a simulation of an international shipping network. Here, the objects and links were superimposed on a map to provide a spatial context for the knowledge base.

One possibility is to have both a graphical and a tabular interface. A good candidate for setting initial parameters and evaluating output is a spreadsheet. The spreadsheet shown in Figure 14-31 illustrates how slot values for simulation instances can be translated into a spreadsheet cell format. Figure 14-32 illustrates a simple graphic layout that might complement the spreadsheet.

Data Collection/Data Base Link

Because simulations are frequently used to examine alternate strategies, it is often desirable to save data for later analysis and comparison. In the same way that we defined graphic image frames, we can create a data collector

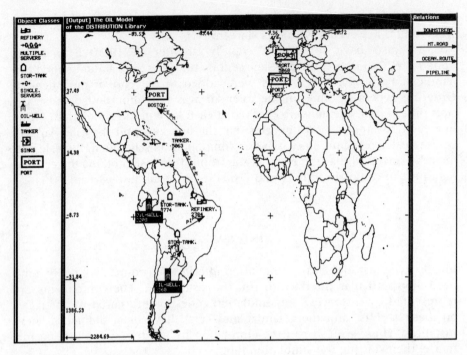

FIGURE 14-30. Global map interface for oil distribution model (Courtesy of IntelliCorp)

FIGURE 14-31. Spreadsheet containing translation of instance slot values

	contents	total cumulative contents	pressure
metal-disk-oiler	batch-48	23	
can-stamper-1	batch-47	10	
washer 1	batch-45	9	normal
can-stamper-2	batch-46	12	
washer 2	batch-44	11	normal
can-coater	batch-49	18	
rinse-pump			normal

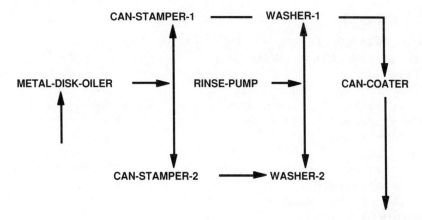

FIGURE 14-32. Partial canning-line flow diagram linked to spreadsheet

frame (Figure 14-33) and use the same mechanism for dynamically collecting data. As was done with the graphic image, we create an instance of the data collector frame, and link it to the monitored slot using a daemon.

In this example, our data collector will write the data directly to a spreadsheet file (or any data base file). Each data collector is mapped to a row in the spreadsheet, with each successive column containing a data sample for incremental time periods. The default row starts with 1—as collectors are added, this will be incremented. The default column is 2 (column 1 is used for the instance name).

Each time the value of the slot changes, the daemon is invoked. The function called by this daemon is shown in Figure 14-34. This function first looks at the monitored slot's data collector facet to find the data collector instance. Then, it checks to see whether the data collector is active (ACTIVE? slot on the data-collector instance). If active, it uses the row and column slots of the instance to find the spreadsheet cell. Finally, it places the new value into the spreadsheet cell. The function updateSpreadsheet is shell and spreadsheet-package dependent, but it will contain a routine that will write into a data file, translating the row and column information into a data location in the format used by the spreadsheet package.

The process just described is a mechanism for actively monitoring changing slot values and dynamically updating a spreadsheet or data base. A more simple alternative would be to create a frame with a slot for each monitored slot. Slots would be removed or added as different slots were monitored. The slot value would be a list containing the monitored instance and slot and the cell row and column. A simple function would iterate through all the slots, getting each monitored slot value and then placing it into the spreadsheet cell.

Frame: **DATA-COLLECTOR**
Parents: **SIMULATION-FRAME**
--Slots--
ACTIVE? : YES
Documentation: When :no, the collector remains attached
   but no data are collected
Constraints: YES NO
COLUMN : 2
Documentation: Used by spreadsheet data collectors to keep
   track of column in spreadsheet to write or read.
   A list of the (component slot last-column-written)
SPREADSHEET :
Documentation: The name of the spreadsheet data will be
   written to
MONITORED-OBJECT :
Documentation: A pair containing--instance slot--of the
   object monitored
ROW : 1
Documentation: Used by spreadsheet data collectors to keep
   track of row in spreadsheet to write or read

FIGURE 14-33. Data collector frame

```
function WriteToSpreadsheet inst,slot,new,old
  put getFacetValue(inst,slot,"dataCollector")
     into CInst
  put getValue(CInst,"spreadsheet") into spreadsheetName
  put getValue(CInst,"row") into row
  put getValue(CInst,"column") into column
  updateSpreadsheet spreadsheetName,row,column
end WriteToSpreadsheet
```

FIGURE 14-34. The writeToSpreadsheet daemon

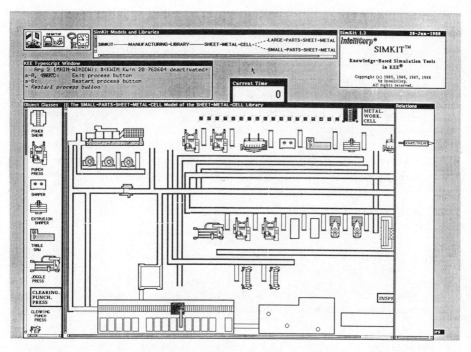

FIGURE 14-35. Flexible cell manufacturing line (Northrop) (Courtesy of IntelliCorp)

Finally, let's take a look at a sophisticated simulation interface. In the factory pictured in Figure 14-35, the arrows of Figure 14-32 have been changed to pictures of conveyor belts. Flow of product along the lines has also been animated by showing the objects as they progress along the conveyors. Finally, the component names have been replaced by graphical icons that visually cue the operators to their function.

SUMMARY

The discovery of layout problems at the plant came about somewhat accidentally, as a result of the simulation implementation, creating in turn a whole new purpose for the simulation. The designers responsible for plant layout and design suddenly became interested in the simulation/expert system combination. What they had discovered was an ideal environment for exploring where to place sensors and generating test and repair scenarios. The simulation allowed them to move components, add and remove sensors, and so on, and the expert system allowed them to test the related fault procedures. They quickly discovered three sensors that could be replaced with a single sensor in a slightly different location on the line and were sold on the project.

The moral of this story is that there are many uses of simulation in the expert system environment: sampling external sensors, testing the expert system rules, training less experienced end users about their domain, and designing extensions to the domain, to name only a few.

The simulation can be as simple as asserting a set of conditions to simulate the states of all objects at the moment when a fault occurs. Or, as described in this chapter, the simulation can be a dynamic model of passing time, with temporal interactions occurring that mimic events that might occur in the real world. The simulation techniques developed in this chapter also provide a mechanism for polling external sensors and other data sources for information to be used in the expert system's inferencing.

READINGS

Birtwistle, G., ed. 1985. *AI, graphics and simulation*. La Jolla, CA: The Society for Computer Simulation.

Faught, W. S., P. Klahr, and G. R. Martins. 1980. An artificial intelligence approach to large-scale simulation. *Proceedings of the 1980 Summer Simulation Conference, Seattle, WA*: 231–236.

Holan, J. D., E. L. Hutchins, and L. Weitzman. 1984. STEAMER: An interactive inspectable simulation-based training system. *AI Magazine* 5, no. 2: 15–27.

Malin, J.T., and R.A. Harris. 1988. CONFIG Project: Adapting qualitative modeling and discrete event simulation to support development of diagnostic systems. AAAI-88 Workshop on Artificial Intelligence and Process Engineering. St. Paul, MN.

Melamed, B., and R. J. T. Morris. 1985. Visual simulation: The performance analysis workstation. *Computer*, August.

Moser, J. G. 1986. Integration of artificial intelligence and simulation in a comprehensive decision-support system. *Simulation* 47, no. 6: 223–229.

Payne, E. C. 1985. The integration of traditional simulation with expert systems and AI knowledge representation. *Approximate reasoning in expert systems*, ed. M. Gupta. North-Holland.

Rosenfield, D. B., W. Copacino, and E. C. Payne. 1985. Logistics planning and evaluation using "what-if" simulation. *J. of Business Logistics*, 6, no. 2: 89–109.

15

INTERFACING TO THE OUTSIDE WORLD

M any times, the expert system must be connected to the external
environment. In some cases, the expert system will require external
data from sensors and other devices or from external data bases. In
other cases, the expert system will need to control the actions of external devices, either to gather more information or to change settings and so on as
a result of the expert system's advice. Finally, we may wish to control external
devices that provide some type of additional support to the user of the expert
system such as multimedia sound and vision.

EXTERNAL DATA INPUTS

Although external data may take many forms, internal translation of the data
for use by the expert system is always the same. Once the data have been
moved into the knowledge-base environment, a transformation is performed
converting the data from a stream of characters into assertions of facts.

Access to software resident on the same computer as the expert system
but in another software environment is done through software within the
knowledge base. In other cases, the data are external to the expert system's
hardware and must be accessed through both software and hardware—a bus
or a serial or a parallel port through either a net or direct interface into the
computer. In either case, access of the data may be direct (to the external
port or other software generating the number) or through shared data files
(the expert system and the external data source can both read and write a
common file but cannot directly communicate with one another).

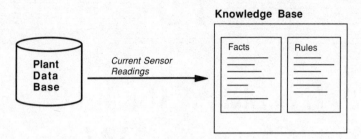

FIGURE 15-1. Separating the knowledge base from the data base

Integrating a Knowledge Base with a Data Base

Two options exist for integrating a knowledge base with a data base. If the data base already exists and will not be redesigned, then the configuration will usually consist of a stand-alone expert system reading information from the data base, converting that information into the knowledge-base format, and then reasoning on the information (Figure 15-1). However, if the data base is being designed in conjunction with the knowledge base (or can be easily modified), then the designer should also consider the option of **embedding** the expert system within the data base. Then, each time key items are changed, the expert system will be invoked—from the users' point of view, they never leave the data-base environment.

A major integration consideration concerns how the two systems will interact: Does the knowledge base request data from the data base (Figure 15-2(a)), or does the data base periodically send data to the knowledge base (Figure 15-2(b))? If the knowledge base requests data, how does it decide when those data are needed? If the data base sends data to the knowledge base, what is the format? Do they communicate on a record-by-record basis—via a network, for example—or by way of a temporary extract file created by the data base?

To simplify matters in our example application, we assumed that the mechanism for moving sensor readings from the plant data base into our canning-line knowledge base used existing utilities in the implementation shell. Our only job was to map the data definitions to the instance slot values (Chapter 14).

Temporal Data

Problems can arise if the expert system's analysis time is longer than the periods between data updates. This can occur if one or more of the following temporal conditions are true:

- The problem domain concerns a highly dynamic phenomenon that changes very rapidly,

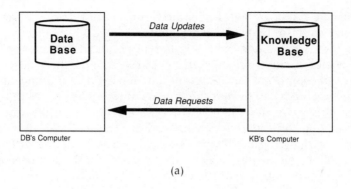

(a)

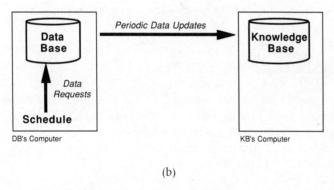

(b)

FIGURE 15-2. Alternatives for linking a knowledge base to a data base

- The data-transfer method for moving data from the data base to the knowledge base is very slow,

- The analysis computation time (within the expert system) is very long.

NOTE: Time measurements are relative to the domain—if changes occur in the domain every second then minutes could be very slow. On the other hand, if domain activity occurs over hourly periods, minutes could be quite fast.

In a highly dynamic situation, for the system to reach a new conclusion it must sometimes be possible to determine the date or time a data item was measured. One extreme method is to time-stamp all observations in the knowledge base, including any conclusions reached by the expert system. More often, we need record the sampling time of only a few key parameters.

Often, specific rule logic will be required for determining to what extent a given conclusion can be believed at a given moment.

Changes in data often occur at different points in time and with different frequencies or rates of change. In some applications, these differing rates of change can complicate the process of transferring data into the knowledge base and deciding when to start the process of reasoning about the changes. In the canning plant, for example, there is a wide range of sampling frequencies among the different sensor readings. Figure 15-3 illustrates this graphically by showing the relative frequencies for updating different sensor readings for a single pump—every few minutes for the sensor monitoring rpm and hourly monitoring of the oil level.

Fortunately, we are able to ignore data-frequency difficulties in the canning plant application, because our analysis concerns mechanical problems that are slow to develop. If we were performing a trend analysis, on the other hand, we might have to take the various sampling frequencies into account.

Using Sensor Data

Sensor data are pieces of information from the external environment that have been converted into digital signals. These digital signals can then be entered into the computer (in the same way that information is entered using a modem or a local area network) and translated into information meaningful to the expert system.

Let's take a simple example of how this might work using a Universal Lab Interface board (Figure 15-4) sold by Creative Technologies. This board has a number of inputs, allowing the simultaneous interfacing of up to eight different sensors to the computer. This is primarily an experimental board, and so has a variety of inputs for different types of devices; e.g. digital in and out, voltage in, and resistive in.

In our example, we'll attach a single sensor to measure temperature. To interpret data from our board requires three steps: hooking the sensors to their environment, writing the functions that will translate the incoming

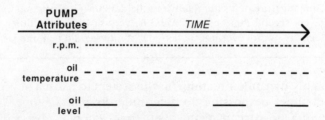

FIGURE 15-3. Examples of different data frequencies from pump sensors

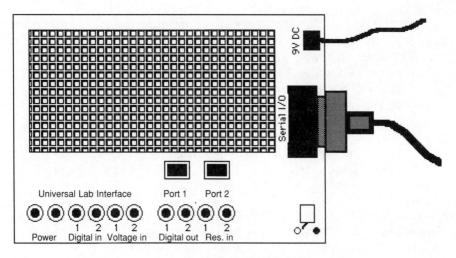

FIGURE 15-4. Universal Lab Interface with sensors

data into a form our expert system can use, and calibrating the sensors. In the case of our sensors, calibration is a combination of two steps: linking the sensor to a set of known values and translating the sensor information into a form that the expert system can recognize.

We have defined a sensor-reading function, Sensor (Figure 15-5). This function makes use of HyperTalk XFNS sendSport (send request to the serial port) and recvUpTo (receive data from the serial port) distributed by the Apple Programmers and Developers Association (APDA™) as part of their package for reading information from a serial port. This program requests information from the serial port and then provides that information to the translation program. Encoded numeric values from this function are then converted into actual temperature values. Rules (or functions) can further convert these values to qualitative measures such as NORMAL or HIGH.

In the test versions of the canning plant system, whenever the rules required unknown slot values during backward chaining, the operator was queried for those values with choice menus. The queries arose during the consideration of FAULT-CONDITIONs: in the queryFinding function and, when a manual observation was required, in the askOperatorWhenUnknown function.

Once the connection and calibration of sensors were finished, the interactive question-and-answer requests for data were partially replaced with procedures carried out automatically, with no operator intervention required.

For example, many of the required slot values were actually qualitative versions of numerical sensor data, such as PRESSURE and TEMPERATURE. In these cases, we were able to access the sensors directly. The sampling frequency was set to that of the most frequently changing data. The incoming data were then filtered

```
Function Sensor Mode
  --USE XFNS drivers to read and write serial port,
  --returning value
  --TELL THE BOARD WHICH SENSOR(S) TO READ
  sendSPort Mode & return
  --GET THE DATA FROM THE BOARD
  --if "check" IS returned the Sensor is not plugged in
  if line 1 of recvUpTo(return,4,empty) = "Check" then
    answer "Check that the Sensor is working properly"
    exit Sensor
  end if
  put (line 1 of recvUpTo(return,9,empty)) into FromSensor
  sendSPort numToChar(3) --Turn off Sensor
  return FromSensor
end Sensor
```

FIGURE 15-5. Function to read sensor data

for each type of sensor, and we asserted only those values that had shown a significant change from the last reading. Rules were added to translate the numerical values into the qualitative measures (e.g., LOW, MEDIUM, and HIGH) used previously (Figure 15-6). Note the new slot, SENSOR-TEMPERATURE. We have separate slots for the sensor readings for two reasons: we get a chance to apply filter rules to see whether significant changes have taken place when the value is updated (one of the disadvantages of qualitative data is that there is no such thing as "1 degree lower than low") and the rules need a slot for both the qualitative and quantitative values.

In some cases, it is difficult to imagine that the user could be bypassed. The analysis of certain pump problems in the plant, for example, requires that the operator distinguish between a "grinding" and "squealing" noise. Even though it might be possible to analyze the pump sounds for certain signatures using pattern-recognition techniques, it is not likely to be cost-effective.

Automatic Accessing of External Data

As we have seen in previous chapters, expert systems can operate in either a data-driven (forward chaining) or a data-requesting (backward chaining) mode. In the case of forward chaining, we would like the data to be sent

---

Rule: **LOW–WASH–TANK–TEMP**
Rule Set: **QUANTITATIVE–TO–QUALITATIVE**
Documentation: When the temperature of a wash tank is
  below 150° then the temperature is LOW.
IF
  ?WASH–TANK IS A TANK
  AND
  THE SENSOR–TEMPERATURE OF ?WASH–TANK IS ?T
  AND
  ?T < 150
THEN
  THE TEMPERATURE OF ?WASH–TANK IS LOW

FIGURE 15-6. A rule for converting numeric information into qualitative values

regularly to the expert system and the inferencing to be driven by the arrival of new data. In backward chaining, we want the rules to access a slot, which in turn requests updated data.

Automatic accessing of external data from within the knowledge base can be implemented in several ways including:

- installing daemons on the slots to be polled automatically

- writing functions that access slot values from the rules

These two options differ considerably. If daemons are attached to slots, automatic accessing will occur every time those slots' values are retrieved. In situations where the slot is pointing at external data, we will need further information on the slot indicating where to retrieve the external data from— for example, we might add a slot facet that specifies the file and the position in that file where the data will be found.

Most expert shells have a facility for firing both a when-accessed (a request for the slot value) and a when-modified (a modification of the slot value) daemon. For automatic polling to occur whenever a slot's value is retrieved (as opposed to modified), a when-accessed daemon must be installed.

Care should be taken when installing a when-accessed daemon during application development. If the daemon requires a considerable time to execute, every request for the slot's value will cause the daemon to execute— often not the desired behavior. The daemons also may cause inadvertent side-effects to occur elsewhere in the knowledge base. Since the execution of daemons is usually transparent, no warning may be given to the developer.

A very common problem is locking into an infinite cycle, when a daemon fires the rules that update the slot that fires the rules, *ad infinitum.*

The other method of accessing external data is to write one or more functions that are called from the rules. In the canning plant application, we could implement automatic polling—and bypass the use of operator-supplied information altogether—by modifying the two operator-query functions, askOperatorWhenUnknown and askOperatorToFind. Because all querying of slot values related to the QC analysis uses only these two functions, no other modifications are required. If we were to do this, we would need to add a facet to each slot that had an external data reference and then access that facet to retrieve the data.

An alternative to adding the facet would be to make the actual slot value be the pointer to the external data. This approach is useful in situations where the shell does not have a facet feature, but can be confusing—a developer inspecting the slot value does not see the real value. With a facet or daemon, the connection to the external data is obvious, but with a function unconnected to the slot it can be difficult to understand or locate the mechanism for the data retrieval.

Finally, for the case of forward chaining, where it is the updates that drive the inferencing (backward chaining requests the updates), we might use a mechanism similar to the simulation loop described in Chapter 14. The simulation function iterates "forever" on a timed cycle. Within that loop, we can insert requests for external data followed by an invocation of the forward chainer. If significant changes have occurred during the data update, forward-chaining rules will then fire.

MULTIMEDIA

The term **multimedia** refers to the control of multiple media devices and tools by the computer. These media include:

- vision: videodisc, animation, digitized images
- sound: CD recordings, synthesized sound

When used in conjunction with an expert system, sound and vision can provide support for users during both the inferencing process, when the rules may request information, and afterward when the rules provide advice.

Video Options

Video can be incorporated into expert systems in several ways. Visual aids can guide the user (in all these cases the user is the end user of the expert system, not the developers) in gathering the information requested by a rule; for example, a rule requesting that an operator determine whether a sprayer is producing an even rinse pattern might first show a short video segment of a properly working sprayer. The expert system might also present users with visual rather than textual choices of hypotheses before beginning backward chaining. For example, instead of textual choice menus, an operator suspecting a quality problem in a can might choose from a menu containing pictures of different can problems (Figure 15-7 shows an example of a menu combining text with picture options relevant to an art historian).

Another use for images is to provide a still picture on which the user can select active regions. In Figure 15-8, the user is diagnosing circuit boards. As the expert system works through the diagnosis, successive pictures shown on the screen illustrate different views of the hardware, with mouse-active indicators pointing to the areas requiring investigation.

At the conclusion of inferencing, the consequent of the rules might provide advice in the form of a short video sequence, for example, a video sequence of an expert maintenance worker fixing a clogged sprayer nozzle.

Video training tapes are nothing new. The problem is their linear, sequential format and the consequent difficulty in cueing to a particular sequence. What is required is for the expert system to immediately show

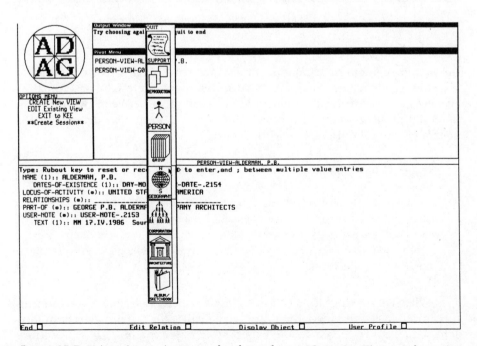

FIGURE 15-7. Using pictures in menus for the end user (Getty Art History Information Program)

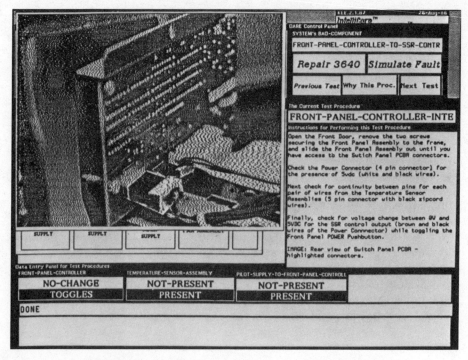

FIGURE 15-8. Circuit board diagnosis (Courtesy of IntelliCorp)

the proper segment or segments of the video for a given situation, building a custom sequence on the fly. In the canning plant, we might wish to show an operator how to repair a machine or distinguish between two different potential problems—for each new failure type, a unique sequence must be generated. Recall our session with George:

> Next, George explained the procedure for shutting down a washer. This procedure was posted, but perhaps not as obviously as it could have been. George also showed how the washer nozzle could be taken off, where the cleaning tank was located, and how to pour the solvent. Finally, he showed us how to re-install the nozzle, then how to restart the washer. Although none of it was very complicated, it was easy to see how an inexperienced operator could make a mistake, especially in the heat of the moment.

What we need to do is capture these sequences of experts performing specialized tasks on video, then provide a facility for rapid playback of random sequences triggered by the expert system, for example, as a procedure in the premise or conclusion of a rule.

Even if motion is not desired, many problems require a large number of still photographs. Again, let's visit George at the plant:

> Finally, George led us directly to a detailed description of the clogging problem, buried inside two operations manuals. The language in the manuals was almost incomprehensible, although the photographs and diagrams were quite useful. The pages containing the most useful photographs and diagrams were well worn with use.

Again, books and manuals present fixed, linear sequences, whereas we need to present the user items ordered with relevance to the problem at hand. To meet this requirement, optical media are available, including such technologies as videodisc (read-only), CD-ROM (compact-disc–read-only-memory), and the newer Digital Video Interactive(DVI). These technologies have the desired features of mass reproducibility and random access under computer control. The advantage of disc media over linear media such as manuals and video tape is the ability to juxtapose or resequence related materials dynamically.

One of the limitations of optical media is the problem of editing and updating—once the disk is written, it cannot be changed. WORM(write once, read many) and erasable discs provide these capabilities, but because of their relatively high price and low portability, they are only practical for very large applications (over 500 megabytes). Thus, they are more suited to mass storage than information distribution.

CD-ROM technology enables developers to cheaply store large quantities of information very compactly (approximately 650 megabytes), but it does not have sufficiently rapid retrieval to provide real-time video playback. Thus, it is particularly useful for systems that have large amounts of text or digitized pictures and sound. CD-ROM is also the oldest technology and consequently has the greatest portability among different hardware. Unfortunately, CD-ROM drives are the slowest optical medium, even slower than a floppy-disk drive, making them impractical for applications that jump quickly to multiple retrieval locations.

Videodisc is suited to both stills and real-time playback sequences, but it is a less available medium than CD-ROM. Videodiscs allow two formats for images and sound: continous (which is not computer accessible) or analog. In the analog format, about 54,000 images can be stored; CD-ROM can store only about 500-4000 images in digital format (CD-ROM is optimized for text and in this medium far outperforms the videodisc). Analog videodisc images can be formatted either as CAV or CLV: CAV (constant angular velocity) provides one-half hour per side, with each of the 54,000 frames internally coded and accessible. Constant linear velocity (CLV) formatted discs have twice as much information per side (one hour) but the computer can access only chapters (large blocks of frames) instead of individual frames.

Applying Video Technology

To incorporate video technology into an expert system requires knowledge engineering similar to writing rules; all aspects of how the expert performs the tasks to be videoed must be scripted in advance. Next, video tapes are made of the required sequences following these scripts. These tapes are then edited and transfered to a video disc. Finally, each still and sequence is logged, with start and end points noted. Using these sequence numbers, a playVideo command can be added as either a line in a function invoked by a rule or as a direct invocation from a rule antecedent (e.g.,request for visual confirmation of a statement) or consequent (e.g., visual instructions complementing the advice being given).

> At the plant, George and other operators demonstrated the various techniques and "tricks" they use for testing for and identifying problems. Once a final tape was made, a master was created, and replicate videodiscs were produced from multiple pressings (like a record), one copy for each workstation at each of the plants. Now, when an operator was requested to fix a clogged sprayer, the video screen would spring to life with a detailed demonstration of George in action.

Animation

Animation can be used to display concepts that are not clear in pictures or words. Often, these are conceptual ideas. For example, an animation might use sensor data to show the changes over time in the temperature of a machine or the trends in economic data. Animation is particuarly effective with data that change over time because of the time element inherent to motion sequences.

Digital video effects fall under the same category as animation. Analog video images are converted into digital data, geometric transforms are applied, and then the digital data are reconverted to analog video at a rate of 30 frames per second (one million bytes per frame).

Sound

Sound can be output in two forms: on a CD controlled by the computer or as a synthesized sound. Sound can also be used as input to control the computer using voice recognition software and hardware, an emerging technology that will find wide usage in situations where the user needs both hands for activities other than interacting with the computer.

CDs are practical if the distribution is going to be large (in the hundreds or thousands). Synthesized sound is more versatile, though often lower in reproductive quality.

Synthesis can be either stored in the computer or generated. Stored sounds are first recorded as an analog signal using a microphone and then digitized and stored on a computer disk. Software in the computer then retrieves the digital information and converts it back to analog, playing the analog signal through either a built-in computer speaker or an external device. Sounds stored in this manner are quite flexible, because they can be edited and altered but require a fair amount of computer storage. Software also exists for generating sounds from scratch including programs that convert written words into speech.

Stored sounds are useful for exactly reproducing a particular sound, for example, the sound a machine makes when the revolutions-per-minute (rpm) rate is exceeding safe limits. Generated sounds are useful when the nature of the sound may vary based on changing data. A perfect example of this is the human voice–speech synthesizers can turn generated text sentences into speech.

SUMMARY

Connections between the expert system and the external environment can take many forms. Using these connections, the expert system can retrieve or update data, manipulate external devices, and control multimedia supplements to knowledge-base information for the user.

Although making the software connections is relatively simple, creating links that meaningfully enhance the expert system can be as time consuming as building the expert system itself. A well-made videodisc supplement to an expert system can cost many thousands of dollars to design and produce. Large data bases require correspondingly large resources to build and maintain. And embedding the expert system within an external environment requires careful thought as to how and when the expert system will be invoked and how it will interface with the front-end application.

READINGS

Ambron, S., and K. Hooper, eds. 1988. *Interactive multimedia.* Bellevue, WA: Microsoft Press.

Apple Computer, Inc. 1988. Multimedia production: A set of three reports. *Apple Multimedia Lab Technical Report* no. 14. Cupertino, CA.

Apple Computer, Inc. 1988. Interactive multimedia design 1988. *Apple Multimedia Lab Technical Report* no. 13. Cupertino, CA.

Feiner, S., S. Nagy, and A. van Dam. 1982. An experimental system for creating and presenting interactive graphical documents. *Trans. Graphics* 1, no. 1.

Meyrowitz, N. 1986. Intermedia: The architecture and construction of an object-oriented hypermedia system and applications framework. *OOPSLA 1986 Proceedings.* Portland, OR, September.

Shneiderman, B. 1987. User interface design for the hyperteis electronic encyclopedia. *Hypertext 1987 Papers.* Chapel Hill, NC, November.

A

GENERIC SHELL PROGRAMMING AND RULE OPERATORS

T his appendix contains descriptions of a subset of generic programming and rule operators for different shells. Each shell contains many
more operators, but this set should serve as a quick guide to assessing
differences/similarities between the examples in the text and the various
commercial shells.

PROGRAMMING OPERATORS

The operators provide access via programming to the data structures in
the knowledge base. KEE and GoldWorks operators are defined in LISP.
ADS uses an internal language KDL which contains somewhat English-
style constructs. LEVEL5 uses an internal language PRL. Blanks in the table
indicate the authors' inability to confirm information (See Table, pp. 358–
359).

RULE CLAUSES IN DIFFERENT EXPERT SYSTEM SHELLS

This section contains a selected set of rule-clause patterns implemented in
different shells. Use these comparisons to translate the examples in the book
into the different expert system shells. In these examples, the following
values are used:

frame: **PUMP**

instance: **PUMP 1, TANK 1**

SLOT ACCESSOR FUNCTIONS

Function Descriptions	Book Examples	KEE 3.1	GoldWorks 2.0	KBMS	NEXPERT 1.1	ADS	LEVEL5
get slot value	getValue	get.value get.values	slot-value slot-all-values	select	getAtomInfo	instance.slot*	instance. attribute
replace slot value	putValue	put.value put.values	setf: slot-value or slot-all-values	update	Volunteer	instance.slot = value	instance. attribute : = value
add value to slot		add.value	slot-add-value	insert	NA1	add value to instance.slot	instance attribute : = value
get facet value	getFacetValue	slot.facet.value	slot-facet	NA2	getAtomInfo 2	NA2	NA2
set facet value	putFacetValue	put.facet.value	setf slot-facet	NA2	NA2	NA2	NA2

INFERENCE ENGINE FUNCTIONS

Function Descriptions	Book Examples	KEE 3.1	GoldWorks 2.0	KBMS	NEXPERT 1.1	ADS	LEVEL5
forward chain	forwardChain	forward.chain	forward-chain	insert 3		forwardChain	demons present
backward chain	backwardChain	query	query	select 3		parameter OR message	agenda present

MESSAGE PASSING

send message	sendMsg	unitmsg	send-msg	OBJECT FUNCTIONS	NA	send OR instance.slot. METHOD*	instance. attribute (METHOD)
create an instance	createInstance	create.unit	make-instance	insert	CreateObject	create	MAKE
create handler		create.slot & put.value fn 4	define-handler		NA		define method
delete instance	deleteInstance	delete.unit	delete-instance	delete	DeleteObject	delete	FORGET
frame instances	frameInstances	unit.descendents	frame-instances	select 5	getAtomInfo 5	for classname classname(->s)**	FIND
frame children	frameChildren	unit.descendents	frame-children	select 5	getAtomInfo 5	NA	FIND
frame slots	getObjectsSlots	unit.slots	instance-all-slots	select 5	getAtomInfo 5	NA	NA

[1] Not Applicable--no multiple value slots

[2] system facets

[3] insert and select activate the chaining mechanism

[4] Handlers in KEE are defined as slot values with Method inheritance

[5] arguments to function determine action type

*In ADS, you get a value by directly referring to it in the form of a compound variable name, the instance name followed by a period, and the slot name. If this same reference is followed by ".METHOD", it invokes the message.

**Classname(->s) sets up a loop where each instance is bound to the variable, and classname is the name of the frame.

slot: **PRESSURE**

slot value: **HIGH**

variable: depends on shell

> KEE,GoldWorks—variables are words beginning with ? (e.g., ?pump).

> NEXPERT—the name of the class is enclosed with |
> (e.g., |PUMP|.pressure checks pressure slot's value for all instances of PUMP).

> KBMS—variables are implicitly bound, and KBMS interprets the clause and determines the instance.

> ADS—a keyword match is followed by the class name (e.g., IF match PUMP with PRESSURE = high). In cases with more than one clause using a pump slot, PUMP is indexed (e.g., IF match PUMP(1) with PRESSURE = high match PUMP(2) with TEMPERATURE = low).

> LEVEL5—Considered variable if does not match instance name.

Test a specific instance of PUMP1 with a slot PRESSURE for a value of HIGH.

> KEE: the **PRESSURE** of **PUMP1** is **HIGH**
>
> GoldWorks: instance **PUMP1** is **PUMP** with **PRESSURE HIGH**
>
> NEXPERT: is **PUMP1.PRESSURE "HIGH"**
>
> KBMS: the **PRESSURE** of **PUMP1** is **HIGH**
>
> ADS: **PUMP (PUMP1). PRESSURE = HIGH**
>
> LEVEL5: **PRESSURE** of **PUMP1** is **HIGH**

Test all instances with a slot pressure for a value of HIGH.

> KEE: the **PRESSURE** of **?instance** is HIGH
>
> GoldWorks: instance **?instance** is **PUMP** with **PRESSURE HIGH**
>
> NEXPERT: is **|PUMP|.pressure "HIGH"**
>
> KBMS: the **PRESSURE** is **HIGH**
>
> ADS: ifmatch **PUMP** with **PRESSURE = 'HIGH'**
>
> LEVEL5: **PRESSURE** of **PUMP** is **HIGH** (*or alternately*, if **PUMP.PRESSURE** is HIGH)

KEE will match all instances in the knowledge base with a pressure slot; preceding the clause shown with the clause "?**instance** is in class **PUMP**" will limit search to instances of frame **PUMP**. In NEXPERT the frame is part of the search pattern. KBMS will match on all instances with a pressure slot; in ambiguous cases, the clause would be rewritten as "the **PUMP PRESSURE** is **HIGH**." In ADS the symbol PUMP is set to each instance name with a pressure equal to 'high'(single quotation marks distinguish a value of high from being a variable named high).

Set a variable value from an instance **with a** slot pressure.

> KEE: the **PRESSURE** of ?**instance** is ?**value**
>
> GoldWorks: instance ?**instance** is **PUMP** with **PRESSURE** ?**value**
>
> NEXPERT: name |objectclass|.**PRESSURE** value (Note: value now becomes a global variable in NEXPERT.)
>
> ADS: ifmatch **PUMP** with **PRESSURE** = value
>
> LEVEL5: **PRESSURE** of **PUMP** := value

"Is there at least one **pump in the class of pumps with pressure high?"**

> KEE: ?**instance** is in class **PUMP**
> find.any (The **PRESSURE** of ?**instance** is **HIGH**)
>
> NEXPERT: is < |**PUMP**| >.**PRESSURE** "HIGH" (Note: NEXPERT uses <> to denote an existential pattern.)
>
> exists (**PUMP** with **PRESSURE** = '**HIGH**')
>
> LEVEL5: **PRESSURE** of **PUMP** contains **HIGH**

"Do all pumps in the class of pumps have pressure high?"

> KEE: for (?**instance** is in class **PUMP**)
> always (The **PRESSURE** of ?**instance** is **HIGH**)
>
> NEXPERT: is { |**PUMP**|}.**PRESSURE** "HIGH"
> (Note: NEXPERT uses {} to denote a universal pattern.)
>
> ADS: for **PUMP**,s
> not exists (**PUMP** with **PRESSURE** <> '**HIGH**')
>
> LEVEL5: not **PRESSURE** of **PUMP** omits **HIGH**

ADS uses the "exists" keyword to set up an iterative loop, within which the user can "program" any number of tests and so on. The form pump is a pointer set to each instance of pump in turn.

Execute an externally defined function *Test-Pressure.*

KEE: LISP Test-Pressure **PUMP1 TANK1 PRESSURE**

GoldWorks: Test-Pressure **'PUMP1 'TANK1 'PRESSURE**

NEXPERT:

Execute TestPressure

@ATOMID = **PUMP1 .PRESSURE** @ATOMID = **TANK1**
   .PRESSURE

LEVEL5: activate "TEST-PRESSURE"
      send **PRESSURE** of **TANK1**
      send **PRESSURE** of **PUMP1**
      return **AGREE**

Test-Pressure is a function that takes two arguments, a tank instance, a pump instance, and a slot name (PRESSURE) (i.e., tank and pump pressure) and returns true if the two pressures are within 90 percent of one another, false otherwise. KEE signifies use of a function with the keyword LISP at the beginning of the clause. GoldWorks uses a two-step process. First, the user must define a **relation** of type LISP, including the function name and the function arguments; that relation can then be used in rules (no keyword required). NEXPERT uses the keyword Execute. In ADS, use FUNCTION to invoke a routine in KDL (the ADS knowledge-definition language) or PROCESS to call external routines.

B

APPLICATION
EXAMPLES: RULES

This appendix contains a more complete set of rules than that presented in the different chapters.

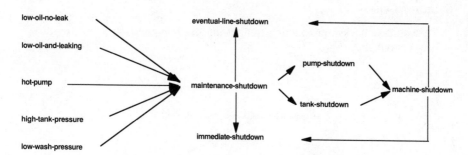

FIGURE B-1. Forward-chaining rules for diagnosis

See Chapter 4 for a detailed discussion of the above rules.

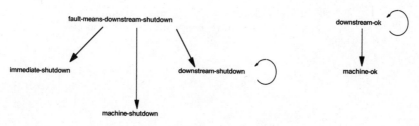

FIGURE B-2. Rules for fault propagation

See Chapter 6 for a discussion of the above rules.

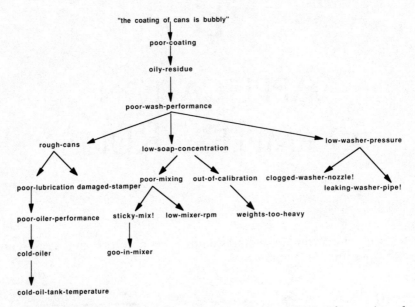

FIGURE B-3. Backward-chaining tree testing the hypothesis "the coating of cans is bubbly"

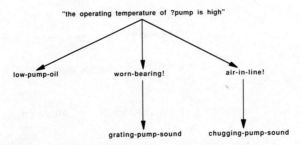

FIGURE B-4. Backward-chaining rules testing the hypothesis "the operating temperature of pump is high"

The following backward-chaining rules (from Figure B-3) show an example of the ROUGH-CANS segment of the rule tree—at this point, we are exploring the hypothesis that the performance is poor for some washer.

Rule: **ROUGH-CANS**
Rule Set: **QUALITY-CONTROL**
Documentation: Ask the operator about the cans outer
    surface to detect problems on the inside surface caused
    by the stamper.
IF
    AskOperatorWhenUnknown "CANS", "OUTER-SURFACE"
    AND
    THE OUTER-SURFACE OF CANS IS SMOOTH
    AND
    ?WASHER IS A WASHER
    AND
    THE UPSTREAM OF ?WASHER IS ?STAMPER
    AND
    ?STAMPER IS A STAMPER
    AND
    THE PERFORMANCE OF ?STAMPER IS POOR
THEN
    THE PERFORMANCE OF ?WASHER IS POOR

Rule: **POOR-LUBRICATION**
Rule Set: **QUALITY-CONTROL**
Documentation: Performance is related to the quality of
    lubrication.
IF
    ?STAMPER IS A STAMPER
    AND
    THE LUBRICATION OF SHEET-METAL IS POOR
THEN
    THE PERFORMANCE OF ?STAMPER IS POOR

Rule: **DAMAGED-STAMPER**
Rule Set: **QUALITY-CONTROL**
Documentation: The stamper surface has to be completely
   smooth, otherwise the can will be grooved.
IF
   ?STAMPER IS A STAMPER
   AND
   askOperatorWhenUnknown ?STAMPER "SURFACE"
   AND
   THE SURFACE OF ?STAMPER IS ROUGH
THEN
   THE PERFORMANCE OF ?STAMPER IS POOR

Rule: **POOR-OILER-PERFORMANCE**
Rule Set: **QUALITY-CONTROL**
Documentation: The oiler lubricates the sheet-metal before
   it is stamped.
IF
   ?OILER IS A OILER
   AND
   THE PERFORMANCE OF ?OILER IS POOR
THEN
   THE LUBRICATION OF SHEET-METAL IS POOR

Rule: **COLD-OILER**
Rule Set: **QUALITY-CONTROL**
Documentation: Low oil temperature causes the oil to be
   too thick, reducing lubrication.
IF
   ?OILER IS A OILER
   AND
   THE OPERATING-TEMPERATURE OF ?OILER IS LOW
THEN
   THE PERFORMANCE OF ?OILER IS POOR

Rule: **COLD–OIL–TANK–TEMPERATURE**
Rule Set: **QUALITY–CONTROL**
Documentation: The oiler must be provided with hot oil
   by the upstream auxiliary tank.
IF
   PROVIDES STAMPING–LUBRICANT ?TANK ?OILER
   AND
   askOperatorWhenUnknown ?TANK "TEMPERATURE"
   AND
   ?TANK IS A TANK
   AND
   THE TEMPERATURE OF ?TANK IS LOW
THEN
   THE OPERATING–TEMPERATURE OF ?OILER IS LOW

This last rule, COLD-OIL-TANK-TEMPERATURE, demonstrates an important concept in the use of pattern-matching rules, the **join operation**. In a join, the rule makes the connection between (joins) two separate data items, in this case an OILER and a TANK. The first clause finds a tank and oiler pair, and the fourth clause checks to see whether the tank's temperature is low, allowing us to make a conclusion about the oiler in relation to its associated tank.

C

HYPERTALK SUMMARY

This appendix contains a brief description of HyperTalk commands and functions used in the book examples.

Procedure Definition

on <name> ... **end** <name>: define a handler
```
on test
  answer "hi there"
end test
```

function <name ... **end** <name>: define a function
```
function test2
  return "hi there"
end test
```

Note: handlers do not return a value. If you place a return in the handler, you can get a return value by using "the result" on the next line.

```
on test
  answer "hi there"
  return "hello"
end test

on test2
  test
  answer the result --> answer will pop-up "hello"
end test2
```

A function returns a value. Using the function test2 from above, we would rewrite test2 as:

```
on test2
  answer test1()
end test2
```

Note that a Function call is followed by (), enclosing the arguments.

Program Control

repeat [with or until]: iterate for a fixed number of times
```
repeat with i = 1 to 10
  answer i
end repeat
```

```
repeat until i = 10
  answer i
  add 1 to i
end repeat
```

if <condition> 1 then <action1> else <action2>:
do action1 if condition is true otherwise do action2
```
if i = 10 then answer i
else add 1 to i
```

exit <name>: quit a loop, handler, or function early
```
repeat with i = 1 to 10
  if item i of x = 0 then exit repeat
  answer 10 / item i of x
end repeat
```

return <value>: return a value from a function
```
function test
  return "hi there"
end test
```

Commands

answer <statement>: pop-up statement in box
```
answer "Data is not available"
```

ask <statement><default>: ask user for input
```
ask "What is pump pressure?" "normal"
```

do <statement>: evaluate a statement
do "1 + 2" --> 3

global <**variable names**>:
make a variable available to all functions and handlers
`global currentSchedule, CurrentLayout`

put <**value**> {**into, before, or after**} <**variable**>:
place a value in a variable name
`put 42 into temperature`
`put "washer2" before washerCheckList`

delete item n of <**variable**>: remove an item from a list
`put "a,b,c" into VAR`
`delete item 1 of VAR --> VAR is "b,c"`

Operators

&: glue two sentences together
`"hi" & "there"`

<**object**> **is in** <**list**>: test to see if object is in a list;
`returns true or false`
`"washer2" is in "wash-mixer,pump4,washer2" --> true`

is,=: test two objects for equality
`x = 43`
`x is 43`

is not, ≠: test two objects for inequality

arithmetic operators `+(plus),-(minus),*(times),/(divide)`

Functions

number of <**list**>: return the number of items in list
`number of items in "wash-mixer, pump4, washer2" -->3`

length <**statement**>: return the number of characters in statement
`length ("hi there") --> 8`   (space counts as a character)

round <**value**>: round numeric value to the nearest integer
`round (100 / 3)   --> 33`

Constants

`true,false,empty,return`

HyperTalk has a few conventions to keep in mind:

- Put all text in quotes (" ").

- Words and sentences within quotes are considered items when separated by commas. For example, "one, two and three, four" has three items: one; two and three; four. Items in a quoted list can be deleted (delete), indexed (item 2 of machineList), extended ("one" & "," & "two and three" become the list "one, two and three"), and augmented (put "zero," before "one, two and three").

- You can build paragraphs in a fashion similar to building sentences, each line separated by a return (return is a HyperTalk special constant). Lines can be indexed, deleted, and so on, for example, `delete line 1 of machineInventory`.

- Lines that begin with two dashes (--) are considered comments.

APPENDIX

D

LISP PROGRAMMING EXAMPLES

Although the Lisp language contains hundreds of functions, we have found that 95 percent of all programming in support of an expert system can be reduced to the following set of Common Lisp functions:

Procedure Definition	defun
Program Control	let dolist loop when if cond case
Manipulating Lists	list reverse cons push append first second third nth delete assoc sort
Arithmetic Operators	plus minus times exponential divide
Logical Operators	equal less-than greater-than unless or and not null member
Input/Output	format string
Other	gentemp unwind-protect defparameter defvar self setq length

Once you are comfortable using these functions, you'll know enough Lisp to program almost any extension to an expert system application. For an in-depth treatment of Lisp programming we suggest Winston's *Lisp* and for a complete reference to all the Common Lisp functions, Steele's *Common Lisp*.

EXAMPLES

This appendix contains examples of code taken from Chapter 9 reimplemented using Lisp.

CHAPTER 9

Diagnose Component

```
(define-handler (component diagnose)()
  ;;-- Is this component not ok?
  ;;-- If it is not, walk up the links
  ;;-- (upstream) to discover faults
  (when (send-msg self :check-component-state)
    (dolist
      (upstream (slot-all-values self 'upstream))
      ;;-- check all upstream components
      (send-msg upstream :diagnose))
))
```

```
(define-handler (mixer diagnose)()
  ;;-- example of local handler which differs from default
  (when
    ;;**** only check if RPM not LOW
    (and
      (not (equal 'low (slot-value self 'rpm)))
      (send-msg self :check-component-state))
    (dolist
      (upstream (slot-all-values self 'upstream))
      ;;-- check all upstream components
      (send-msg upstream :diagnose))
))
```

Propagate State

```
(define-handler (component propagate-state)
                (&optional new-state)
  ;;-- self is a component being updated with a new state
  ;;-- value called either at top-level or by update-
  ;;-- state...if given set
  ;;-- current state to new-state else new-
  ;;-- state to the current state
  (if new-state
    (setf (slot-value self 'state) new-state)
    (setq new-state (slot-value self 'state)))
  (dolist (downstream (slot-all-values self 'downstream))
    (format t "~&Propagate-state from ~a to ~a"
        (gw-name self) downstream)
    (send-msg downstream :update-state self new-state)  ))
```

```
(define-handler (component update-state)
                (upstream-component upstream-state)
  ;;-- invoked by 'propagate-state' to update self with
  ;;-- new state  and then pass the change downstream
  (let ((new-local-state
        (send-msg self:calculate-new-state
                upstream-component upstream-state)))
    (when new-local-state; proceed if value returned
        (when *nav-trace*
                (format t "~&Setting ~a to ~a" self
        new-local-state))
      (setf (slot-value self 'state) new-local-state) )
    ;;-- this will cause another cycle, with
    ;;-- propagate-state being called with the upstream-
    ;;-- component's downstream
    (send-msg self:propagate-state new-local-state)   ))
```

```
(define-handler (component calculate-new-state)
                (upstream-component state-type)
  ;;-- find the components state constraints
  ;;-- specific handlers (e.g., pump) will modify this
  ;;-- upstream-component will be used by these specific
  ;;-- handlers Arg upstream-component may be used in other
  ;;-- versions of this handler
  (declare (ignore upstream-component))
  (default-calculate-component-state self state-type) )
```

A handler returns the result of the function it calls.

```
(defun default-calculate-component-state (component
   state-type)
  ;;-- Return the value which the state slot of a component
  ;;-- will be ;;-- set to, decide this component's state based
  ;;-- on STATE-TYPE. If COMPONENT is in a fault state,
  ;;-- it stays in that state
  (let ((current-state (slot-value component 'state)))
   (cond  ((equal current-state 'fault) 'fault)
          ((or (equal state-type 'fault)
               (equal state-type 'shutdown)) 'shutdown)
          ;;-- Return OK if OK now???
          ((equal state-type 'ok) 'ok)
     )))
```

APPENDIX

E

IMPLEMENTATION
NOTES

This appendix is divided into sections designated by the chapter heading where the illustrated concepts are introduced. The purpose of the appendix is to provide users with a mapping between the terms used in this book and the equivalent terms in each commercial shell. For example, we discuss frames, which are designated as units in KEE, classes in ADS, and objects in KBMS. In this appendix we have used the following shell versions:

- IntelliCorp—KEE 3.1
- Neuron Data—NEXPERT OBJECT 1.1
- Gold Hill—GoldWorks 2.0
- Albathion—Entrypaq 1.0
- Aion—ADS
- AICORP—KBMS
- Information Builders, Inc.—LEVEL5 OBJECT

KEE is IntelliCorp's expert system shell running on a number of platforms, including the Symbolics, TI Explorer and Explorer for the Mac, Sun, and 386 machines. NEXPERT OBJECT is Neuron Data's expert system shell running on hardware including the Macintosh, PC, DEC workstations, and UNIX workstations. EntryPaq is a small demonstration expert system shell that illustrates the concepts discussed in this book (EntryPaq can be ordered with the coupon at the back of this book). Gold Hill's GoldWorks currently is running on the PC, Macintosh, and SUN. Aion's ADS runs on the IBM mainframe and the PC. AICORP's KBMS runs on the IBM mainframe and the PC. IBI's LEVEL5 runs on IBM PC, Apple Macintosh, DEC VAX, IBM mainframe, and SUN. Note that this list only provides a partial list of platforms for some shells.

FIGURE E-1. Rules

	Entrypaq	KEE	GoldWorks	KBMS	NEXPERT	ADS	LEVEL5
Variables	?name	?name	?name	referential binding	implied by syntax	text without quotes	implied by syntax
How	None	Graphical derivation tree	text		Graphical derivation tree	text	Graphical tree
Why	None	Simple text explanation	text	user defined text		text	user defined graphic or text
Agendas	None	agenda	agenda	agenda	agenda	agenda	agenda

CHAPTER 4–Rules

In Chapter 4 rules are introduced. Figure E-1 contains descriptions of rule language features such as the form in which variables appear in rules.

In the demo disk (EntryPaq), KEE, and GoldWorks, a **variable** is specified in a rule by prefacing the variable name with a question mark(?). KBMS logically parses the clause, maintaining internal variables and letting users implicitly reference them. In NEXPERT, you cannot set **variable values** within the rules. However, you can create global variables or new objects (in effect global variables) whose values can then be tested in subsequent clauses. ADS specifies any word not enclosed in quotes as a variable. See Appendix A for more details.

Once a derivation is completed, the user can discover **how** a conclusion was reached by requesting that the system display the derivation of a solution. KEE and NEXPERT both provide graphs showing the fired rules in the order fired, indicating failed and successful paths. Other shells, such as GoldWorks, provide text describing the rules that successfully fired with the supporting facts or related rules.

When a request for information is made from a rule, the user has the option of asking **why**. Shells either show the context of the question (e.g., KEE provides the related rules in the context of the current chaining) or print predefined information provided by the application developer.

Agendas contain the rules to be fired in the order in which they will fire. In some shells, agendas can be both inspected and modified (modification consists of changing rule-firing order and/or deleting rules from the agenda). Some shells allow the user to write an algorithm for placing rules on the agenda (difficult).

CHAPTER 5–Objects

In Chapter 5 objects are introduced. Figure E-2 provides translations for the definitions of objects and their attributes, including interfaces to the rule system, in various shells.

Figure E-2. Objects

	Entrypaq	KEE	GoldWorks	KBMS	NEXPERT	ADS	LEVEL5
Frames	Backgrounds	Units	Frames	Objects	Classes	Classes	Classes
Instances	Cards	Members	Instances	Occurrences	Objects	Instances	Instances
Slots	Fields	Slots	Slots	Attributes	Properties	Slots	Attributes
Facets	Invisible Fields	Facets (user & system)	Facets (user & system)	sort of*	(system)	Properties (system)	Facets & Properties
Multiple Values in Slots	Yes	Yes	Yes	sort of*	No	Yes	Yes
Refer to Slot Values in Rules	Yes	Yes	Yes	Yes	Yes	Yes	Yes

* Extensions of slots can be done with relational links, which the rule system can interpret in a fashion similar to multiple values and facets.

Facets extend the descriptive capabilities of slots. All systems have some predefined system facets the value of which the user can set, for example the name and the value of the slot. Other possible system facets might be daemons, documentation strings, and confidence factors. In addition, many shells provide facilities for allowing users to extend the facets with their own definitions; for example, in the book we use facets to cross-reference objects that represent the slot's value graphically.

Multiple values allow representation of more complex concepts than single values, for example the fact that an attribute of Nancy—the cars she owns—might include a pickup truck and a sports car. If a variable is used in a frame-matching premise clause, all values in the slot will be tested in turn, in the same way that multiple instances are tested. In situations where multiple values are not supported, you could create multiple copies of the same instance (with some numbering scheme in the name to distinguish them) and place one value in each slot (this would be somewhat unwieldy when there are a number of multiple value slots required for an object).

CHAPTER 6–Graphics

Chapter 6 introduces object graphics. Images that change **dynamically** provide users with both graphic input and output capabilities. These images can thus be used in the design of both developer and end-user interfaces. Dynamically changing images are associated with an instance's slot; changes in the image change the internal knowledge base value, and changes in the internal value cause the image to automatically update (Figure E-3).

Figure E-3. Graphics

	Entrypaq	KEE	GoldWorks	KBMS	NEXPERT	ADS	LEVEL5
Graphic Objects	Frames & Instances	Frames & Instances	Frames & Instances	Not available for development at this time.	Not available for development at this time.	Not available for development at this time.	Frames & Instances
Graphical Layout Editor	Graphic Toolkit	KEEPictures	Graphic Layout Tool				Display Editor
Graphic Customizing	Yes	Yes	Yes	Delivery graphics character-based or third-party add-on package.	Delivery graphics character-based or third-party add-on package.	Delivery graphics character-based or third-party add-on package.	Yes
Dynamically Changing Images	Dynamic Images	Active Images	Graphics Toolkit				System Display Classes

CHAPTER 8–Object Programming

Most shells provide a capability for extending the shell language using a programming language. Because all of these shells have an object component, they all provide object programming capabilities (Figure E-4).

Message passing capabilities provide the user with facilities for extending the shell features with a programming language, either a language defined for the shell (e.g., ADS) or a standard language such as LISP or C. Messages defined in a programming language are attached to a frame or slot and inherited by the instances. KEE, GoldWorks, and ADS allow the user to define arbitrary message names, while KBMS and NEXPERT limit the user to writing new definitions for a fixed set of system-defined message names (for example, the message that is sent when a slot value is modified). Related to messages (some shells such as KBMS and NEXPERT define messages to be what we discuss here as daemons), **daemons** can be defined to fire when a slot value is modified (e.g., when-modified) or accessed (e.g., when-accessed).

Inheritance occurs between frames and instances for slots and all their attributes. Because handlers are defined on frames and slots, they also inherit. In some shells (e.g., KEE), handlers can be modified with before and after **wrappers** (additions to the handler code that are added at lower levels in the inheritance hierarchy). Users can often select from a set of predefined inheritance types (e.g., override the parent's value—usually the default—or the union of parent and child values) or define their own. Inheritance can be set for each slot and also for each slot's facet.

CHAPTER 9–Backward Chaining

Chapter 9 introduces a backward-chaining paradigm to the example application and shows how the rule language can be extended by user-defined operators (Figure E-5).

In some shells, such as KEE and GoldWorks, **backward chaining** can be invoked on a hypothesis by using a command followed by the hypothesis clause. In other shells, backward chaining is invoked through the interface and may include "opportunistic chaining," where the system may alternate modes as it makes new assertions.

External function calls from within rules allow developers to extend the expressability of the rule language. Primarily, this allows the rules to mimic experts who, in addition to evaluating simple facts, often use complex calculations in determining solutions to problems. For example, a rule might need a calculation concerning taxes done as part of a set of clauses determining a user's tax liability. These calls can take the form of direct function calls preceded by a keyword (KEE, NEXPERT) or messages sent from the rule clause to an instance (functions can also be called indirectly as when daemons are fired by requests for slot values). In GoldWorks, instead

FIGURE E-4. Object programming

Object Programming	Entrypaq	KEE	GoldWorks	KBMS	NEXPERT	ADS	LEVEL5
Object Programming	Methods	Methods: Method slots	Handlers: define-handler	System Messages	System Messages	Methods	Methods
Inheritance*	Static	Dynamic	Dynamic	Dynamic	Dynamic	Dynamic	Dynamic
Daemons	daemons	Active Values: avput avget	daemons: when-modified when-accessed	Attributes when-assigned when-needed	If-Change	daemons & immediate-fire rules	daemons when changed when needed

*Inheritance may apply to slot values, slot facets, and messages associated with frames and instances.

FIGURE E-5. Backward chaining

	Entrypaq	KEE	GoldWorks	KBMS	NEXPERT	ADS	LEVEL5
Backward Chaining	No	Query	Query	automatic*	yes*	yes*	Yes
External Function Call in Rules	Yes	LISP	LISP relation	Yes	EXECUTE	FUNCTION	METHODS ACTIVATE
User Input Rule Queries	Built-in menu	ask.user	ask relation pop-up frame	Formatter	Built-in	Built-in menu	Default queries

*Opportunistic forward/backward chaining

of a preceding keyword, a user first defines a relation (type LISP) and uses the relation name followed by arguments in the rule clause. In ADS, users can just use the name of their function if it is defined in KDL (the internal language) or the keyword FUNCTION for external calls. In KBMS, functions can be defined using an internal language and the function call becomes part of an English-like sentence.

Rules in most shells can **query the user** to request missing information. Some shells precede a clause with a keyword that will request information that cannot be found in the frame system (KEE); others allow the building of input screens that appear to the user as forms (KBMS).

CHAPTER 11–Rule Control

In Chapter 11 various techniques for controlling the order and conditions under which rules fire in are discussed. Each shell provides the user with tools to determine rule groupings and orderings (Figure E-6).

Priorities enable users to resolve conflicts in situations where two rules (or rule sets) can fire at the same time. Shells implement these priorities for individual rules, sets of rules, or both using numeric values to define the order in which the rules will fire. KEE implements **priorities** as a weight slot on the rule frame—in addition to putting a numeric value in the weight slot, you select a new agenda mechanism specific to priorities by changing the function in the rule's DC.RULE.ORDER.FUNCTION slot to one that looks for priorities. In similar fashion, GoldWorks provides attributes on both rules and rule sets where priorities can be set. In KBMS, priorities are set for a collection of rules; all of those rules will fire before or after other rule "packets," depending on the result of a user-defined priority function.

Certainty or **confidence factors** attempt to mirror real-life uncertainty about outcomes, for example, the fact that inflation is increasing is "somewhat" an indicator that the stock market may go down. Various approaches

FIGURE E-6. Rule control

	Entrypaq	KEE	GoldWorks	KBMS	NEXPERT	ADS	LEVEL5
Priorities	No	Rule Weights	Both Rule & Rule Set Priorities	Packet Priority Function	Inference Category	Rule Priorities	Order
Certainty Factors	No	Programmable by the user	Certainty Factors	Programmable by the user		Certainty Factors	Certainty Factors
Rule Sets	Yes	Rule Classes	Rule Sets	Packets		States	Rule Groups

including Bayesian mathematics and fuzzy arithmetic are used to interpret these factors. In line with the on-going controversy surrounding **certainty factors**, many shells, such as KEE, only provide guidance to users on establishing their own certainty or confidence factors. GoldWorks provides specific attributes for holding the values and a sample mechanism for manipulating them. At the other end of the spectrum, ADS provides both the facility for specifying certainty factors and the Bayesian algorithms for interpreting them.

Rule sets are collections of rules that have group properties, including the ability to be activated/deactivated as a group and the assignment of priorities on the order in which the entire group will fire in relation to other groups. In KEE, rule sets are defined by creating a rule class and making each rule an instance of that frame (in KEE, rules are implemented as frames with slots for the various attributes of the rule). In a similar fashion, both GoldWorks and KBMS define a new entity (rule set and packet, respectively) and place the rules within it. In all three cases, the rule set contains attributes distinct from the rules contained within it.

APPENDIX
F

DESCRIPTION
OF KNOWLEDGE BASE

This appendix contains an illustration of the frame hierarchy and a set of tables describing how some of the slots are defined in the knowledge base. The tables include only the slots defined for that particular frame. The table for the PUMP frame, for example, contains entries for only four slots, yet the PUMP frame inherits slots from all of the frames (MACHINE, COMPONENT, and FACTORY-ELEMENT) that lie above PUMP in the frame hierarchy.

HIERARCHICAL FRAME STRUCTURE

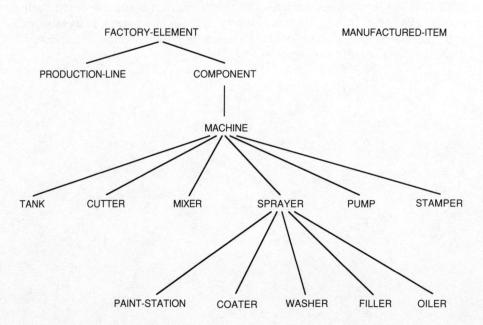

SLOT DEFINITIONS

Frame: FACTORY-ELEMENT

Slots	Documentation	Allowed Values
MAINTENANCE	Tells you when a machine needs to be worked on	UNNEEDED SOON IMMEDIATELY
SHUTDOWN	Tells you when a machine must be turned off	UNNEEDED SOON IMMEDIATELY

Frame: PRODUCTION-LINE

Slots	Documentation	Allowed Values
COMPONENTS	All the components in a particular line; allows us to have several lines loaded simultaneously	Instance of COMPO-NENT
FAULTY-SYSTEM	Contains the factory system that has caused a fault in the line	Instance of SYSTEM

Frame: COMPONENT

Slots	Documentation	Allowed Values
DOWNSTREAM	Materials flow from this component to the component or components in this slot	Instance of COMPO-NENT
FAULT	Identifies fault for this component, if any	Instance of FAULT-CONDITION
ON-CRITICAL-PATH	Indicates whether or not there is an alternative to this component or, alternatively, whether shutting down this component implies the entire plant should be shut down	YES NO
PERFORMANCE	Describes how a machine is doing currently	GOOD FAIR POOR
STATE	The current state of a component	OK SHUTDOWN FAULT
UPSTREAM	Materials flow to this component from the component or components in this slot; this is the inverse of components in the DOWNSTREAM slot	Instance of COMPO-NENT

Frame: MACHINE

Slots	Documentation	Allowed Values
OPERATING-TEMPERATURE	Internal system temperature	LOW NORMAL HIGH
PRESSURE	Internal system pressure	LOW NORMAL HIGH

Frame: TANK

Slots	Documentation	Allowed Values
APPEARANCE	The upper surface of the liquid inside	NORMAL FOAMING

Frame: PUMP

Slots	Documentation	Allowed Values
OIL-AMOUNT	What shows on the oil gauge	LOW NORMAL HIGH
OIL-LINES	Is oil leaking out anywhere?	INTACT LEAKING
RPM	What shows on the gauge	LOW OK HIGH
SOUND	Auditory cues to a potential problem	CHUGGING GRATING SMOOTH

Frame: SPRAYER

Slots	Documentation	Allowed Values
NOZZLE	The state of the sprayer head—often clogged with gunk	OPEN CLOGGED

Frame: WASHER

Slots	Documentation	Allowed Values
APPEARANCE	Are there leaks anywhere?	OK SOAP-MIX-ON-FLOOR RINSE-MIX-ON-FLOOR
CONTENTS	What the washer holds	WASH-MIX RINSE-MIX
SOAP-CONCENTRATION	The concentration of the mix	LOW NORMAL HIGH

Frame: MANUFACTURED-ITEM

Slots	Documentation	Allowed Values
COATING	Should be smooth and even, with no breaks or irregularities	UNEVEN BUBBLY STREAKED MISSING OK
INNER-SURFACE	A rough surface results from problems with stamping	SMOOTH ROUGH
ODOR	It's easy to smell trace amounts of oil and soap on the cans, even after the coating has been applied	OILY SOAPY NONE
OUTER-SURFACE	An irregular surface results from problems with stamping	SMOOTH IRREGU-LAR
RESIDUE	Crud on the cans, left for a variety of reasons, which (among other things) makes the contents taste bad; cannot really detect residue after coating has been applied, however	OILY SOAPY NONE

INDEX